QUEST

**Searching for Germany's Nazi Past
A Young Man's Story**

**Ib Melchior
and
Frank Brandenburg**

★

PRESIDIO

Copyright © 1990 Ib Melchior

Published by Presidio Press
31 Pamaron Way, Novato CA 94949

Library of Congress Cataloging-in-Publication Data

Melchior, Ib.
    Quest : searching for Germany's Nazi past : a young man's story /
by Ib Melchior and Frank Brandenburg.
      p. cm.
    Includes index.
    ISBN 0-89141-397-9
    1. National socialism. 2. Germany-History-1933-45.
3. Bormann, Martin, 1900- .   4. Brandenburg, Frank, 1963-
5. National socialists-Interviews. I. Brandenburg, Frank, 1963-
. II. Title.
    DD256.M455 1990   90-7814
    943.086-dc20   CIP
Typography by ProImage, San Rafael, CA
Printed in the United States of America

To Cleo—
my most treasured reader.

FOREWORD

This book is a true and fascinating account of a young German boy determined to find out the truth about the Holocaust that took place during the Third Reich under its dictator, Adolf Hitler.

Motivated by the belief that a nation that cannot face its history cannot deal with its future either, he decided to set out on his own and interview as many people as he could find who had served in positions of responsibility during the Nazi regimen.

When I read the manuscript of Frank Brandenburg's story as written by Ib Melchior, I recalled my own youth as an American boy in Montana. I, too, had found it hard to believe what we were being told about what was happening in Germany, and other parts of Europe, as Hitler's army occupied nation after nation. Like Frank Brandenburg, I, too, was determined to find out the truth. What intrigued me most was what allowed people to carry out such criminal acts.

Years later, as Commandant of Spandau Allied Prison, I had the opportunity to interview some of the top Nazi war criminals myself. Nevertheless, this present account has answered many of the questions I have been trying to answer for years. It is indeed an important, highly informative document of modern history that should be read by everyone.

Frank Brandenburg's quest, his interviews and investigations, provide a grim look into the innermost thoughts and feelings of individuals who played dominant roles in the Third Reich. His observations hold a warning for both the present and the future, a warning to be contemplated by those who cannot lay aside their fascination for power.

I know Frank Brandenburg. His was an astonishing adventure. I can vouch for his credibility and support the veracity of his search.

Eugene K. Bird
Col. U.S Army (Ret.)
Former U.S Commandant
Spandau Allied Prison
West Berlin

INTRODUCTION

I am privileged to have the legendary author, screenwriter, and director Curt Siodmak among my friends, and when, early in 1987, he called me from his scenic farm in Three Rivers on the slopes of the Sierra Mountains in California, and told me that he was sending a young man from Germany to see me, I was at once intrigued. I have always admired the author of the classic *Donovan's Brain* and numerous other tales crackling with imagination, and I was certain that when Curt told me it would be worth my while to talk to the young man, it would indeed be an interesting experience.

I was not disappointed.

Frank Brandenburg, twenty–four years of age when I met him, had a fascinating and exciting tale to tell. His story will be told in this book, but it will not be diminished by revealing the gist of it here.

In January of 1979, sixteen–year-old Frank embarked upon an incredible, dangerous, and adventurous quest. He had just seen the American television film, "The Holocaust," which had been broadcast over one of the lesser TV channels in Germany, and what he saw and heard had left him profoundly appalled and disturbed. He could not believe that what the program showed could be true; he had never known that such things happened in his country, which he loved. The existence of work camps called concentration camps had been mentioned only sketchily, with nothing about a "holocaust," so Frank determined to find out the facts for himself: to track down the people still living who had been closely associated with the Third Reich and the Nazi Party, who were—in fact—responsible for the policies, ideologies, and subsequent actions carried out during the years of Adolf Hitler.

Frank did his research.

And now he was searching for someone to write the story of his quest, and Curt Siodmak had suggested he ask me.

At first I said no. I had never before worked with any kind of collaborator on any of my books. But as Frank told me more and more of his adventures and the astounding revelations he discovered, I became convinced it was a story worth telling.

Frank realized that in order for the report to have any significance it would have to be written as fact, and that he would have to use his own name in the telling. I agreed, but I was disturbed. The conversation between us went something like this:

I: Have you considered the danger in which you are placing yourself? divulging all this?

Frank: I have. I want to do it. I think it is important for the German people—for everyone—to know.

I: You are not playing with small–time operators, Frank. These are dangerous people. Powerful people.

Frank: I know.

I: And you still want to go ahead? to use your own name?

Frank: Yes. I do.

And so I agreed to write the book, which we decided to call simply *Quest*.

I knew the pitfalls of writing a factual book, especially one with historical subject matter. Although my own factual writing has been limited to a series of magazine articles written several years ago, I knew the risks inherent in quoting others or accepting second–hand information. The most troublesome phrase in the English language is: "Do you know what I mean?" The answer invariably is "yes" although in all too many cases what is perceived by the listener has quite a different meaning to the speaker.

Even prominent chroniclers of history are apparently not immune to the risks of erroneous quoting. I have in my files a letter from Flugkapitän Hanna Reitsch, a German test pilot *par excellence*, the only pilot to have flown a V-1 buzz bomb to evaluate its flight. As one of the last persons in the Berlin Führerbunker to see Adolf Hitler before his suicide, she has been quoted copiously in many books on the subject of conditions in the Bunker at that time, among them one by the prominent British historian and author H. R. Trevor–Roper, who quotes her in detail in his book *The Last Days of Hitler*. The *New York Times* said of the book, "It is a rich source of new information." But Hanna Reitsch writes:

"I can only tell you that it is a shame for England to use as a 'historical scientist' a man like Trevor–Roper in a highly reputed university like the Christ Church College in Oxford. He wrote his book, *The Last Days of Hitler*, not as a historical truth written by a historian but as a Secret Service man (politician) using third-hand sources, including a so-called 'eyewitness report of Hanna Reitsch.' I have never written it, I have never seen it, I have never signed it."

Although I fully believed in Frank's veracity, I owed it to my publisher and my readers to safeguard against such pitfalls and risks as completely as possible. Frank's story was so unusual that I felt I had to find corroboration beyond reproach, in addition to the tapes, correspondence, documentation, and photographic material Frank had given me. I found this corroboration and endorsement of Frank in the persons of an eminent lawyer of international repute, Dr. Robert M. W. Kempner, U.S. staff prosecutor at the Nürnberg Trials in 1945–46 of Göring, Hess, *et al.*, and Col. Eugene K. Bird, U.S. Army (Ret.), former U.S. Commandant of Spandau Allied Prison in Spandau, West Germany, that held the Nazi war criminals, notably Rudolf Hess. Both Dr. Kempner and Colonel Bird were extremely helpful to Frank during his quest.

During World War II Dr. Kempner was expert counsel to the U.S. Department of Justice, the OSS, and to the secretary of war on law enforcement, and intelligence techniques of European dictatorships and foreign organizations in the United States. In 1961 he served as counsel to the Israeli Government in the Adolf Eichmann case. He is the author of a dozen books and the recipient of several honors and decorations.

Colonel Bird is the author of *Prisoner Number 7: Rudolf Hess* (1974), and I am indebted to him for the foreword to this book.

Finally, this account of Frank Brandenburg's experiences is as factual as extensive research and exhaustive, in–depth interviewing could make it. No names (except where specifically noted), no places, and no events have been altered or fictionalized.

The dialogue throughout the book is based on what Frank remembers, as well as on his notes and tapes. If not verbatim, it is factual as to substance and meaning. The descriptions of both people and places are taken from photographs in Frank's possession and from his recollections.

The adventures, revelations, and observations are Frank's.

I

He barely managed to slam the door shut before the huge black German shepherd dog could sink its fangs into his arm. As soon as he had begun to step out of his car, the two big dogs had come charging from behind a woodpile in snarling fury. It had been a near miss.

Heart pounding, twenty–three–year–old Frank Brandenburg sat in his car, watching the ferocious dogs clawing and scratching at the car door. When he had asked for directions to the house of Franz Lechner in the little village of Stoizendorf north of Vienna, a mere ten miles from Austria's border with Czechoslovakia, the villagers had cautioned him. Stay away from the Lechner place, they had warned him, nodding their heads gravely. The man is a loner. He is dangerous.

They had said nothing about the dogs.

He looked at the frenzied beasts hurling themselves in rage at the car again and again, their furious barking obliterating all other sounds.

He placed a shaking hand on the gear shift—and slowly removed it. No, dammit!—he would stay. It was June 16, 1986, and time was running out for him. Automatically he touched his jacket. He felt the hard bulge of the little tape recorder nestled in his inside pocket. Yes, he would stay. He'd come too far these last eight years to let a couple of dogs scare him off now. He had to talk to the man, Lechner. He had been told that Lechner knew the facts about the fate of Reichsleiter Martin Bormann, a fate still an enigma to the world today. He had been told that Lechner had knowledge no one else possessed. He admitted to himself that he was afraid of dogs. Especially the two brutes outside. But he knew he would never forgive himself if he left now, without accomplishing what he had come for. Because of a couple of dogs. He simply *had* to talk to the man.

He leaned on his horn.

At the sound the dogs doubled their efforts to get at him.

Frank watched the house. Surrounded by a forbidding stone wall, it stood in shunned isolation at the outskirts of the village. A large, massive gate gave access to the courtyard and buildings beyond. It was closed.

He kept honking the horn and watching the gate, trying to ignore the clamoring dogs. When the gate finally opened, a man stepped through it onto the road.

Frank abruptly stopped his honking. He stared at the man.

Was that Franz Lechner?

The man was clad in dark, soiled trousers held up by a pair of grey suspenders, and a light blue shirt open at the neck, only partly buttoned and so carelessly tucked into his pants that a flash of pale skin showed above his fly. On his bare feet he wore scuffed clogs and his dirty-blond hair was unkempt.

He cried a short, guttural command to the dogs. Instantly they stopped their barking and ran to sit watchfully behind their master.

Keeping his right hand in his pocket, the man slowly walked up to the car, as Frank rolled down the window.

"What do you want?" the man growled, his hostile stare fixed on the young driver.

For a moment Frank's heart stood still. In a surge of apprehension he realized that he hadn't really thought out how to approach the man—and the reality of it was much different from what he had expected.

"Get out!" the man ordered brusquely.

Eyeing the two big dogs that warily watched his every move, Frank got out of the car to stand in front of the man who might be Franz

Lechner. The man was half a head shorter than he, yet he gave the impression of looking down on the young intruder.

"What do you want?" the man asked again.

"Are—are you Herr Franz Lechner?" Frank managed.

"Yes." The man nodded curtly. "How do you know?"

"I—I—" Quickly Frank pulled a small photograph from his jacket pocket and handed it to the man confronting him. "Do you know that man, Herr Lechner?" he asked.

Lechner took the photograph and glanced at it. His eyes grew hooded. He stared hard at the photograph. It was a small portrait of Reichsleiter Martin Bormann. Both he and Frank knew that hardly any pictures of Bormann existed.

"Where did you get that picture?" Lechner asked with slow deliberation. He stared at Frank. "What do you want with me?" he asked once again—this time his voice tensely insistent. "Who are you?"

Frank's thoughts raced. He had to win this man's confidence. At least his tolerance. Or—this time—he would not make it into the car before the dogs would be upon him.

"I—I was told you were helpful to him," he said, his lips dry. "Many years ago. I—"

"Who told you that?" Lechner snapped at him. "Why are you here? How did you get that picture?" The questions slammed into him.

"From—from our family album," Frank blurted out. It was where all family pictures were kept, was it not? It was in his home. "I— I want to find out what really happened to—to my uncle!" The words seemed to tumble out by themselves. "I am the nephew of Martin Bormann."

He had not meant to say it. He had not planned to say anything like it. It—just came out. Suddenly his clammy hands grew icy cold. Would Lechner know? Would he know it was a lie? Would he know if Martin Bormann had no nephews?

Lechner stared at him. For a moment he stood in silence. Desperately Frank tried to read the man's thoughts. He could not.

"Come," Lechner finally growled.

He turned to walk toward the heavy gate, followed by Frank. And by the two watchful dogs.

Inside, Lechner slammed the massive door shut and barred it. Frank looked around.

The cobblestoned farmyard was ill–kempt and in bad disarray. Broken farm equipment and other debris and trash lay strewn about in piles, and a few scraggly hens pecked listlessly at the remains of a dungheap. The farmhouse, built of square stone blocks, stood to the right, heavily festooned with row upon row of dried corncobs hanging on the walls, through which grimy, multipaned windows looked out onto the squalid yard. A broom lay on the ground next to the door, but from the look of the place, it was never used.

They walked toward the house. Lechner was watching Frank closely. Suddenly he stopped. His hand shot out and slapped the pocket in Frank's jacket that held the little tape recorder.

Frank stopped dead in his tracks.

Lechner's eyes narrowed.

"A gun?" he rasped. "You carry a gun?"

Frank managed a shrug. "One must protect oneself, no?"

Lechner's lips stretched in a thin, mirthless smile. "Quite so," he agreed. He removed his right hand from his pocket. "I, too, have a gun, young man." He pointed a small, snub–nosed automatic at Frank, and gestured toward the house. "Inside," he said. "Inside."

Followed by the two wary dogs, the men entered the house.

The *Bauernstube* was sparsely and simply furnished. Lechner motioned to a straight–backed wooden chair standing at a large table that obviously had seen years of use.

"Sit!"

Frank sat down.

Lechner took a seat directly opposite him. Ceremoniously he placed his gun on the table and his hand next to it. He fixed his pale blue eyes on Frank.

"Now," he said tonelessly. "Now we find out why you are here...."

II

Frank sat staring at the gun. It loomed larger and larger, quickly filling his world with its silent menace.

Silent—for how long?

How had it come to this? It was not what he had anticipated when he first began his quest for knowledge, for facts and information.

How then?

It had all begun more than seven years earlier, as he sat shocked and sickened in front of his television set. The set had a thirteen–inch black–and–white screen, but the images seemed to wash across it larger than life and in searing color as he sat mesmerized, staring at it in his room in the family home on *An den Osterstücken* in Hildesheim, West Germany. What he saw and heard horrified him. It filled him with a mixture of resentment and disbelief. And questions. Mostly questions.

Could it be true? Could it have been so? Could such things have happened?

In *his* country? *His* people?

The program he was watching was an American–produced miniseries and it was broadcast over NDR, Norddeutscher Rundfunk, Program III, one of the lesser television stations in the Bundesrepublik, because the two larger networks were too apprehensive of it. He had turned it on more out of curiosity than with a purpose.

It was called "The Holocaust."

The year was 1979. Frank Brandenburg was just three weeks past his sixteenth birthday. He was watching a re–enactment of events that had taken place in his country more than thirty–five years earlier. He was watching a terrible account of the macabre and gruesome misdeeds perpetrated on some of his fellow countrymen during the time of Adolf Hitler's Third Reich. And he was appalled. Deeply shaken.

Could such atrocities really have happened?

How was it possible for an ordinary, uneducated Austrian fanatic to lead the German people—*his* people—so terribly astray?

What *were* the facts? He had to know.

The subject of the Holocaust, of the concentration camps, of the barbarism rampant in the Third Reich had been taught only in passing in his school, in a superficial mix of World War II, the Third Reich and its accomplishments, and the Jewish and Polish problems. So Frank's first step in what was to become his quest was to seek out his parents and put his questions to them.

Karl–Peter Brandenburg, a straightforward, uncomplicated man, owned and managed a large, successful nursery and landscaping firm, Gärtnerei Brandenburg, located on a few acres of land next to a neat and well tended cemetery, the Südfriedhof, in Hildesheim. Besides seven huge greenhouses, the largest nearly two hundred feet long and thirty feet wide, the area contained great open nursery areas, and spacious business facilities. The Brandenburg family lived in a large, white, two–story house with a black tile roof surrounded by trees. Here Frank was born on January 4, 1963.

Ilse Brandenburg, Karl–Peter's wife and Frank's mother, a pretty, soft–spoken woman, had been only three years old when the war came to an end, and obviously had no first–hand knowledge to give her son about events that took place during the time of Adolf Hitler. Karl–Peter had been less than eight years of age in 1945. He, too, could answer none of his son's questions. In fact, the whole subject made him uneasy. It was nothing he wanted to rake up and dwell upon.

The family also included Frank's paternal grandfather, Wilhelm, and his grandmother, Wilhelmine, always affectionately called Mimi, and Frank's sister Ulrike, three years younger.

Although not a Nazi Party member, Wilhelm had served in the NSKK—the Nationalsozialistisches Kraftfahrerkorps—the Nazi Motor Transport Corps. The primary function of this organization was to assist the police in traffic control and provide motor transport units and training services to supplement the transportation and training services of the armed forces. Frank already knew that the NSKK members wore brown shirts and black breeches, with the national eagle emblem mounted on a wheel enclosing a swastika, worn on the cap or on a black crash helmet. He had seen a picture of his grandfather wearing such a uniform.

But Wilhelm's duties had never exposed him to the horrors Frank described and about which he sought information, and he was loath to talk about the Nazi days. So here, too, Frank could find no answers to his questions.

The Brandenburg family belonged to the Evangelical Lutheran Church in Hildesheim, and although no mention of the Holocaust or similar subjects had been made during Frank's confirmation class, he approached his pastor with his questions. However, once again he was disappointed. The pastor professed to know little about the subject, and Frank was admonished not to dwell on such things. There were more important matters to pursue.

He went to his father's secretary, Fräulein Gertrud Bury, a lady of sixty–two, who obviously had lived through the times of Adolf Hitler, and of her he asked his questions about the Holocaust. She threw up her hands in dismay. "*Junge, Junge!*" she exclaimed. "You are treading on forbidden ground. It could be a dangerous thing to pursue. No one today wants to talk about all that. Leave it be."

Finally he went to his teacher at school, the Freiherr–vom–Stein Realschule, a woman who told him that there was no time to discuss all the unpleasantness of the past and reminded him that "you, young man, you have more important things to learn."

He talked to his friends, but none of them showed any interest or curiosity. It was something that might or might not have happened long ago. What could they do about it? "Let the past sleep," they advised him. "Let the past sleep."

But Frank had become even more disturbed than before he began his quest, and as he encountered obstacle after obstacle he became more and more determined to learn the facts. A whole chapter in his country's past was being kept from him, as if swept under a collective rug by everyone. "Let the past sleep"? He could not accept that philosophy. He felt that everything, even unpleasant things, must be examined in the light of day. If the unsavory past was allowed to wake up by itself, it might wake not like a lamb, but like a lion.

But—what *was* that past?

No one seemed able—or willing—to tell him.

He had, of course, already acquired several books on the subject, books he had not known existed before. But reading them had frustrated him even further.

Had the Holocaust taken place?

Inside the Third Reich, by Reichsminister Albert Speer, stated that it had. After reading the book Frank was full of questions, and he wrote a letter to Speer, who had been released from Spandau prison recently. He got a reply: Speer was too busy to answer his questions. Frank was disappointed but not discouraged. He kept on reading.

Hitler's War, by David Irving, was inconclusive on the subject, he thought.

The Auschwitz Lie, by Thies Christophersen, called the Holocaust an outright lie, concocted and perpetuated by the Allies.

And a pamphlet by Diplom Politologe Udo Walendy, published by Verlag für Volkstum und Zeitgeschichtsforschung—Publishers of National and Contemporary Historical Research, as *Historical Facts no. 15*, showed on page 34 a photograph of a crematorium at Birkenau with the caption: "Crematorium III at Birkenau, north side. Door with peephole. Includes chimney *erected after the war* [italics added]. There is no connection for smoke to pass from the ovens in the crematorium to the chimney. *Built in 1947* [italics added]. Photo 1980." And the pamphlet went on to say that the reports about concentration camps and extermination camps were falsified, as well as the photographs accompanying them.

A yes. A maybe. A no. Contradictions.

No concise picture, no truth emerged from his readings, and that was exactly what Frank sought. The truth.

The printed words he had read were contradictory, expressing either extreme with equal persuasion.

In his research he had run into several irreconcilable puzzles, in addition to the widely divergent reports on the Holocaust, and one of these especially intrigued him.

The enigma of Reichsleiter Martin Bormann.

Had he died in Berlin? Why did the reports of knowledgeable, reputable scholars differ so greatly?

Frank had learned a lot about Martin Bormann, known as "the Brown Eminence" because he always wore a brown uniform. During the reign of the Third Reich, Bormann had been one of the least visible Nazi leaders, least known to the world. After the Reich's collapse and the mystery surrounding his fate, he had become one of the most talked–about, most written–about Nazi personalities.

Martin Bormann, a short, squat man, was forty–four years old when he disappeared in Berlin on May 1, 1945. A school dropout and ex–convict, he had been sentenced to one year in prison as an accomplice of Rudolf Hoess in a particularly brutal murder of a political opponent. (Hoess was later to become the notorious commandant of the Auschwitz extermination camp.)

After serving briefly in an artillery regiment in World War I, Bormann in 1918 joined the Freikorps Rossbach in Mecklenburg, the same rightist organization to which Hermann Göring and Rudolf Hoess belonged. At twenty years of age he joined the Society Against Presumptuousness of the Jewry, and he was one of the first to join the NSDAP, the Nazi Party.

He became Reichsleiter of the NSDAP in October 1933, and was elected as a Nazi delegate to the Reichstag. From 1933 on he was chief of cabinet in the office of Deputy Führer Rudolf Hess. After Hess's ill–fated flight to England, Bormann was named head of the Party Chancellery, and in April 1943 became secretary to the Führer, positions he quickly consolidated until he exercised virtually total control over who saw Hitler and on what subjects. He was a witness to everything the Führer did or said. By then he was the most hated and feared man in the hierarchy of Hitler's Germany.

A master of intrigue and manipulation, he possessed an uncanny ability to capitalize on Hitler's foibles and personal idiosyncrasies, turning them to his own advantage. He was a relentless defender of Nazi orthodoxy and a fanatic anti–Semite who always championed the most extreme and most ruthless measures in the treatment of the Jews.

Bormann was sentenced to death *in absentia* for crimes against humanity at the Nürnberg Trials. Even the briefest summary of these crimes is horrifying.

In the six years from 1939 to 1945, Martin Bormann had been an "authoritative collaborator" in the murder and extermination of inmates in mental institutions, of Polish, Czech, and Russian prisoners of war, and of Jews. In this way he collaborated in killing at least five million people, one million a year.

Martin Bormann was definitely alive on May 2, 1945. After that, as Frank read the various reports, the picture became totally contradictory. On that day, the day after Hitler committed suicide in the Bunker, Bormann led a group in an attempt to break out of the beleaguered Führerbunker under the Reich Chancellery. It was the third such group to make the attempt. In his group were only a few high–ranking Nazis: Gen. Hans Baur, Hitler's personal pilot; the State Secretary, Dr. Werner Naumann; Dr. Ludwig Stumpfegger, one of Hitler's private physicians; and Martin Bormann himself. The others in the fifteen–man group were battle–seasoned soldiers.

Bormann was seen by SS-Standartenführer Erich Kempka, Hitler's personal driver, as the Reichsleiter made his way through the rubble–strewn streets of war–ravaged Berlin. Kempka reports seeing him and Dr. Naumann take cover behind a Tiger tank, the lead tank of a column of tanks that was moving toward a tank obstacle. Bormann and the others were on the left side of the tank when it received a hit on the right side and seemed to blow up. Kempka was rendered unconscious by the blast and when he came to he found that he had been temporarily blinded, so he did not actually see Bormann, Naumann, and the others killed, nor did he see their bodies. But he was convinced Bormann was dead.

But another SS officer, SS Sturmbannführer Joachim Tiburtius, had quite a different story to tell during his three years as an American prisoner of war. He, too, told of the tank being blown up, probably by a *Panzerfaust* fired from a window. He told that he had walked side by side with Bormann, and that he and Bormann had taken shelter on the left side of a tank, which then had received a direct hit on the right side. It had been at about 0200 hours on May 2nd. After the explosion the other tanks withdrew, and when the group of refugees started to move on, Bormann was still at his side, still in uniform.

And he testified that he then lost contact with the Reichsleiter, but ran into him again later at the Hotel Atlas, and that Bormann had changed into civilian clothes. They had begun to move on when he again lost contact with him.

"But the Reichsleiter had just as good a chance to escape as I did," he said. "And I am here."

And shortly thereafter an Italian named Luigi Sivestri, who knew Bormann by sight, swore he saw him in Bolzano in Italy on the tenth of May.

For the next couple of years reports surfaced of Bormann's having been seen alive in various European countries: in Italy, where he was supposed to be living as a monk in a monastery; then in Spain, Portugal, and Switzerland; in Austria, Yugoslavia, and Norway; and in Germany itself. Even in Australia. Bormann was sighted in a dozen or more countries in all, and in 1948, Walter Rapp, chief of the Evidence Division under Brig. Gen. Telford Taylor, who had been a wartime interrogator and an attorney at the war crimes trials, stated that he had proof that Bormann was alive and in Russian hands. It turned out that the driver of the tank behind which Bormann and the others had taken shelter had survived and was alive and well, and in 1950 Dr. Werner Naumann, who Kempka had been convinced died with Bormann in the Tiger tank explosion, surfaced and testified that Bormann had survived the blast also. The search for Bormann was stepped up.

Three years later the Italian publication *Il Momento* reported that Bormann had died the year before in Rome, while posing as an Alsatian tourist named Martin Robert, and had been buried in the Verano cemetery, outside Rome on the way to Tivoli. And in 1954 a German court declared Martin Bormann dead.

Then in 1960, after the capture of Adolf Eichmann in Argentina, Tuvia Friedman, chief of the Documentation Center on Nazi Crimes in Haifa, Israel, was quoted as stating that Eichmann had declared that Bormann was still alive and living in South America, a statement that was corroborated by one of Eichmann's sons, who said that his father had always spoken of Bormann as being alive. Shortly thereafter the Hesse state prosecutor, Fritz Bauer, launched a global manhunt that included all the South American countries in which Bormann had been sighted: Brazil, Bolivia, Paraguay, Josef Mengele's favorite hideout; Chile, Peru, and Argentina, where the largest group of ex–Nazis had congregated. And in 1964 the War Crimes Office in Frankfurt, obviously convinced that Bormann was still alive, posted a $30,000 reward for his capture.

In 1971 Reinhard Gehlen, Hitler's wartime spymaster against the Russians, who after the war had gone to work for American intelligence services, published his memoirs and claimed that to his knowledge Bormann, who had been spying for the Russians, had been in Russian hands and had died in 1968. At the same time several authors writing on the subject, such as Ladislas Farrago, who claimed to have definite knowledge that Bormann was still alive and living in South America, and the *Frankfurter Rundschau* in Frankfurt even published his address in Brazil. The puzzle that Frank was painstakingly trying to put together became even more muddled. The more he read, the more confused he became.

What *had* happened to Martin Bormann?

Then on December 8, 1972, two skeletons were found in Berlin by a cable–laying crew working near Invalidenstrasse close by the Wall, a spot only half a mile from the site of the Führerbunker. After examination, one of the skeletons was declared to be that of Martin Bormann, and the find gave new impetus to the mystery. Both skeletons had splinters of what might have been cyanide capsules lodged in their jawbones, indicating suicide. Dr. Hans Jürgen Spengler of the West Berlin Forensic Institute was convinced that the remains were those of Martin Bormann, and Dr. Reidar F. Sognnaes, professor of oral biology and anatomy of the UCLA School of Dentistry and Medicine, agreed when he was able to match the teeth found with the skeleton with descriptions obtained fifteen years earlier from dental assistants who had worked on Bormann's teeth. Powerful evidence, perhaps, but Frank also learned that Bormann's actual dental records, crucial to such identification, along with the records of other high–ranking Nazi officials, had been lost in a plane crash during the war, when a plane carrying them to a safe depository was shot down.

Many public officials cast doubts on the identification, such as several prominent Berlin police officials, who pointed out that the remains had been found in an area that had been meticulously searched already with no result, and they pointed out the convenience of the find at the exact time when German authorities were under pressure to produce Bormann—or a Bormann corpse. They pointedly suggested that certain officials were overanxious to come up with a dead Bormann so that they could tie up a bothersome loose end. And several scholars joined this skepticism, among them Ladislas Farrago, who claimed Bormann was even then living in luxury in Argentina; Stewart Stevens, a former *Express* foreign editor, and Simon Wiesenthal, Nazi hunter and head of the Jewish Documentation Center in Vienna, who said he still believed Bormann had escaped Berlin and reached Latin America, where he might still be alive.

However, Horst Gauf, the Hesse state prosecutor at the time, had accepted the identification of one of the skeletons as being that of Martin Bormann, officially pronounced him dead, and ordered all search activities discontinued, while at the same time other German law enforcement agencies renewed their efforts to find the missing Bormann.

Understandably, Frank was thoroughly confused. And intrigued. Each source, each expert on the fate of Martin Bormann sounded equally convinced and convincing. Each had impressive credentials. And each had a different story. A Russian prisoner of war...living in luxury in Argentina or Brazil...died as a tourist in Rome...seen in Australia...killed in Berlin during the breakout attempt...living as a monk in Italy...committed suicide...a seemingly endless list. All the stories seemed well documented, but only one could be true.

It had been one of the enigmas of the Third Reich that had spilled from the pages of the many books he had read in his determination to learn the facts. But after many months of reading, of supporting his expensive thirst for knowledge, which quickly exhausted his savings, his allowance, and the extra marks he earned by selling off some of his childhood possessions—toys, children's books, a cuckoo clock, and other belongings that had become expendable now that he had put aside childhood things, his "shop" being an old rug on a busy street in Hildesheim—he realized that reading books would not give him the answers he sought.

It was not enough.

How, then, could he learn whether the shocking deeds and actions he had seen in "The Holocaust" were true? if such inhuman concepts and acts were part of a dead or sleeping past—or were still part of the present? or the future? or it it were all made up?

He had to know. He had to break through the wall of silence he had battered his head against. And he realized he had to do it by himself.

He felt compelled to gain the knowledge he sought by any means at his disposal—the means of a sixteen–year–old boy, still attending school.

He had decided to get the facts, the truth, the realities from the people who had lived them, orchestrated them—the survivors of the Third Reich hierarchy.

And now—seven years later—it had brought him here, to the *Bauernstube* of Franz Lechner. And the gun on the table before him....

Seven years. It seemed a long time in the life of a twenty–three–year–old youth, and at the same time no time at all because so much had happened.

Unbidden, the memory of the day he had taken his first big step in his quest flashed into his mind. It had been his eighteenth birthday, Sunday, January 4, 1981, the day he came of age, the day he would be in full charge of his life. The decision had come suddenly, as he sat at the dinner table with his family.

"Tonight," he had announced calmly, "Tonight I am taking the night train to Munich."

His parents had been astounded. "*Um Gottes Willen!*—for God's sake, Frank. Why?" his father had asked.

"In all the books I have read," Frank explained, "Munich is the place where it all started. The whole Nazi movement. They even call it the cradle of Nazism."

He looked earnestly at his parents. "I want to see that cradle. I want to see if I can find out what that cradle held."

He had had no way of knowing that the events of the next few days would catapult him into the past.

III

Frank found Munich to be everything he had imagined the city to be. The town was founded in the eighth century on the banks of the Isar River; it was steeped in history. Renowned for its wealth of Baroque, Rococo, and neoclassical buildings, this "cradle of Nazism" still held many architectural mementos of the early days of the Nazi movement, too, including a couple of buildings erected during Hitler's ambitious but largely unrealized reconstruction program.

Frank went to see the house on Prinzregentenstrasse where the Führer had had his private apartment in the early days, and he had a spaghetti dinner in the Osteria Bavaria, an Italian restaurant in the Schwabing district of Munich, where Hitler had often dined. The owner showed Frank the table at which Hitler always sat, and while Frank ate, he wondered if Hitler might have used the very same cutlery he was using.

And he paid a visit to the Hofbräuhaus, often confused with the Bürgerbräukeller, torn down after the war, where Hitler had staged his notorious Beer Hall Putsch in November of 1923 in an attempt to start an insurrection in Germany against the Weimar Republic. The

Hofbräuhaus had not been damaged in the bombings and air raids that destroyed more than forty percent of the city.

He went to see the site of the Brown House, headquarters of the Nazi Party, which had been located on Briennerstrasse on Königsplatz, opposite the Glyptotek. Both the Brown House and the Glyptotek had been severely damaged during the war, although the museum's Egyptian, Greek, and Roman treasures had survived. The Brown House had been razed at war's end. From his reading Frank had learned that the Brown House was formerly the Barlow Palace, and boasted one hundred rooms. The building had been purchased by the party in 1930, the interior had been redone and the exterior refaced, and Adolf Hitler himself had designed and supervised the remodelling for party purposes, from the swastikas on the windows and the buff walls to the red carpets and green lamps. The house by then resembled the embassy of a major power, which in a sense it was; it was officially opened as the headquarters of the NSDAP on January 1, 1931.

Here had been the offices of Heinrich Himmler and Joseph Goebbels, and, on the first floor, those of Adolf Hitler. Frank had read descriptions of those offices, in which the fate of Germany had been plotted.

On the wall in back of Hitler's desk chair had been a portrait of Frederick the Great, the Prussian warrior king who was a hero to Hitler; on a pedestal in a corner stood a bronze bust of Benito Mussolini; and another portrait of Frederick the Great with a copy of his death mask adorned yet another wall. Opposite the desk hung a large painting of a World War I battle in Flanders. It had been said that it was the battle in which Hitler had fought and been wounded. Here in the Brown House the "blood flags" from the Putsch had been kept, to be used in Party ceremonies. They would be brought out to touch new Nazi flags, symbolically imbuing them with the vital force of the Party.

For Frank it had been a strangely sobering experience. The history of the world had been traumatically and eternally influenced by the decisions made in that building.

But, like a regular tourist, he had also visited the famous Frauenkirche with its twin cupola–capped towers, the landmark of Munich; the Feldherrnhalle, the Hall of Marshals, a copy of the Loggia dei Lanzi in Florence, standing on the Odeonsplatz at the south end of the Ludwigsstrasse, and he had, of course, watched the remarkable *Glockenspiel* atop the New Town Hall on Marienplatz. Fascinated, he had looked on as the spectacle unfolded: the golden rooster crowing the start, the trumpeters opening the tournament, the standard–bearers heralding the knights; the first charge—and miss, the second charge—and the unhorsing of the red knight, the red–coated folk dancers, the queen's blessing, and the rooster signalling the end of the pageant.

The next morning Frank was abroad early. He wanted to visit the Bavaria Film Studios, located in a peaceful wood in the Isar Valley on the southern outskirts of town. Although he had never seen them, he knew of the many motion pictures produced in Germany prior to 1945 with Nazi themes, glorifying the Nazi ideology, and he had seen stills from some of them, among them *SA Man Brand* and the UFA film *Hitler Youth Quex*. He knew that some of these films had been shot at the Bavaria studios, and he wanted to see the place. Some of the old sets might even be standing.

Frank took the tram to Geiselgasteig, where the studio was located at Bavariafilmplatz 7. He hoped there would be some kind of tour of the studio, but his hopes were quickly dashed when in answer to his query the burly guard at the studio gate told him to get lost. Only studio personnel could enter the studio grounds.

Disappointed, Frank walked back to the tram station. As he stood waiting, a tramcar arrived and a large group of people dismounted, all of them boys about his own age, thirty or forty of them, accompanied by a couple of older men. They at once started to walk toward the studio. Frank watched them walk away.

Should he?

Even before the question had been consciously formed he made up his mind. He caught up with them and as unobtrusively as possible he joined the group, keeping quiet, trying to look as if he belonged.

A special group, he thought. A cinematography class or something, which had made special arrangements to see the studio. They had arrived just at the right moment for him. At the gate, the guard overlooked him in the crowd—and he was on the studio grounds.

What now?

The best way not to call attention to himself right away would be to stick with the group. He did. And quite unexpectedly he found himself standing in line before what looked like a ticket taker's window. He wanted to ask one of the other boys what was going on, but he was afraid he would give himself away and be thrown out on his ear before he saw anything. So he kept quiet, trying to look as nonchalant as possible, doubting that he succeeded completely. And when he finally found himself face to face with an elderly woman wearing large horn–rimmed glasses, sitting behind the window, his heart was thumping in his throat.

"Name?" the woman asked briskly.

He told her.

"Age?"

Again he told her.

"Height?"

Puzzled, he answered her.

"Address?"

He hesitated only briefly before telling her.

"Getting them from the north country now, are we?" she muttered, as she recorded the information on a list. She peered up at Frank through her large spectacles.

"Two doors down," she said. "On your right. Next!"

Frank poked his head through the second door on his right. It was a barbershop. Four chairs, three of them occupied by boys from the group, the fourth one empty.

"Take a seat," one of the barbers told him, pointing to the empty chair. Automatically Frank sat down. At once a barber's cloth was fastened around his neck, and the insistent buzz of a pair of electric clippers filled his ears.

He tried to look in the mirror before him, but the busy barber obscured his view. Less than two minutes and it was over. Frank stared at the mirror, as the barber removed the cloth with a flourish.

He hardly recognized the image that stared back at him from the mirror. On both sides of his head the hair had been shorn so short it was barely visible, and it ended in a tuft of hair perched high on top of his head.

The barber pointed to one of the boys just leaving the shop. "Follow him," he said. "He knows where you go." He turned to the door and called, "Next!"

Frank followed the boy across the studio street to a small building. Inside, a man handed him a bundle of clothes. On top was a brown blouse with a red armband around the left sleeve. Frank recognized it at once. A white band circling the red, a black swastika on a square white field.

Hitler Youth!

And he knew now with certainty what he'd come to suspect—he

was in the movies! He was an extra about to take part in some Third Reich motion picture.

Makeup was next, and a bowl of hot soup to ward off the cold. Frank was enjoying himself immensely.

All the boys, now looking exactly like their counterparts in reality had looked forty years before them, were herded onto a big bus, which took them to the center of town, to the Haus der Deutschen Kunst— the House of German Art, and here they waited for the first scene in which they would participate. They were admonished not to leave the area, for obvious reasons, and to keep together as a group.

Frank was fascinated. This was a lot better than a studio tour. He began to ask questions, of his fellow "Hitler Youths," of anyone who would listen. He was no longer afraid that anyone would throw him off the set.

It was an American television production in which they would appear. An ABC special, he was told, based on the memoirs of Reichsminister Albert Speer, and called "Inside the Third Reich." Inwardly he marvelled. He had finished reading that book only a few days before. A man standing in conversation with another man at a big camera crane was pointed out to him. It was the American director. Chomsky was his name.

Frank had cornered one of the assistants from the German film crew and was asking him questions about the production when he noticed a man in the full regalia of a German lieutenant general. He was drinking a Coca–Cola out of the can.

"Who's that supposed to be?" Frank nodded toward the man.

"That's General Baur," the assistant said. "Hans Baur. He was Hitler's personal pilot."

Frank knew about Flugkapitän und Generalleutnant Hans Baur. One of the few people trusted by Hitler. One of the last to see him alive in the Führerbunker. The man to whom Hitler gave his most treasured possession just before killing himself, the portrait of Frederick the Great, the only painting to hang in his office in the Führerbunker. Hans Baur, one of the survivors of the Nazi hierarchy, as he may have looked forty years before, now portrayed by a German actor, drinking a Coca–Cola.

"I guess he does look like Baur did at that time," the assistant mused. "Although it's hard to tell. Baur is eighty–four now. And looks it."

Startled, Frank turned to him. "You've *seen* him?" he burst out. "I mean the *real* Baur?"

The man nodded. "Once. It was at the studio, I think. I guess it was in connection with this movie. But he hasn't been around since."

"He's here? General Baur is here? In Munich?"

"Yes."

"Do you know where? Do you know where he lives?"

The assistant shook his head. "*Keine Ahnung*—no idea."

Frank was excited. Baur was in Munich. He had to find out where. This was his chance to make contact with one of the close associates of Adolf Hitler. He looked around. Half a block away, still within the cordoned–off area, stood a telephone booth. He turned to the assistant.

"Are we about to go on?" he asked. "Do you think I'd have a few minutes?"

The assistant sagely surveyed the set. "More like a couple of hours," he said drily. "Waiting around is what you do most of in this business."

"Thanks."

Frank made for the telephone booth. A thick telephone book for Greater Munich was lying on a shelf. A broken chain with which it had been fastened to the wall dangled from it.

There were seven Hans Baurs listed. One was a lawyer, one was a manufacturer, and two had middle initials. That left three men listed simply as Hans Baur. One of them could be Hans Baur, Lieutenant General, Ret.

If he were listed at all.

Frank fished some coins from his pants pocket, grateful that he had had the foresight to transfer them from his own trousers to his Hitler Youth shorts. He placed them on the shelf before him and dialed the first Hans Baur. Surprised, he noticed that his hands were clammy.

He let the phone ring. There was no answer.

He made the second call. A woman answered, a young voice.

"Is this the residence of Herr Hans Baur?" Frank asked.

"It is."

"Is Herr Baur at home?"

"I'm sorry. My husband is in the Tyrol. On a skiing trip with his club. Who may I say called?"

It was obviously the wrong Baur, and Frank could taste his disappointment. Flustered he stammered, "Oh. I—I'm sorry. Nothing. It's—uh, nothing. I have the wrong number," he finished hastily, "please excuse me."

"Of course," the woman said pleasantly.

"Wait!" Frank blurted out. "Perhaps—perhaps you could help me?"

"How?"

"I—I'm trying to locate a Hans Baur, Flugkapitän Hans Baur. Would you by any chance know how I can reach him?"

There was a pause. "We have had a few calls like this before," the woman said, her voice suddenly cool and distant. "We do not know Herr Flugkapitän Hans Baur, nor where he can be reached. All I know is that he is supposed to live in Herrsching am Ammersee. Goodbye." And she hung up.

Herrsching! Only a few miles from Munich.

There was, of course, no telephone book with listings for Herrsching in the booth. He called information.

"Please," he said. "Do you have a listing for a Hans Baur in Herrsching am Ammersee?"

There was a pause.

"We have only one Baur listed," the operator informed him in her clipped, official tone of voice.

"Is that Hans Baur?"

"I do not know. The listing is only H. Baur. Do you wish to have the number?"

"Please."

The operator gave it to him. He dialed it. The phone rang several times. Frank was just about to hang up when a man's voice answered.

"*Baur hier.*"

Frank's heart leaped.

"Herr Hans Baur?"

"Yes. Who is calling, please?"

"Is this Flugkapitän, Generalleutnant a.D. Hans Baur?"

There was a pause, then: "This is Flugkapitän Hans Baur. Who is this please?"

Frank took the receiver from his ear. In awe he stared at it.

It was the magic instrument that would connect him with the past—a past he felt compelled to know.

IV

The forty–minute trip by S–Bahn, Munich's rapid transit system, to the picturesque little town of Herrsching on the Ammersee, a small lake some thirty kilometers southwest of Munich proper, seemed to Frank to take an age.

 After he had introduced himself to Baur on the telephone and briefly explained his interest in the Hitler era and his desire to know more about it, the retired general had readily agreed to see him and had invited Frank to visit him. A time had been set for the following day, Wednesday.

On his lap he held a large box of chocolates, a gift for Baur. It was Lindt chocolate, the same kind he had brought his girl, Herta, on their first formal date.

The incongruity of bringing the same gift to a former Nazi general as he had brought his girl never entered his mind. But his thoughts flew back to Herta. She had been his special girl for about a year now.

He had come to know Herta Brettmann* through his younger sister,

* Not her real name.

23

Ulrike, when Herta was seventeen years old and both girls were attending the Pädagogium Bad Sachsa in the southern Harz. He had liked her at once, her winning smile, her twinkling eyes, and most of all her natural honesty and total lack of hypocrisy. Born in Bremen, Herta still lived there. Their relationship had quickly grown to more than mere friendship, and were it not for his trip to Munich, they would have been together.

The Bavarian villa on Neuwiddersberg in which Hans Baur lived was painted white and had brown shutters. A big, well kept garden with a fountain led to the front door.

Tightly clutching his box of chocolates, Frank rang the bell.

The man who opened the door startled Frank: an old man, half a head shorter than Frank, with a pronounced beer belly, a jowly face and white hair thinly bordering a receding hairline. Clad in a wrinkled brown sweater, unpressed brown pants, and an open shirt, Hans Baur at eighty–four was a far cry from the dashing young officer, resplendent in the uniform of a lieutenant general of police, proudly shaking the hand of the Führer in the photograph Frank had seen.

"General—Baur?" he asked hesitantly.

"Herr Brandenburg," Baur said cordially. "Come in. Come in." He spoke with a pronounced Bavarian accent. He held the door open, and Frank entered a little hallway. From an adjoining room a little brown dachshund came running. It stopped short when it saw Frank and eyed him suspiciously. Then it came over to investigate his shoes. Frank thought it looked like his own little dachshund, Gritti, at home in Hildesheim. A woman followed the dog into the hall.

"My wife," Baur introduced her to Frank.

Frank politely acknowledged the introduction. He suddenly felt foolish clutching the box of chocolates. Impulsively he held it out to Frau Baur. "*Bitte, gnädige Frau*," he said. "With my compliments."

The woman beamed. She took the chocolates. "Thank you, young man," she said. "Thank you very much." She turned to her husband. "You have such considerate friends, Hans," she smiled.

"Come," Baur nodded. "We shall go into the living room, yes?" He led the way, walking with a decided limp.

Frank looked around, curious to see what kind of house a former Nazi general would live in.

The room was L–shaped, the short leg of the L serving as Baur's office. It was a neat, unexceptional middle–class home except for a few things. In Baur's office stood a bronze bust of Adolf Hitler, and on a table were displayed about a dozen framed photographs showing a younger Baur with such Fascist dignitaries as Rudolf Hess, Martin Bormann, Benito Mussolini and, of course, the Führer, as well as King Boris of Bulgaria.

On a wall, prominently displayed, was an engraving of Hitler, surrounded by paintings and photographs of old planes, World War II vintage. Scale models of such aircraft crowded Baur's desk. In the living room, prominently displayed on a wooden pedestal, a large bronze eagle, wings outspread in imminent flight, perched on a massive marble rock. Frank eyed it with curiosity. Baur noticed his interest.

"A gift," he said proudly. "From Lufthansa. From 1931. I was with them before I became the Führer's chief pilot." He pointed to a silver plaque mounted on the marble rock. "It says: To the tried and true Flugkapitän Baur in grateful acknowledgement of his services on the occasion of the one hundredth flight across the Alps." He chuckled. "It *was* rather spectacular, my young friend. Rather spectacular."

They all sat down in the living room.

Frank had no idea how to start. It was the first time he'd ever met an important former Nazi official, someone who was part of the history of the Third Reich, someone who once held real power in the land. And he was awed.

He had, of course, read about General Baur, but, he felt suddenly, not nearly enough.

He knew of Baur's close relationship with Adolf Hitler, and he knew of his distinguished achievements as an artillery observation pilot during the first World War. Rejected as an infantry volunteer at the age of seventeen, Baur had pulled every string in sight to get into the Artillery Flying Corps, and when his little observation plane had finally been armed, he had shot down nine French infantry fighter planes on his various sorties, after his observation duties had been successfully concluded.

Frank had been aware of Baur's service with Lufthansa even before he had seen the eagle award in Baur's living room; he had known that Baur had piloted Hitler around Germany on his election campaign tours during the early thirties, and that this fact had earned him the post of the Führer's chief pilot, a post he had held for thirteen years.

Baur leaned forward and looked expectantly at Frank.

"Now, young man," he said pleasantly. "What do you want from me?"

Frank looked back at him. He rather liked the man. A friendly grandfatherly sort of man, he thought, not at all what he had expected. He had to start. He plunged in.

"Adolf Hitler," he said. "You knew him well. What was he like?"

"*Unser Vati*—our Dad—was one of the greatest men the world will ever see," Baur said, a smile of fond memories curving his lips. "A true genius."

"Some people have called him—a monster," Frank ventured.

Baur chuckled tolerantly. "There has been much falsehood written about *unser Vati* by people who have never met him, much less known him," he said, a touch of mild admonition in his voice. "But the Führer was no stranger to me. I spent much time with him. He trusted me. He was truly a remarkable man, a kind and considerate man."

Frank took a deep breath and plowed on.

"But—what about all the stories I've read? The atrocities that took place in the concentration camps?" Frank asked, becoming increasingly bold. "Mass murders. Gassings. They say that Hitler knew all about that. Millions killed, they say." He swallowed. "They—they call it the Holocaust."

For a moment Baur contemplated Frank.

"My dear boy," he said kindly. "You *are* naive."

"How so, Herr General?"

"There were work camps, of course. Relocation camps for the many unfortunates made homeless by the indiscriminate Allied bombings, both in Germany and her sister countries. There were camps for certain criminals, as there are camps or criminal detention facilities in every country."

"But—I've seen pictures," Frank protested. "And a film. I've read books about what they call extermination camps. Like Auschwitz. And Bergen–Belsen. Books with pictures of people. Jews. Terrible pictures."

"It is true that many of the inmates of those camps were Jews," Baur shrugged. He leaned forward in his chair and looked earnestly at Frank. "The Jew is a curious creature, my young friend," he said softly. "He either hogs everything for himself at the expense of others, or he wallows in self–pity and degradation, both mental and physical."

Again he shrugged. "Of course one can get photographs of Jews that look—uh, terrible." Slowly he shook his head. "The horror stories you have heard about extermination camps, about mass killings and torture and atrocities are all lies, my boy, lies made up by enemies of Germany. Lies to discredit the Fatherland, so that it will seem right and just to the rest of the world to heap humiliation on our country."

He fixed his eyes on Frank's.

"Those camps you saw photographs of, those showcase camps one can still visit today, they were all built by the Allies *after* the war was over," he said earnestly. "They are nothing but manufactured false evidence against us."

Again he shook his head slowly, rather sorrowfully.

"Your Holocaust, my dear boy, is a lie. It never happened!"

Frau Baur, who had remained silent during their conversation, suddenly spoke up.

"I think our young visitor might like a cup of coffee," she announced cheerfully. "Don't you think so, Hans?" She smiled at Frank. "And some *Apfelstrudel*, yes? It is freshly made. I shall get it, while you two go on with your nice little talk."

She left the room.

"If you read as much as you say you have," Baur went on, "then you must also have read books that told you what I have just told you, is that not so?"

Frank nodded. "Yes. It is. But—"

Baur spread out his hands expansively. "Well then, there you are!"

Frau Baur returned with a large carved wooden tray. "I think you will like the *Strudel*, Herr Brandenburg," she said pleasantly. "It is my own recipe." She smiled at him as she placed the cups and saucers and some little flowered plates on the table. "A little extra of the really yummy things."

With a pair of silver tongs she placed a generous piece of strudel on Frank's plate. She showed him the beautifully sculpted tongs.

"A gift," she said proudly. "From the Herr Reichsminister Dr. Joseph Goebbels. He gave us such a lovely set of silverware. So sweet of him, *nicht wahr?*—not so?"

Frank nodded. He picked up his spoon to stir some cream into his coffee. It had the same ornate pattern as the tongs. Part of the Goebbels set, he thought. He had a sudden nervous urge to giggle. Here he sat, a little nobody from Hildesheim, stirring his coffee with a gift from Joseph Goebbels, the notorious Nazi minister of propaganda, the man responsible for the deluge of dogma aggrandizing Hitler's Third Reich!

The spoon suddenly felt hot in his hand. The coffee must be scalding, he thought. Better be careful, or he might burn himself. He put down the spoon and turned to Baur.

"Herr General," he said. "Why do you think Dr. Goebbels and his wife decided to—to die in the Bunker, with all their children, rather than to escape?"

Baur slowly shook his head. "Every man must make his own decisions," he said. "Every man has his own reasons for making them. He must live with them. Or die with them."

"And you, Herr Baur, you decided to break out."

Baur nodded. "I would have stayed with *unser Vati*, had he had need of me," he said. "But he had ordered me to stay with Reichsleiter Bormann."

"During the breakout?"

"Yes. And for as long as the Reichsleiter needed me."

"For what?"

Baur shrugged. "I do not know. I only know that the Führer had given Bormann special orders—a special mission. But I do not know what it was."

"What really did happen during the breakout?"

Baur got a far–away look in his eyes, as he transported himself back to that fateful day. His mouth grew tight and twitched almost imperceptibly a couple of times.

"As I told you," he began, his tone of voice curiously flat, "*unser Vati* had ordered me to stay close to the Reichsleiter." He knit his brow. "I never did like Martin Bormann," he said. "No one did. He always treated me well, but he was *eine undurchsichtige Persönlichkeit*—an opaque personality. Mistrusted. But it was he who determined the order in which we were to travel. Our group had only a few members of importance, the rest of the fifteen were ordinary soldiers."

He paused for a moment, lost in memories. Frank kept silent. He did not want to derail the man's train of thought.

"Naumann, the state secretary from the propaganda ministry, was to take the lead; Bormann would follow him," Baur continued. "After him would come Dr. Stumpfegger and then I." Unconsciously he hunched his shoulders. "I had the painting of Frederick the Great, the

Führer's favorite painting, which he had given me before he died, I had it rolled up and strapped to my knapsack. We all ran out together, but we had hardly reached the street when we were fired upon. Heavy small arms fire. We made it to the Weidendamm Bridge and then ran along the Ziegelstrasse, strung out in a loose file."

He stopped and looked directly at Frank.

"It was an inferno, my boy," he said softly. "An inferno. Pray God you will never see its like." He took a deep breath before he went on. "Berlin, our beautiful city, was dying," he said heavily. "Anyone who lived through that terrible experience will never forget. The images of horror, suffering, and destruction will return to him forever. Buildings had collapsed into the streets, vehicles were burning in the rubble, smoke and fire were everywhere. Power lines were down, lying twisted across the paths through the wreckage. There was no way of knowing which were live, which were not. Any moment I expected to be electrocuted. And we could hear the screams of the wounded even over the din of the enemy fire, which seemed to come from every window, every doorway, every place of hiding." Again he sighed. "We were quickly scattered," he finished. "I lost sight of Reichsleiter Bormann. I never saw him again. I saw no one again. But I am convinced that the Reichsleiter died in the hail of fire."

"Why do you think so?" Frank asked.

"Bormann is dead," Baur repeated with finality. "He wore a simple brown public official's uniform without insignia. He is most certainly dead, and buried in some mass grave along with all the others lying dead in the streets. His face was little known in those days. No one would have recognized him. He is dead."

"State Secretary Naumann survived," Frank protested.

Baur nodded. "I have heard of this. To this day it is inconceivable to me how."

"You survived."

Baur grinned disarmingly. "Barely, my boy," he said. "Barely." He slapped his leg. "And part of me did not."

Frank was about to ask how it happened, how Baur had lost his leg, when the ex–general continued.

"It was beginning to grow light," he said. "We were making our way along the S–Bahn tracks. We received heavy fire from the Reichstag building. We were running through a courtyard. We did not know that Russian sharpshooters had the portal under observation. I suddenly felt a violent blow slam into both my legs. I fell. And I screamed, my boy. I screamed.

"Someone dragged me into a burning building that offered some shelter. The front had been shot away. The bullet had gone clear through my right leg and shattered the left. Someone put a splint of scrap wood and old cardboard on the shattered leg and bandaged the other one. Only then did I realize I had also been wounded in the chest and in one hand."

He paused for a moment and looked at his wife sitting at his side. She reached for his hand and held it.

Frank sat spellbound.

"The building was burning fiercely," Baur went on in his strangely unemotional voice. "The others had all left, and I thought I would burn to death. I could not move. I had my pistol—and I was about to end it all, when the fire began to subside. I stayed there, lying on the floor, hoping that the bullets ricochetting through the ruins would not find me, listening to the cries and screams of the wounded and dying all around me. Finally a Russian soldier appeared. After relieving me of my watch and my beautiful Walther pistol, he had me taken to a field hospital."

"And the Russians operated on you?"

Baur shook his head.

"No," he said slowly. "They did not. When they learned my rank, my position, they interrogated me. They demanded I sign statements. For one week—seven long days and seven long nights—they interrogated me."

"Without tending to your wounds?" Frank was appalled.

"With a minimum of care, my dear boy, a minimum of care. They left the bullet embedded in my bone. They just encased the whole leg in plaster of Paris." He grinned. "I guess they didn't want to look at the mess while they were questioning me. They didn't even tie off the veins. The plaster was quickly bright red."

"Then—how—?"

"I was finally, grudgingly, taken to a hospital. In Posen. But the doctors could no longer save the shattered leg. It—it had to go. Unfortunately they had no instruments. No scalpels. No surgical saws. Nothing." He looked at Frank. "They took off my leg with somebody's pen knife."

He patted his artificial leg. "But—I survived. I survived to spend more than ten years as a prisoner of the Russians. Ten years of beatings and floggings, until I could no longer stand, even with crutches—on the single straw shoe I had been given for my good leg."

"But—why?" Frank asked. "What did they want?"

"Something I could not give them," Baur said soberly. "Nonexistent facts about something that never happened." He shook his head as if still incredulous at what he had had to endure for nothing. "They thought I knew something I did not know. Could not know. They thought that if the Führer *had* escaped from the Bunker *I*, as his chief pilot, would have flown him out. The Americans thought that, too."

"But—how could they?" Frank asked, perplexed. "How could they think that? You were still in Berlin. You were caught in Berlin."

"*Ganz richtig, mein Junge*—quite right, my boy. But they were idiots. They insisted I had returned to Berlin. To provide an alibi." Again he shook his head. "They believed it was the Führer's double who had been taken from the Bunker, to be burned and buried in the Chancellery garden."

"Hitler's double? Hitler had a double?"

Baur nodded. "It is quite probable. But only a handful of his closest associates knew of this. I know only that they found a man in Breslau who looked and sounded exactly like the Führer. And General Rattenhuber, who at that time was head of the Reich Security Service, asked me to broach the subject to the Führer of occasionally using a double at an appropriate occasion."

"Did you?"

"I did."

"What did the Führer say?"

"He laughed. He said he was not Stalin. He did not need a double."

"Then—nothing came of it."

Baur shrugged.

"All I *know* is that Rattenhuber later on said to me, 'Baur, we have him. He is here.'" He looked at Frank out of the corner of his eye. "I do not *know* if Hitler's double existed, or if he was ever used, or on which occasions. I only *believe* so."

"Could you have flown the Führer out of Berlin? Even at that late hour?"

Baur nodded emphatically. "Even on the night of April 29th, the day before *unser Vati* left us forever, I could have flown him to safety.

He had summoned me. To tell me to leave—and, as I said before, to stay with Reichsleiter Bormann. I told the Führer then that I could still get him out. I told him I could still fly him to—to anywhere he would want. He refused to leave the last bastion of his Third Reich."

He looked soberly at Frank. "Perhaps, had he known what was in store for me, he would have let me stay, he would have let me follow him, as I always had."

"But—when you *did* try to escape, it proved impossible. The Russians captured you. Would that not have happened to Hitler as well?"

"The breakout was more than a full day later. The situation had changed enormously."

Frank nodded. "The Russians kept you for ten years," he said. "Why so long? Other prisoners of war came home much earlier. Why so long?"

"I was declared a war criminal. I was a special case," Baur said, a sardonic smile on his lips. "They expected to change history with me. They expected me to tell them that Adolf Hitler was still alive. They expected me to tell them where he could be found." He shrugged. "I did tell them. In the ground in the Chancellery garden. But they did not believe me.

"I was dragged from prison to prison, from camp to camp, each with a new set of interrogators determined to make me tell them about something that never happened. I was constantly beaten. I was deprived of sleep. I was tortured. They even tried to bribe me. But, of course, I could tell them nothing.

"During those ten years I often regretted I could not have stayed with *unser Vati* and shared his fate, his ultimate sacrifice for the Fatherland. It was what I had wanted to do. Finally I could stand no more. I made up my mind that I *would* follow the Führer—one way or another, my boy, one way or another."

He sighed again. "But it is not easy to do away with yourself when you are being watched constantly. They found the little knife blade I had honed carefully from a small piece of scrap iron, and when I decided to stop eating they force–fed me. Day after day a thick, rough tube was forced through my nostrils or my throat until everything was like bloody raw meat. Even the Russian doctor, listening to me scream, had tears in her eyes as she carried out her orders. At last the pain was too much for me and I lost consciousness. While I was out they fed me through that damned tube. Even that way out was denied me."

The remembrances were obviously beginning to take their toll. Baur turned away from Frank, who sat in silent engrossment, watching him. He stood up and walked over to the bust of Adolf Hitler. For a moment he stood motionless before it. Then, without turning away from it, he spoke.

"He was a great man," he said solemnly. "A great man, my boy. One of the greatest the world will ever know." Slowly he turned to look at Frank. "If history had been written by anyone other than the enemies of the Reich *unser Vati* would have gone down in history as a giant among men."

He walked back and sat down next to his wife. He looked straight at Frank.

"If only you could have known him," he said, "you would have agreed. His trials were far greater than mine, his resolve much stronger."

He took a long look at his wife, who sat beside him, head bowed, hands in her lap on top of the box of chocolates she had been nibbling.

"I am proud that I behaved myself as he would have wanted me to," Baur said, "when I was in the hands of the enemy." He frowned lightly. "Only once did I waver in my determination. When they threatened to use my wife against me..."

Frau Baur looked up. She reached over and put her hand on her husband's knee.

"No, Hans," she whispered. "No."

Baur placed his hand on hers. Gravely he nodded. *"Doch, Schatzl."* He used the Bavarian idiom for "darling." "He should know who the barbarians really were. He should know...."

V

Baur, we have a little surprise for you!' an MVD officer said to me one day," Baur went on, his face grim. For the first time Frank detected a suppressed anger in his voice.

"'Your wife will soon be sent here. If you insist on keeping your mouth shut, then—before your very eyes—we will tear her pants down. If that is not enough, we will flog her. And if you still refuse to talk, we will turn her into an army whore! Talk now—and we will forget all that.'"

Baur stopped. He swallowed hard. Frank did not dare say a word—or look at either Baur or his wife. He kept his eyes averted.

"By the grace of God they did not get their hands on her," Baur said softly. "Or on my daughter, which they had threatened to do." He looked up at Frank, his eyes dark. "*You* talk about a holocaust, a holocaust that never happened. I talk about real barbarism."

He sat up, erect, his posture suddenly reminiscent of a bygone military bearing. He seemed to shake himself mentally, as if to dislodge the past.

"You told me you were researching the Hitler times," he said. "You must have heard what I have told you about the so-called Holocaust from others."

Frank shifted uneasily on his chair. "Well, you see, Herr Flugkapitän," he stammered. "I *am* doing the research, but—but you are the first person I have talked to."

Baur stared at him for a brief moment, then he laughed out loud. The little dachshund that had gone to sleep at his feet startled awake, and looked dolefully at Frank, the stranger in the midst of her world who must have been responsible for disturbing her nap.

"We must remedy that, must we not?" Baur boomed heartily. "I know a few people who I am certain can be of help to you."

Frank picked up. "That would be most helpful of you, Herr Flugkapitän. Most kind."

"Let me see," Baur mused. "There is Rudel. Hans Ulrich Rudel, our most decorated war hero. I am sure you know of him."

Frank nodded eagerly.

"And von Below. Nicolaus von Below, the Führer's Luftwaffen-adjutant. He was in the Bunker with us." He thought for a while. "There are others," he said. "Important personalities. They value their privacy. I will find out if they will talk to you, and I will write you."

"I am most grateful, Herr Flugkapitän."

"*Schon gut*—that's fine. I shall give you the addresses of Rudel and von Below. I think you will find them both interesting to talk to." He turned to his wife.

"*Mutti*, don't you think our young friend would like to have a piece of your *Apfelstrudel* to take along on his trip back to Munich? There will be plenty left for us."

Frau Baur smiled brightly. "But of course," she said. "I shall wrap up a nice large piece for Herr Brandenburg."

Munching on his strudel as he sat in the S–Bahn, Frank was elated. He had had no trouble getting to talk to General Baur, and he felt he had learned a lot. And from someone, someone important, who was actually part of it, actually *there!* From the horse's mouth, as the saying went. Although Baur had reminded him more of an amiable St. Bernard.

It would be easy, he thought. His quest for real, first–hand information would present no problems. No problems at all.

He had enjoyed his motion picture acting job, and on top of it all, the 170 DM he had earned as a Hitler Youth for a day would come in handy in his future search for the truth about the real Hitler Youths, and the rest of the spawn of the Third Reich. It had been a *prima* trip.

And it was only the beginning.

He had decided which of the two men whose names Baur had given him to call on first. Rudel lived in the Tyrol in Austria, von Below in Detmold in Westphalia, only about seventy–five kilometers from Hildesheim. An easy hour's drive. He would call von Below on the telephone first, as he had done with Baur, and then drive over to see him.

He had only sketchy information about Hitler's Luftwaffe adjutant. He knew that Col. Nicolaus von Below had been with Hitler at the Wolfsschanze—the Wolf's Lair, the Führer's headquarters near Rastenburg in East Prussia—on July 20, 1944, when the bomb meant to kill the Führer exploded in the conference room. It had been von Below, a bloodied and deafened von Below, whom Hitler had sent to the telephone exchange to summon Göring and Himmler to the headquarters, and it had been von Below who had closed down the exchange and forbidden any operator to go near the equipment, so that news of the assassination attempt could be delayed until the official version had been decided upon.

And Frank knew that von Below had served the Führer faithfully for eight years and had been present in the Führerbunker in Berlin while Hitler had been in residence there, not only as the Führer's Luftwaffe adjutant, but as of May 1944, also as Munitions Minister Albert Speer's liaison officer. Von Below had belonged to the inner circle of Hitler's associates, and had been present at the Führer's marriage to Eva Braun and the following reception for a few intimates. He had finally left the Führerbunker around midnight of April 29th, the last officer to leave before Hitler's suicide, entrusted by the Führer with one of the three executed copies of his personal last will and testament.

A few days later Frank made a telephone call to Nicolaus von Below.

The former Luftwaffe adjutant to the Führer listened politely to Frank's explanation of his interest in matters pertaining to the Third Reich, and how Flugkapitän, Generalleutnant a.D. Hans Baur had been gracious enough to tell him how to make contact with the Herr Oberst von Below.

Von Below was courteous and correct, but he firmly declined any request to meet with Frank or allow him to visit his home in Detmold. He even doggedly yet diplomatically turned away any attempt by Frank to question him via the telephone.

"Perhaps at a later date more convenient to you, Herr Oberst," Frank tried.

"Perhaps, Herr Brandenburg," von Below answered noncommittally.

"One last question, please," Frank said. "Could you by any chance suggest others with whom I might be able to talk? Or meet? The Herr Flugkapitän Baur gave me a few such names. It was most helpful."

There was a moment's silence.

"I shall consider your request, Herr Brandenburg, and be in touch with you by letter."

It was a tactful but unmistakable dismissal.

Frank was disappointed, but far from discouraged. A minor setback, that was all. And he rather enjoyed overcoming setbacks. It always gave him a feeling of accomplishment.

He thought back to the time at the Freiherr-vom-Stein Realschule when he had tried to get his school to devote some informational instruction and discussion to what had occurred during the reign of the Nazis. His suggestion had fallen on deaf ears, as had his request that his class be allowed a field trip to the notorious concentration camp, Bergen–Belsen, which was located near Celle not far from Hildesheim. He had not allowed himself then to take no for an answer. He had persuaded two of his classmates to work with him on a term paper entitled "The Persecution of the Jews in Hildesheim," which would have to be discussed in class, as was every term paper. Later, he had also written to several elected German officials, asking them to state their opinions on the Third Reich for an article to be published in the school paper, the *Abitur Zeitung*. Not one of the politicians had responded to the question, although they had all stated how valuable their contribution could be for Germany's future. The article was left unwritten, but the term paper had generated some discussion as well as earning a good grade for Frank and his two friends. It had all been quickly forgotten, however, by everyone. Except by Frank. What he had learned while doing research for the term paper strengthened even further his resolve to learn the facts and the truth first–hand. He had told himself, it may not be easy but you must stay with it.

He had not given up then, and he had no intention of doing so now.

He was in the midst of planning his next step when a few weeks after his telephone conversation with Luftwaffe adjutant Col. Nicolaus von Below, a letter on von Below's personal stationery arrived. Frank's mother, Ilse, who brought him the letter, looked at it in raised–eyebrow curiosity. But she said nothing.

Eagerly Frank opened the envelope.

A brief note included two names: SS-Obersturmbannführer Richard Schulze–Kossens, Waffen SS adjutant to the Führer; and Chief Press Officer Heinz Lorenz, of Goebbels' Propaganda Ministry, both of them living in Düsseldorf. Both of them minor personalities, Frank felt. But at least Lorenz, as Hitler's permanent representative for the Reich press, might be an informative contact. Frank had seen the man's name frequently in his research, and he knew that because of his position he had been in the thick of things, and had often been the first harbinger of news of—to Hitler, at least—momentous events.

It was Lorenz who, during the eve of Sunday, December 7, 1941, had burst in on one of Hitler's after–dinner gatherings to announce the bombing of Pearl Harbor by the Japanese, and that the U.S. and Britain were at war with Japan. Hitler had been elated. He had slapped his thighs in glee and cried, "This is the turning point! Now it is impossible for us to lose the war!"

It was he who had brought Hitler the news, heard on a BBC broadcast as reported by Reuters, that Reichsführer SS Heinrich Himmler had offered to surrender Germany to the Allies. Hitler had been infuriated and had raged against his erstwhile trusted friend.

And it was Lorenz who had brought the Führer the news that the American and Russian armies had linked up near Torgau on the Elbe River—and had promptly quarreled over who was to occupy what territory. Hitler had been gratified and encouraged. It was obvious to him that it showed great disunity among the Allies. They would soon be at each others' throats, he had felt. No time for Germany to give up now....

Lorenz had been instructed to take down verbatim all the historic war conferences of the final days in the Bunker. He had attended them all and he had carried out his orders as best he could. His notes, begun the afternoon of April 23d, 1945, had, however, been fragmentary. Perhaps in person he would have more to tell.

And Lorenz had been one of the men trusted by the Führer with carrying important final instructions to Admiral Doenitz in Flensburg, who had been chosen to be Hitler's successor. Miraculously Lorenz had escaped Berlin, but he had never delivered the documents entrusted to him; he simply kept them in his desk drawer. Only because he talked too much and boasted of the "secret papers" in his possession were they discovered by the Allies.

Yes, Frank thought. Chief Press Officer Heinz Lorenz would make a most interesting subject for his quest.

He decided this time not to call without preparation, but to write first instead. In a book he had found a photograph of several high–ranking Third Reich personalities, including Lorenz, posing with Hitler at the New Year's celebration at the Berghof in 1938. He had it copied and enlarged and sent it along with a letter requesting a meeting. In due time he got his reply.

It was not what he had expected.

VI

The letter was brief and to the point.

"*Sehr geehrter Herr Brandenburg*," it began, "Most honored Mr. Brandenburg..."

And it went on: "Please understand that I cannot comply with your request as a simple matter of course; I should first like to know something about your background.... How do you come into possession of the photograph? Do you know on what occasion the photo was made and when? Why do you assume that I am pictured in that photo?

"And further, as to your person: do you collect these photographs from the Third Reich for historical purposes? Have you any connections with right radical or so–called neo–Nazi circles?

"Please answer these questions truthfully....I should not like to become involved in some kind of affair because of the possible circulation of photos from the Third Reich. I look forward to your response with interest."

Frank sat staring at the letter. It was not at all what he had expected. Not at all. Suddenly the tables had been turned. *They* wanted to know about *him*. It was something he had not anticipated. The Baur meeting had been so simple, so easy. But after von Below, and now Lorenz...

Was he going to be able to pull it off? Was it worth it?

He leaned back in his chair. Gritti, his little dachshund, somehow sensing his mood, jumped up on him, licked his hand, reassuringly curled up, and snuggled down in his lap.

Absentmindedly he patted her. "Gritti," he said. "What do you think? It is not going to be as easy and straightforward as I thought. But then hardly anything is. And I do want to learn everything I can. First–hand. It is important to me. But that means getting close to a lot of people who might not want you to get close to them, right? Should I chuck it? Or should I go on?" He smiled down at the contentedly dozing dog. "Wag your tail," he said. "Once for no, twice for yes."

He scratched the dog affectionately behind her ear. Gritti sighed with well–being—and her tail wagged several times.

"Can't make up your mind either, eh old girl?" Frank chuckled. "That was either a whole bunch of nos, or a whole bunch of yesses. Guess it's still up to me to decide where to go from here." He sighed. "But one thing is sure," he went on. "Lorenz is a bust. He'd never open up—with his attitude."

He knit his brow in thought. He let his eyes roam the room. His room. Located on the top floor of the family home, it was small and shaped like a lean–to with a slanted ceiling.

His eyes moved past the little TV set which he could watch from his bed and on which he had first seen "The Holocaust." When? Ages ago...past the four–foot–tall potted plant he had had since it was only a foot tall...past the framed pictures of antique automobiles on the walls and the two colorful oil landscapes and the signed Dali lithograph...past the big yellow ceramic sun with its broad smile, almond–shaped eyes, and radiating rays, and the family pictures, including a framed photograph of his great–grandfather on his grand-mother Mimi's side, in the uniform of an officer in World War I, and sporting a huge *Schnurrbart* moustache...past the plane and tank models, vintage World War II, and the bookcase with his books and stamp albums coming to rest on the framed motto his parents had brought him from Austria when he was eleven. He read it. For the umpteen hundredth time...

Ein bißchen mehr Friede
und weniger Streit,
Ein bißchen mehr Güte
und weniger Neid,
Ein bißchen mehr Wahrheit
immerdar und viel
mehr Hilfe bei Gefahr!
Ein bißchen mehr „Wir"
und weniger „Ich",
Ein bißchen mehr Kraft,
nicht so zimperlich!
Und viel mehr Blumen
während des Lebens,
Denn - auf den Gräbern
sind sie vergebens.

A LITTLE MORE PEACE
AND LESS CAUSE TO FIGHT,
A LITTLE MORE KINDNESS
LESS LEANING TOWARD SPITE,
A LITTLE MORE TRUTH
ALWAYS AT HAND,
AND MUCH MUCH MORE HELP
ANY THREAT TO WITHSTAND.
A LITTLE MORE "WE"
AND LESS OF THE "I,"
A LITTLE MORE STRENGTH
NOT JUST "LET IT GO BY."
AND MANY MORE FLOWERS
WHILE STILL WE'RE ALIVE,
THEN—PLACED ON OUR GRAVES,
THEY NEED NOT SURVIVE.

More kindness. More helpfulness. More truth. He believed in that. He also knew that most of the people whose lives he wanted to touch would not....

More strength not to let it go by? He sat up, startling Gritti, who once again began to lick his hand.

No. He would *not* let it go by! He would continue his quest—wherever it might take him.

He had two names. Those of the Waffen SS adjutant to the Führer, SS Obersturmbannführer Richard Schulze–Kossens, given to him by von Below, and the super–ace, Oberst der Luftwaffe Hans Ulrich Rudel. Either of these two men might be able to further his quest, if in no other way than to steer him toward someone else, someone of greater importance.

Rudel lived in the Tyrol, Schulze–Kossens in Düsseldorf, much nearer. His choice was dictated by geography–and by his pocket book. Besides, he was preparing for his *Abitur*—his graduation—and could not afford to undertake the fairly long trip to Austria.

Frank knew little about Schulze–Kossens outside of the fact that the officer had been on Foreign Minister Joachim von Ribbentrop's staff during the negotiations in Moscow in 1939, which resulted in the infamous Hitler–Stalin Pact; he was, in fact, the last surviving German officer present at that meeting.

Frank decided to write a letter to the ex–adjutant to the Führer. For days he labored over it, rewriting it several times to make certain he would not be turned down again. At last it was ready. He took it personally to the post office to send it. When he returned home the mail had arrived. There was a letter for him. The sender's name and address were on the back of the envelope:

Flugkapitän a.D. Hans Baur
8036 Herrsching/Ammersee
Neuwiddersberg 38

He tore it open.

It was a brief note. It contained three names and addresses and the puzzling non sequitur *"Bormann ist tot und gefallen*—Bormann is dead and fallen."

That's it, Frank thought. The man who broke out of the Bunker with Bormann himself says he is definitely dead.

End of case...or was it?

And there was something else. Something that had been nagging at the edges of his mind ever since his talk with Baur. Something about someone else who was supposed to be "definitely dead." What was it? What the hell was it?

It suddenly flooded his mind. Baur's letter had apparently served as the catalyst.

The Führer! Adolf Hitler!

Baur had told him that for years the Russians had kept him imprisoned, interrogated him, tortured him, to get him to tell them if he had flown Hitler from Berlin to safety.

Why?

Why had they gone to such lengths of brutality when they had told the world they possessed the Führer's body? retrieved from the Chancellery garden? If that had been the case they would have known that Hitler had not escaped. It they were certain they *did* have the body. If they were certain...

Reluctantly he put it aside. For now. He knew it would keep on nagging him.

He frowned at the letter before him. And now, Baur was insisting that Bormann had died. Briefly he wondered why Baur felt compelled to stress that assertion again. He had already stated it quite firmly during their meeting. He wondered if Baur's protestations could be

described by the observation expressed by the Queen in William
Shakespeare's *Hamlet*, when she watches the Player Queen belaboring
a point: "The Lady does protest too much." Did the General protest
too much? What did he really *know?*

Baur had not actually seen Bormann killed, either by enemy fire
or in the tank explosion. He only assumed he had died. Furthermore,
Naumann, who had been with Bormann and also close to the blast
when the tank was hit, had survived. And so had Baur himself. Then
why not Bormann, too? Could it be that declaring Bormann dead was
the best safety measure that could be taken to protect him if he *were*
alive? He wondered.

But he dwelled on it only briefly. He was studying the three names
supplied him by Flugkapitän Baur:

> Ministerialdirigent Heinrich Heim
> Ungererstrasse, Munich

> Reichsstatthalter, Gauleiter Rudolf Jordan
> St. Paul Strasse, Munich

> SS Oberstgruppenführer Karl Wolff
> Wilhelminenstrasse, Darmstadt

Excitement built in him as he stared at the last name on Baur's list.
SS Oberstgruppenführer Karl Wolff, who had had a rank exceeded
only by that of Field Marshal. One of the truly important personalities
of the Third Reich: general of the Waffen SS; Chief of the *Lebensborn*,
the Nazi breeding homes; chief of the Bureau of Ancestral Investigation; chief of the SS Hauptamt, the personal staff of Reichsführer
SS Heinrich Himmler, and his personal adjutant; Höchster SS und
Polizeiführer—Highest SS and Police Chief—for all of Italy, a position
created especially for him by Himmler and Hitler; and mainspring of
Operation Sunrise, which resulted in the surrender of all the German
forces in Italy. Frank had seen Wolff's photograph many times during
his research. Whenever there had been a picture of Hitler and two
high–ranking officers, it seemed that one of those officers was always
SS Oberstgruppenführer Karl Wolff. He was a man never in the
limelight but always there.

Darmstadt was only about thirty kilometers south of Frankfurt am
Main, a comfortable four–hour train ride from Hildesheim. Frank had

written a letter to the general. He had watched his mailbox impatiently for weeks, but had received no reply. Finally he had followed up his letter with a telephone call, and General Wolff had consented to see him.

He had prepared for his visit carefully. In a book about Adolf Hitler he had found a color photograph taken in 1937 of an *Erntedankfest*— a Harvest Thanksgiving Celebration—in a town called Brückeburg near Hameln on the Weser River, which showed Karl Wolff with Himmler, Bormann, and Hitler, surrounded by an enthusiastic crowd of gaily dressed, "Heil–Hitlering" people. He had copied it and enlarged it to poster size to bring as a gift for the general. It rested safely, rolled up in a three–foot cardboard tube.

On the day of his appointment he went directly from his school to his grandmother's flower stand, where he was scheduled to help out before taking the train to Darmstadt later in the day. In a canvas bag he had his school books, a change of underwear and clothing, his toothbrush, his camera, and his tape recorder. He was all set for his important meeting.

The woman who opened the door in answer to Frank's ring was in late middle age and quite plain, with straw–blonde hair worn in a straight bobby-cut. "*Servus, Herr Brandenburg*," she said, to Frank's surprise using the colloquial Bavarian greeting. "Please come in."

She watched him with curiosity as, juggling his three–foot cardboard tube and stuffed canvas bag, he stepped into the small hallway. The Wolff apartment was warm. Perhaps a little too warm. Frank was glad. It was a cold autumn day and there had been something wrong with the heating system in the railroad car. He was frozen. It had been a shivering experience changing from his dirty clothing into his fresh underwear and shirt in the chilly, cramped railroad car toilet. He had managed, though, and his soiled laundry was crammed into his bag. But he had gotten so cold that for warmth he had huddled down in his coat as best he could, once back in the compartment. Perhaps that was why he had dozed off. Unfortunately, before he did he had forgotten to turn off his tape recorder after checking the batteries— and they had gone dead. Luckily the machine had a cord attached. All he had to do was plug it in.

"I am Edeltraut Ziegmann," the woman said, "a friend of Karl Wolff's." She gestured toward the living room. "This way, please."

Frank entered the room.

Under a golden chandelier too large for the room several oil paintings hung on the walls, all dwarfed by the life–size, gold–framed, full–figure painting of General Wolff himself, resplendently impressive in full SS-Obergruppenführer uniform, which dominated the room as the presence of its subject must have done in earlier days.

Frank gazed in awe at the commanding figure.

Unbidden, what he knew about the man swept through his mind.

Karl Friedrich Otto Wolff was born in Darmstadt, the very town in which he now made his home. As a lieutenant of the Guards in World War I he had earned the Iron Cross, both first and second class, and from 1918 through 1920 he had been a lieutenant in the Freikorps Hesse.

In 1931, in the infancy of the NSDAP, he joined the Party, and already two years later he had become an important SS leader. He served for a brief time as adjutant to the National Socialist governor of Bavaria, Gen. Ritter von Epp, before becoming Heinrich Himmler's personal adjutant.

Wolff rose rapidly in the ranks of the SS, reaching the powerful rank of SS-Oberstgruppenführer in a scant eleven years, being awarded the Golden Party Badge as well as several decorations along the way up, and ultimately being appointed to many posts of top importance.

In 1943, in the middle of the war, Wolff became military governor of Northern Italy and plenipotentiary to Mussolini; but in 1945 when he became convinced that Germany would lose the war, he established contact with Allen Dulles of the OSS. In secret meetings held behind the Führer's back, an operation code–named Sunrise, he negotiated the early surrender of all German troops in Italy, six days before VE–Day.

Because of this action he was not tried at Nürnberg, where instead, unlike other high–ranking officers, he was allowed to appear as a witness before the court in full military uniform. However, in 1946 he was sentenced to four years hard labor by a British tribunal. He spent only one week in prison.

After his release he established an advertising agency in Cologne that became very successful, and from his considerable earnings he built himself a magnificent two–story villa with a broad lawn that swept down to the shore of the idyllic Starnberger Lake just north of the Bavarian Alps. Wolff was often respectfully referred to as that rarity, "an SS general with clean coattails."

But in 1962, as evidence against him surfaced, he was arrested, and in 1964 he was sentenced by the Munich County Court to fifteen years penal servitude for his complicity in the murder of at least 300,000 Jews sent to the Treblinka death camp, and for his participation in the shooting of partisans and Jews behind the front near Minsk, where he had been present as Himmler's chief of staff.

Because of his "otherwise blameless life" and his contribution to shortening the war, his sentence was commuted and he was released in 1971 after serving only half his time.

Frank tore his eyes from the painting. He looked around the room. A far cry from the splendors of the Starnberger villa, he thought.

He was suddenly aware of a man sitting in a chair across the room. He got up as Frank looked at him. A slight man with a receding hairline and a strangely elongated face, it was obviously not General Karl Wolff.

Edeltraut Ziegmann introduced him. "Herr Brandenburg, this is Herr mmmu–mmmum." She mentioned a name, but Frank did not hear it. A little taken aback, he wondered—who were these people? Where was Wolff? He was about to ask to have the name repeated when the man made a short, quick bow in his direction and Edeltraut Ziegmann said, "Please have a seat."

They all sat down, the Ziegmann woman near the man with the unintelligible name, facing Frank.

The so–far–nameless man eyed the long, unwieldy cardboard tube Frank was holding awkwardly on his lap along with his bag.

"May I ask, Herr Brandenburg," he said pointedly, "what is in that—that container?"

"It is a picture," Frank answered him. "A rolled–up picture. A little gift for the Herr General.

"May I see it?"

"Of course." Frank handed him the tube.

While the man and Edeltraut examined the tube, hefting it and peering at the folded–in ends, Frank put his bag on the floor next to his chair. As he did, he noticed an electrical outlet in the floorboard. *Prima!,* he thought, *Just what I need.* Quickly he opened his bag, pulled out the tape recorder cord, and plugged it in. A quick glance told him the recorder was going. On record. He left the bag open.

The man handed the tube back to him. "Thank you," he said.

"*Bitte*—you're welcome," Frank said politely. Again he was about to say that he had not understood the man's name, when Edeltraut Ziegmann spoke.

"How old are you, Herr Brandenburg?"

Frank was taken completely off guard. He stared at the woman.

"Nearly—uh, twenty, *gnädige Frau*," he stammered. It was only a small lie. After all, he would be twenty in a little over a year.

The woman smiled at him. "I see," she said. To Frank her voice dripped with doubt. "And how did you come to know General Wolff's address? and telephone number?"

"Flugkapitän, General Hans Baur gave the information to me," Frank explained, on safer ground. "When I visited him in Herrsching."

"I see," the woman said again. She exchanged a brief glance with the nameless man. "And why do you wish to speak with General Wolff?"

"I am interested in the time of the Third Reich, Frau Ziegmann," Frank quickly explained. "I am doing research on it." He warmed to his subject. "I have read a lot about it, but everything is so—so contradictory. So confusing. It is difficult to learn the facts. The truth. So I thought—I thought, if I could get to talk to someone, someone important and knowledgeable, someone who *really* knows, then I could learn a lot." He looked ingenuously at the woman. "Someone like Flugkapitän Baur. Or General Wolff."

"Do you pursue your—your interest alone, Herr Brandenburg? or do you have—associates?"

"Oh—alone."

"Are you a journalist? A reporter?"

"Oh, no. I—"

A sudden audible click came unmistakably from Frank's bag. Both the man and the woman started, their eyes darting toward the bag.

"What was that?" the man exclaimed sharply.

"Oh—I'm sorry. It's nothing," Frank said. "It's just my tape recorder. The tape ran out." He tried to hide his embarrassment by bending over the bag. "I'll—I'll just turn the tape."

"Tape recorder!" the man and woman exclaimed in unison.

Frank looked up. "I'll only be a second."

The man rose to his feet. He walked over to the bag and unceremoniously pulled the cord from the wall socket. "I must ask you, Herr Brandenburg," he said stiffly, "*not* to do any tape recording while you are here."

"Of course," Frank agreed. Flustered, he began to stuff the cord into his bag. "Please excuse me."

"What else do you have in that bag?" the man asked.

"Oh, nothing," Frank mumbled. He looked up at the man looming over him. The man stood silent, fixing his eyes expectantly on Frank.

Frank felt himself blush. Dammit! "It's—it's only my—uh, my laundry," he said sheepishly. "And some books. And—my camera." He deliberately left out the toothbrush.

Edeltraut Ziegmann and the nameless man exchanged glances once again. The man sat down.

"You said that Flugkapitän Baur gave you General Wolff's address," Edeltraut Ziegmann said.

"Yes," Frank answered her, grateful to change the subject away from his dirty laundry.

"Did Baur give you any other names?" The man had an unpleasantly high–pitched voice.

"Yes, Sir." Dammit, he wished he knew the man's name. But it was too late to ask now. He felt uncomfortable.

"Who?"

"Ministerialdirigent Heinrich Heim," Frank answered. "Reichsstatthalter, Gauleiter Rudolf Jordan and Luftwaffenadjutant Nicolaus von Below. And Rudel," he added. "The Luftwaffe ace, Oberst Hans Ulrich Rudel."

"Did you see any of them?"

"No, Sir. Not yet." He did not want to talk about his turndowns by von Below and Lorenz. "Not yet. But I intend to."

"You will find Colonel Rudel quite a formidable man, Herr Brandenburg. I can vouch for that."

Frank quickly turned toward the new voice. He knew at once.

The voice had to belong to SS Oberstgruppenführer Karl Wolff.

VII

The man who stood in the door to the living room was tall and well built, and he carried himself erect and with assurance. His hair was silver, his face craggy with deep wrinkles or character lines that bore witness to his eighty–one years of hard living. His mouth was straight and thin–lipped, his grey–blue eyes disturbingly penetrating. He wore a dark suit with an open shirt. In the photos Frank had seen of him, taken forty years earlier, he had cut an imposing figure. He still did.

Karl Wolff walked over to Frank and offered him his hand—a large, strong hand. Frank shook it.

Wolff turned to the anonymous man. "Thank you," he said. "That will be all."

Even that short sentence, spoken in a low, authoritative voice, made it obvious to Frank that he was in the presence of a man used to giving orders—and having them obeyed.

Wolff turned back to Frank.

"I must apologize to you, Herr Brandenburg," he said disarmingly. "Twice. First for not answering your kind letter." He spread his huge hands. "You must forgive me. But letter writers seem to be legion. Especially these days. One simply cannot answer them all." He gestured

51

hospitably toward the sofa in the living room. "Please," he said pleasantly. "Sit down."

Frank took a seat on the sofa. Wolff sat down beside the Ziegmann woman.

"And secondly," he went on, with a little smile, "for subjecting you to that little—interrogation." He shook his head regretfully. "Unfortunately it is necessary to be cautious."

Frank looked puzzled.

"You could have been—a Mossad agent, Herr Brandenburg. Israeli agents are everywhere." Wolff laughed amiably. He grew sober. "Fact is, I *have* had threats. More than once. That is the other not–so–pleasant side of the coin."

He leaned forward toward Frank. "Now, young man," he asked, "how can I be of help to you?"

Frank fought to regain his composure. The strange interlude of questioning and Wolff's rather melodramatic appearance had unnerved him. He felt a pang of misgiving. He hoped he would be able to cope better in future confrontations. He would. After all, he was still new at it. But—how to begin? He quickly decided to use the "Holocaust" film approach again, and he told Wolff about seeing the motion picture on television—and expressed his desire to know the facts.

Wolff solemnly pursed his lips. He nodded pensively.

"The concentration camps did exist, my boy," he said slowly, as if carefully weighing his words. "It cannot be denied. Most were work camps, resettlement camps, to which men and women were transferred, evacuated from specific areas to offer some relief from intolerable situations." He frowned. "But, in other camps, certain—people *were* afforded special treatment, their numbers reduced, as it were. But not to the highly exaggerated extent claimed by some elements today." He fixed his penetrating eyes on Frank. "Personally I had nothing to do with these—these camps. But I am convinced that what the Führer had in mind when they were established was the correct thing for Germany and the German people."

Frank watched the earnest man sitting opposite him. He listened to his words, and a word he had read in a fascinating book, *1984*, came to his mind. Doublespeak. According to General Wolff, the inmates, or victims, of the concentration camps had been evacuated or transferred, removed from intolerable conditions—not arrested, abducted, or deported; and they had been resettled, afforded special treatment, and their numbers reduced—not killed or murdered, not shot or gassed.

"But—" Frank began. Wolff held up a hand, silencing him.

"I know what you are about to say, young man," he said, his face grim. "I have heard it too often before. Yes, I was convicted and imprisoned for the very crimes you wish to know about." His eyes bored into Frank, as if willing him to believe the words spoken at him. "You must not believe everything you hear or read—or sometimes even events that happen. Often they are not what they appear to be. My sentencing? My imprisonment? My—guilt? It all came about at a time when Germany, responding to the pressures of international Jewry, belatedly conducted a rash of so-called war crimes trials. They needed warm bodies to convict. Preferably warm bodies of importance. I fitted that need, and I was available. But guilty? No! I was guilty only of doing my duty. I never had anything to do with the elimi-nation—the killing of Jews. My duties involved many things, but never that. Not that, young man."

He spread his hands. "However, the court elected to believe the lies put out by the international Jewish community. It was the fad of the times—and I became one of its victims."

Frank regarded with wonder the distinguished elderly man sitting across from him. What he said seemed so logical, so plausible. Could it be true? Wolff seemed so straightforward, so believable, a man easy to like—and trust. Were his hands clean? Or had he been guilty of the crimes he had been accused of? It is, of course, possible to be guilty, he thought, without dirtying one's hands. Or coattails.

"In reality," Wolff went on, "I helped many Jews leave Germany when life here became—difficult for them. That is a known fact. One of them, as a matter of fact, was the world–renowned banker, Baron Louis de Rothschild. That is even part of the Nürnberg trial records. Does that sound like the deed of a war criminal?"

Not knowing what else to do, Frank shook his head. "No, Herr General," he muttered. But he couldn't help wondering what the super–wealthy Rothschild might have given Wolff in return for the favor. He'd love to know. But it was not something he could ask about.

He suddenly remembered the picture he had brought as a gift for Wolff. He hauled the tube out from behind the chair where it had joined his bag. He handed it to the general.

"Please," he said. "I took the liberty of bringing you a small gift. I hope you will like it."

"How very thoughtful of you," Wolff said. He did not, however, seem surprised. He opened one end of the tube and pulled out the enlargement. He spread it out on the table, placing an ash tray at each end to keep it from rolling up. For a moment he sat staring at it, a strange, faraway look on his face.

"Those were wonderful days, my young friend," he said quietly, his voice unsteady. "Wonderful days." He looked up at Frank. "How very, very thoughtful of you," he said again.

"It is my pleasure, Herr General."

Wolff gazed at the picture again for a brief moment, as Edeltraut leaned over to take a look. Then Wolff took a deep breath and seemed to shake himself mentally. He turned to Frank.

"There must be something besides the Jewish question that you would like to know about," Wolff suggested. "What might that be?"

Frank gave a little cough. "There is, uh, one thing, Herr General." He struggled to keep from blushing. "It is about the—the *Lebensborn.* Since I read about them, I have wondered. You—you were head of the *Lebensborn* operation." He swallowed. "Some of the books I have read called them Nazi stud farms. One even Himmler's Whorehouses." Dammit, he *was* beginning to blush. "What—what were they really like?"

Wolff pretended not to notice Frank's embarrassment.

He smiled at him. "Not what you have read about them, I am certain," he said. "And probably not what a young man's imagination might make of them. They were the creation of Reichsführer SS Heinrich Himmler. He was always most interested in keeping the Aryan blood line of the German people pure. In 1936 the SS became the sponsor of the *Lebensborn*, and three years later the Reichsführer issued his famous edict."

Frank looked puzzled. "Famous edict?"

Wolff nodded. "Issued to the SS. Charging them with the responsibility of fathering children before going into combat. Married or not." He thought for a moment. "I think I remember what he said: 'winning victories by our swords and our blood makes no sense, unless they are succeeded by the victories of children and the occupation of new land.'" He looked at Frank. "So, to facilitate the 'victory of children,' pure Aryan children, he created the *Lebensborn*. They were homes, usually situated in beautiful surroundings, in the mountains, at lakesides, where young Aryan men and women could meet, and, without the encumbrance of marriage and the resulting responsibilities, produce beautiful, healthy babies of pure ancestry. Superior children for the Reich. And for the Führer. That is why the program was called *Lebensborn*—Fountain of Life. The young mother was given the best of care all through her pregnancy and the birth of the child, before her child was placed in a clean, well run, state–subsidized *Lebensborn* institution." He smiled at Frank.

"The *Lebensborn*, however, were not places rampant with lechery and debauchery. There was no smoking. No drinking. And the rules were strict. Once a young man, usually a rising young SS officer or non–com, once he had picked out a girl to be the mother of his child, there was no playing around. It was not some sexual free–for–all, despite what you may have read in your sensation–seeking publications."

"Were the men only from the SS?"

Wolff shook his head. "From among the racially pure and healthy. Of course the SS men were the cream of Germany's youth, so most of the fathers were SS. But there were young men from the Navy and the Wehrmacht as well."

"And where did the girls come from?"

"From all walks of life. Many from the BDM; others were young women who wanted to serve their fatherland. Still others were selected young girls from occupied countries who were healthy and looked particularly Aryan. And the *Lebensborn* supplied other services, Frank." He gave Frank a quick look. "May I call you Frank?"

"Of course, Herr General," Frank said, pleased.

"They also served as homes for other children. Children of sound racial background who could be reclaimed from parents who were undesirable, for political or other reasons. The *Lebensborn* would provide homes and care for such children as they were being rehabilitated. And there were children from occupied territories, such as Poland, for instance, who possessed the right characteristics and were racially suitable for removal from their parents and integration into German life through the *Lebensborn*. As you can see, these institutions, these homes had many worthwhile functions."

"You were Reichsführer SS Himmler's personal adjutant for many years—"

"Ten."

"—for ten years. What was it like?"

"Hard work, Frank," Wolff smiled. "Work that carried great responsibilities. Demanding work, although not all the time. There were opportunities for other activities at times. The Reichsführer SS thought it of great importance to keep physically fit. He demanded that all his SS personnel take part in some form of sports. He himself played tennis, usually doubles. And always with a good partner. The Reichsführer SS did not like to lose." He smiled at Frank. "I was quite often his partner. In that, too."

"One more thing, Herr General," Frank said. "Reichsführer SS Himmler did not survive the war, of course, but others did. I am interested if you, Herr General, know if Reichsleiter Martin Bormann survived?"

Edeltraut Ziegmann suddenly sat bolt upright. She glared at Frank.

"*Bormann ist tot!*" she cried, her insistent voice growing more strident with each cry. "He is dead! He is dead! He is dead! There is nothing more to say!"

Wolff leaned over and gently patted the woman's hand.

"*Schon gut, Edeltraut*," he said softly. "*Schon gut.*" He turned to Frank. "There are some things that it is not wise to discuss," he said. He stood up. The interview had come to an end. Frank rose too.

"Thank you, Herr General," he said. "It was kind of you to see me."

Wolff took Frank's hand in both of his. It disappeared in the big man's grasp.

"It was my pleasure, Frank," he said. He seemed to mean it, and Frank believed him. He turned to the Ziegmann woman.

"*Gnädige Frau*," he said politely, making a short bow.

She responded with a slight nod.

Wolff walked Frank to the door, past the imposing painting of himself.

"Perhaps we shall meet again," he said. "Perhaps another time we shall discuss—other matters. When we know each other a little better, yes?"

"I should be honored," Frank said. "You are most kind."

"Nonsense," Wolff dismissed it expansively. "It is my pleasure."

Frank was turning to leave when Wolff stopped him.

"One more thing," he said, keeping his voice low, as if to prevent it from carrying into the living room. "If you are that interested in Reichsleiter Bormann, you might try to talk to Heim, Ministerialdirigent Heinrich Heim. He lives in Munich. In the Schwabing district. On Ungererstrasse, I believe." He looked closely at Frank. "He was Bormann's adjutant—had an honorary rank in the SS. SS-Standartenführer—SS Colonel, I believe, and I understand he has several papers written by the Reichsleiter in 1945 which he tells me have never been seen by Allied authorities." He eyed Frank. "I understand Hans Baur also mentioned him to you."

Frank had a quick thought. Wolff *had* been listening as the Ziegmann woman and the man the general called Otto had questioned him. Wolff nodded confidentially at him.

"You might find Heinrich Heim—interesting."

The train ride back to Hildesheim gave Frank a chance to compose his notes and evaluate his meeting with SS-Oberstgruppenführer Karl Wolff, while it was still fresh in his mind.

It had been an ambivalent meeting, he felt. Wolff was charming and enormously likable. It was difficult—no, impossible—to believe that he had been party to the murder of hundreds of thousands of innocent people. Yet, unless a terrible miscarriage of justice had taken place, that was exactly what he had done.

And it had been an ambiguous meeting. He had been fascinated by meeting this ex–member of Hitler's inner circle and listening to what he had to say, but Wolff had really said nothing. Nothing new, anyway. Nothing that really shed light on anything. He had made it sound important. But had it really been? He decided not. Wolff had been expansive in his display of cordiality, but reserved in his imparting of hard information.

However, Frank had a strong hunch that his contact with Wolff ultimately would yield significant information.

And there was the matter of Heim. Ministerialdirigent Heim. Both General Baur and General Wolff had mentioned him as someone worth seeing. He decided to make a second trip to Munich as soon as he could.

Spring had come to Munich, and the Münchners had shed their winter overcoats as they walked the streets, now empty of snow; and in Hildesheim the Michelsengymnasium was closed for a short vacation. It was a beautiful, sunny day as Frank stood before the address Heim had given him when Frank had called him for an appointment. "'My office," the Ministerialdirigent had called it.

It looked more like an old *Luftschutzkeller*—an old air raid shelter left over from the war, Frank thought, with a massive iron door and bricked–up windows.

In fact it was.

Christmas and New Year had passed quietly and uneventfully in Hildesheim. Frank had had a long talk with his uncle and godfather, Norbert Renczewitz, who had been a party member and a Wehrmacht Feldwebel—Sergeant—in the war, and had fought on both the western and eastern fronts. Wounded at Stalingrad, he had been one of the last men to be evacuated before the German military collapse. Norbert had never before talked with Frank about his war days, and Frank was fascinated. "The most gruelling days of my life," his uncle had said. "The most gruelling days of any man's life." In response to Frank's inevitable question about the Holocaust, his uncle had grown reticent. He believed it did happen, he had said, but he did not know about it until after the war. "It was the only thing the Führer did that was wrong," he had said regretfully. About Bormann and his possible survival he had professed to have no knowledge—and no opinion.

Frank looked at the forbidding iron door. The man behind it, the man who had been Reichsleiter Martin Bormann's personal adjutant and had belonged to the inner circle of Hitler associates, would know. He felt certain of it.

He knocked on the door. Each knock boomed hollowly.

Ministerialdirigent Heinrich Heim opened the door himself. An unimpressive man, Frank thought, with white hair and pale blue eyes, and a fleshy, jowly face that looked surprisingly robust for his eighty–one years. Clad in a simple, almost shabby slate–gray suit with a black tie not quite drawn up, he stood aside to let Frank in.

Frank entered the room. The first thing he saw was a picture that hung on the wall facing him—a color photograph of a man.

He gaped at it.

It was the last person in the world whose picture he had expected to see.

VIII

The place was indescribably cluttered. Untidy stacks of papers, documents, and file folders covered every available surface. Dozens of legal binders leaned in disarray against books and pamphlets. File boxes filled to overflowing were stacked haphazardly in the corners, and electrical cords, draped over battered filing cabinets and disorganized bookcases, converged on a littered, white–painted desk with an orange clamp–on lamp.

The unpainted concrete walls had art posters and pictures clipped from magazines tacked up wherever they were bare of the many exposed pipes, ducts, and electrical conduits that ran both vertically and horizontally along them. A few panel boxes, one of them an open fuse box, were also mounted on the walls, and displayed in a prominent spot was the startling color picture, cut from a magazine—a portrait of a smiling Elvis Presley!

Frank was astounded. Why would the former adjutant to the second most influential man in Nazi Germany have a picture of Elvis Presley on his wall? Was he a fan? The kind of musical performance that was Presley's trademark hardly seemed to fit Ministerialdirigent Heim. Did he know him personally? or what? Frank was dying to know, but he didn't have the nerve to ask. Not yet.

At Heim's invitation he stepped into the chamber. The heavy iron door clanged shut behind him. For a split second he feared it would stay shut permanently, imprisoning him forever in the cluttered, claustrophobic cubicle.

"You must forgive the bit of untidiness," Heim said apologetically. "There is so much to do." He cleared some papers off a small stool. "Please sit down." He walked to a chair behind his white desk.

Frank looked around the room. Except for a few books on Third Reich or World War II themes there was nothing to indicate Heim's important Nazi past. Yet Frank knew the man had been one of the very early Nazi Party members.

Still apologetic, Heim swept a hand across the amassed filing binders. "Legal records, Herr Brandenburg," he explained. "Even though I am now retired from my practice, there is so much to do, putting everything in order." He smiled tentatively at Frank. "You seem to find my office somewhat unorthodox?"

"Oh, no," Frank protested quickly. "I mean—it *is* unusual. It *is* an old *Luftschutzkeller*, is it not?"

"It is."

"But, why, Herr Heim, why are you still in an air raid shelter? It— it does seem odd." Involuntarily he glanced at Heim's shabby suit, a glance that did not go unnoticed by the Ministerialdirigent. "It— *is* unusual."

"You wonder about my premises, young man. And about my simple clothing." He smiled, a mirthless smile. "In my home I have more than twenty of the best suits money can buy." He grew sober. "But I elect to stay here, and to wear what I do—in memory of the disgrace of having lost the war!"

Again he smiled his mirthless smile. "As a matter of fact, I rather like it here. I call it my cave."

He fixed his pale eyes on Frank. "But I am certain you did not come here to discuss my premises or my sartorial preferences, Herr Brandenburg. Why did you wish to see me?"

"My interests are about the time of the Third Reich, and I know that you were one of the first to join the NSDAP."

Heim nodded slowly. "That is correct."

"What made you join?"

Heim did not answer at once. Instead he opened a drawer in his desk, rummaged around in it and came up with a small card. He handed it to Frank. "You might like to see this," he said.

Frank took the card. It was dog–eared and discolored, but it was obviously a membership card in the NSDAP, no. 1782, for Heinrich Heim, dated 1920 and signed by Adolf Hitler. Gingerly, Frank turned it over in his hands. Heim had indeed been one of earliest Nazi Party members.

"*Hoch interessant*," he said. And he meant it. He gave the card back to Heim. "Have your—opinions of Adolf Hitler and what he stood for changed since that time?"

Heim slowly spread his hands before him. "One man can never agree with another completely," he said.

Frank tried again.

"How did you and Hitler—disagree?"

"One can disagree with another without cavilling specifics," Heim answered after a short pause. "It is sometimes a matter of esoterics."

Whatever he meant by that, Frank thought. Aloud he said, "About what the Allies call the Holocaust?"

Heim steepled his fingers before him and slowly tapped his finger tips against each other.

"I had no knowledge of what has been claimed about what you call the Holocaust, young man," he said deliberately. "I did not learn of these claims until after the war."

"Do you believe them to be true?"

"I do not think that even A.H. had knowledge of anything like what is claimed to have happened."

It was quickly becoming obvious to Frank that he would get no direct answers from Heim. The man's cautious lawyer mind apparently prevented him from saying anything that could not at some time, in some way, be explained away if need be. He decided to change his questioning to something he knew Heim could not circumvent.

"General Wolff told me," he said, "that you had in your possession some documents written by Martin Bormann, which have not been seen publicly or examined by Allied authorities."

"Did he." It was an acknowledgement rather than a question.

"Yes. Do you?"

Heim contemplated Frank pensively. Again he steepled his fingers and tapped the finger tips. Finally he said, "As you undoubtedly know, young man, M.B. gave me the task of compiling and recording the speeches and remarks made by A.H. at various meetings and func-tions."

There it was again, Frank thought. Not Martin Bormann or Adolf

Hitler, but M.B. and A.H., as if referring to them by initials rather than by names made Heim less their intimate. He had a momentary recollection of his mother spelling out words she did not want him to understand. He suppressed his sudden impulse to laugh.

"Yes," he said. "And I have seen the book that was published on your work, about Hitler's monologues. But I understood you had certain material which was not published in that book. Is that correct?"

Again Heim studied Frank for a moment before he spoke. He takes his time, Frank thought, still like a lawyer censoring what he wants to say to be certain no rash mistakes are made.

"My reports span the time from 1941 through 1944," Heim said at last. He tapped his finger tips together. "But I do have a few pages, fifty or sixty of them, notes dictated by M.B. for the month of February 1945—just before—the end."

"About the Führer's speeches?"

Heim nodded slowly. "About the speeches of A.H."

"Have they been published?"

"To the best of my knowledge, no."

"But you did not use them in your book?" Frank asked. "*You* did not show them to—to anyone?"

Heim shook his head. "I did not."

"Why not?"

For a moment Heim regarded Frank speculatively. Then he shrugged. "My reasons are unimportant," he said. "Suffice it to say I did not."*

"You were very close to Reichsleiter Bormann, were you not?"

"I was his adjutant for three years."

"Do you think the Reichsleiter survived the breakout from the Bunker?"

Heim fell silent. Finally he stood up, walked to a bookcase, extracted a records box, opened it and pulled out a sheaf of papers about an inch thick. He walked over to Frank and gave him the papers.

"This is a copy of the notes M.B. gave me," he said. "Quoting the speeches of A.H. during February 1945."

Frank took the papers. They were typewritten. The first page was headed: *FHQu Berlin*—Führer Headquarters, Berlin—*4 Februar 1945*.

* Bormann dictations from the month of February 1945 were published in 1981 by Albrecht Knauss, Hamburg, under the title, *Hitler's Politisches Testament*.

He leafed through them. One sentence caught his eye: "One day Germany will emerge from this struggle stronger than ever! But England weaker and more contemptible...." And another: "I deliberately spared the British at Dunkirk, but Churchill was too stupid to recognize my gesture of goodwill."

Fascinated he looked up at Heim. "May I have these pages? Long enough to read them?"

"You may keep them." Heim walked back to his chair at his desk.

Frank was delighted. He did not expect to find any earth–shaking discoveries in the notes dictated by Bormann—certainly not since Heim had given them to him. But it would be intriguing to read the thoughts expressed by Hitler only a few weeks before his suicide.

"What do you think of what the Führer had to say in the many conversations you, yourself, quote in your book? and what he says here?" He tapped the Bormann notes. "What is your opinion of his ideas?"

"They were nothing short of brilliant, young man. Nothing short of brilliant."

Emboldened by Heim's generosity and sudden candor, Frank decided to pose his Bormann question again.

"Herr Heim," he said. "You did not give me an answer about Reichsleiter Bormann having survived. Do you think he did? Do you know?"

Heim sat silent for a brief moment, his eyes closed. Then he rose from his chair.

"There are some things it is unwise to discuss," he said.

He walked around the desk to Frank, who had also stood up.

"Perhaps—perhaps you will call me, or visit me again. Later. Perhaps we can then—talk again."

To Frank the implication was clear. Heim would check him out. At least with General Karl Wolff.

"Meanwhile," Heim said quietly. "Perhaps it would be best if you kept our conversation and what I have told you confidential, yes?"

Frank nodded. "Herr Heim," he said. "You have been most generous with your time. Could you perhaps suggest someone else with whom I could talk about the old times?"

Heim frowned in thought. Frank had a mental image of a long series of names flashing through Heim's mind like the symbols on a slot machine until one or two "safe" ones clicked into place.

"I know Henriette von Schirach," Heim said slowly. "The widow of Reichsjugendführer–Reich Youth Leader—Baldur von Schirach. She lives here in Munich."

He looked at Frank. "And, of course, there is Albert Bormann, M.B.'s brother, Gruppenführer Albert Bormann. He, too, lives here. I can give you his telephone number."

"I should be most grateful," Frank said.

At the door they shook hands. Over Heim's shoulder Frank could see the picture of Elvis Presley, smiling from the wall. He had to ask.

"Herr Heim," he said. "Forgive me, but why do you have a picture of Elvis Presley on your wall?" He pointed to the photograph. Heim turned to look at it.

"Oh," he said. "That. The granddaughter of a friend of mine gave it to me. It was obviously one of her treasures. I thought it a pleasant enough young man, and I put it up to please her."

He turned to Frank.

"Who *is* Elvis Presley?"

Frank had trouble falling asleep. It wasn't the strange hotel room, nor the big–city noise rising from the streets below.

It was excitement.

It was working! His quest was paying off!

Already he had talked to several high–ranking personalities, men who had been influential in the affairs of the Third Reich, who had known the Führer intimately, and who had been important in his concepts and stratagems. And already he was beginning to form an image of the time and how those individuals felt and thought about it.

He couldn't get Heim's bleak air raid shelter—his cave—out of his mind. Perhaps it was because it reminded him of a depressing version of his own bunker.

The bunker had been named thus by his bemused family, who were somewhat at a loss to understand his preoccupation with an unsavory past and its survivors. As Frank's collection of books and memorabilia from the Nazi era grew, he needed more space for the paraphernalia of his search for information than was available in his own room on the second floor of the Brandenburg home. He shared this second floor with his grandparents, while his parents and his sister occupied the ground floor, and it had soon become apparent that he had to look elsewhere for space to expand.

He had found it in the basement.

Down there was a large, windowless fruit cellar that was never used. Frank had cleared it out, covered the concrete walls with wood scrounged from a lumberyard, and covered the cement floor with remnant carpeting. From an aunt he had acquired some old furniture—two hundred years old, she had told him—which included a grandfather clock, a large oak cupboard, and a sturdy bookcase. It would be his workroom, his special place to keep all his books and other research material, and the mementos he continued to pick up. He had thought it a fun idea to call his place the bunker.

The Bormann dictates given him by Heim would be kept here, as would the photos of the people he had met. Or wanted to meet.

The bunker was actually quite commodious. Opposite the only door to the place stood a round table with three chairs, and in the corner the grandfather clock. Along the wall to the right stood the bookcase, and on the left was a little desk and chair. On the wall behind the chair hung a portrait of Adolf Hitler, and next to it, on a small side table, stood a globe and an old radio he had picked up at a flea market. Once called a *Volksempfänger*—a People's Receiver—it was built into a black wooden box and had swastikas embossed on the tuning knobs.

Against the wall opposite the door stood the large oak cupboard, and to the left of it a projection screen had been mounted on the wall, on which Frank could watch his collection of old films and short subjects from the Hitler era.

Already he had acquired a few unusual Third Reich mementos.

On his desk lay a leather letter folder with four pictures of Minnesingers in color on the cover. Inside was an affidavit notarized by a notary public in Berchtesgaden that the folder had been recovered from the Berghof and had belonged to Adolf Hitler. On the table rested a silver spoon and fork that Frank had been given by the owner of Hitler's favorite restaurant in Munich, the Osteria Bavaria, and which undoubtedly at one time or other had been used by the Führer.

On a shelf in the big cupboard stood his Hitler and Third Reich stamp collection and several models of tanks and planes of World War II vintage. On his desk stood a tape recorder on which he would play music by Wagner.

On the wall hung two framed and autographed photographs of Wolff and Baur, with room for more to come.

Somehow—in a sort of incongruous way—the place was intriguing and cozily campy, in contrast to Heim's cave, which had been dreary and disturbing.

He was up early the next morning and waited impatiently for a decent hour to call Albert Bormann. Finally, a little after ten, he made the call.

As he listened to the rings at the other end of the line, he grew increasingly excited. In a brief moment he would be talking to Gruppenführer der NSKK—the Nazi Motor Transport Corps—the general who had been one of Hitler's personal adjutants and at one time Leiter von der Privatkanzelei des Führers—Chief of the Führer's Private Chancellery—the younger brother of Martin Bormann.

It was the closest he could get to talking with the enigmatic Reichsleiter himself.

He could hardly wait for the phone to be answered.

The photograph of Martin Bormann that Frank showed to Franz Lechner.

Frank Brandenburg.

Flugkapitän, Generalleutnant
Hans Baur.

Frank Brandenburg with Franz Lechner at Lechner's farm in Stoizendorf,
Austria.

Hans Baur with Frank Brandenburg.

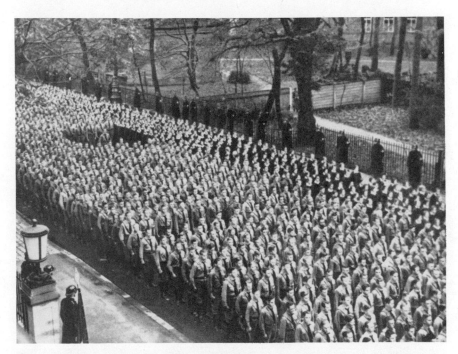

Hitler Youths marching past the Brown House in Munich, 9 November 1935; a scene duplicated in "Inside the Third Reich."

Oberst Nicholaus von Below,
Hitler's Luftwaffe Adjutant
with the Führer. (Bildarchiv
Preussicher Kulturbesitz)

Boarding airplane during 1932 election campaign. *Left to right*: Press Chief
Putzi Hansftängl; Adolf Hitler; Julius Schaub, Adjutant; Heinrich Hoffman,
photographer; Flugkapitän Hans Baur, and Wilhelm Brückner, Adjutant.

SS Oberstgruppenführer Karl
Wolff with Reichsführer SS
Heinrich Himmler. (Bildarchiv
Preussischer Kulturbesitz)

Heinz Lorenz. (Ullstein)

Frank Brandenburg with Karl Wolff.

Heinrich Heim with Frank Brandenburg.

IX

He was a little taken aback when a woman answered.

"*Bitte*," he said. "May I speak with Herr Albert Bormann?"

"Who is calling?" The voice was cautious.

"My name is Frank Brandenburg," he told the woman.

"I am Frau Bormann. What do you want to talk to my husband about?" Still the wariness.

"I—I am doing research on the Third Reich, Frau Bormann," Frank explained. "And I should very much appreciate a few minutes of your husband's time. At his convenience."

There was a slight pause.

"I wish you people would leave us alone." The woman's voice was flat and cold. "My husband will have nothing to do with raking up the past. Nothing. He will not talk to you."

There was a click, and the phone went dead.

Frank sat staring at the receiver—resentfully, as if it were at fault. Slowly he replaced it in its cradle.

It was his first real rebuff and he felt as if he had been slapped. He frowned.

He really wanted to talk with Albert Bormann. If anyone knew the facts of Martin Bormann's fate, his brother would. Later. He would try again later. In a less direct way.

Meanwhile, he was in Munich, only a short train ride from Kufstein in Austria, less than a hundred kilometers to the southeast, where the Luftwaffe ace Rudel lived. He would take advantage of being so close and try to make an appointment to see him, as General Baur had suggested.

Luftwaffen Oberst Hans-Ulrich Rudel tilted his head back and laughed easily. "It was a *film, lieber Herr Brandenburg*," he said. "Merely a clumsy motion picture, designed by those who wish us ill to show Germany and the Nazi movement in a bad light. You must remember, our enemies hate National Socialism because it exalts the superior qualities of the German people. That—'Holocaust' spectacle of yours, it had *nothing* to do with reality, nothing at all. Those— extermination camps pictured on the screen never existed in reality. What you saw was nothing but fanciful fiction, and one must be careful not to take as truth such a distortion of fact made solely for exploitation. The concentration camps as depicted by the Allies are a myth. A lie."

Frank sat watching the famous Luftwaffe ace, the most decorated German soldier in World War II and a venerated hero and champion of the Third Reich, as he talked.

As Frank had presented himself at the beautifully landscaped, two–story Tyrolean villa named "Refugium," built on a hillside above the Stimmer Lake in the evergreen–clad mountains, and identified himself on the security system speaker at the front door, Rudel himself, casually clad in a short–sleeved, open–necked white shirt and light blue slacks, had opened the door.

Still a handsome man at sixty–five, Frank had thought. He had followed his host into a pleasant, light, and airy room with a grand view filled with dozens of skiing, tennis, and flying trophies, show-cased decorations and medals, and several large paintings of Rudel himself.

Hans-Ulrich Rudel had had an adventurous life after attending the Luftkriegsschule—Aerial Warfare School—at Wildpark–Werder near Berlin in 1937. Upon graduation, he was assigned to the Luftwaffe as an artillery spotter, and in 1939 he was promoted to lieutenant and joined a Stuka formation fighting in Poland. He was assigned primarily to hunting tanks. Frank had been curious to know exactly what the famous and feared name Stuka meant, and he had learned it was a contraction of *Sturzkampfflugzeug*—dive bomber.

Unequalled by anyone, Axis or Allied, Rudel's war record had been phenomenal. He was the first pilot to sink a battleship, the Russian *Marat,* named after the assassinated French revolutionary, Jean Paul Marat, and he was also credited with sinking two cruisers, a destroyer, and seventy landing craft, and with the destruction of 519 Russian tanks in over 2,500 combat missions.

Rudel was shot down thirty times, but never by an enemy plane, always by antiaircraft fire; and he never parachuted to safety, he always rode his plane down. He was wounded five times, and in March 1944 he was captured by the Russians after being shot down, but he managed to escape.

In January of 1945 he had been awarded a medal created especially for him. Frank had read what the Führer himself had said on the occasion: "You are the greatest and bravest soldier the German people have and have ever had. Therefore I have decided to create a new, most high, decoration for bravery, the Golden Oak Leaves with Swords and Diamonds to the Knight's Cross. I hereby award it to you and at the same time promote you to Colonel."

It had undoubtedly been Rudel's most cherished hour, but a month later he was again shot down, and as a result of a wound he had to have his right leg amputated. Yet he continued to fly and at war's end commanded the renowned Immelmann Squadron.

After the war Rudel had fled to Argentina along with so many of his friends and comrades, and there he became a popular and prominent member of the Nazi community, enjoying the protection of the Peron government. There he also founded Der Rudel Klub to help former Nazis, and became head of the Nazi rescue organization known as the Kameradenwerk.

Throughout his stay he acted as an important contact man between Nazis in exile and those still in Germany, and on his return home in 1951 he became a patron of the ultranationalistic Freikorps Deutschland and publicly expressed his unwavering admiration for Adolf Hitler, thus becoming the idol of the neo–Nazi movement.

In 1956 he returned to South America, living for a while in both Brazil and Paraguay, where he befriended President Stroessner.

Even now, as he sat opposite Frank explaining away the atrocities committed in the Nazi concentration camps, Rudel was a highly controversial figure—and a totally unrepentant Nazi.

"So you see," he finished. "Much of what you hear, *mein lieber Herr Brandenburg*, is untrue. Lies."

"With all respect, Herr Oberst," Frank ventured. "A lot of evidence to the contrary has been offered."

"Manufactured evidence, Herr Brandenburg. It is ridiculous even to think that mass murder on the scale claimed by our detractors could have taken place without everyone knowing it. And *I* certainly did not know it, and I am certain the Führer, himself, had no knowledge of it. Not surprising, of course, since it did not happen."

"You knew the Führer well?"

"I should have liked to know him better. He was a genius. A true genius. One of the greatest geniuses the world has ever known. Mark my word, *lieber Herr Brandenburg*, one day the world will recognize this. One day the world will speak in a different way about the Third Reich and its goals and accomplishments than it does today. I promise you!"

He stood up. "But I am being a poor host," he exclaimed. "You were kind enough to bring me a bottle of wine. A good German wine. The least we can do is sample it."

He brought two glasses from a cupboard, opened the bottle of Rhine wine Frank had brought, and poured.

"*Zum Wohl!*" he toasted, hefting his glass.

Frank returned the toast. He only sipped the wine.

"Herr Oberst," he said. "You spent several years in South America. After the war."

Rudel nodded. "Good years," he said. "Spent with good friends."

"Friends from Germany?"

"Many of them."

"How did they get out of Germany? How did they get there?"

"They used the various escape routes."

"I have read about such escape routes," Frank said. "A little. What were they like, exactly?"

"Are you interested? In how we took care of our own? Really interested?"

"I am."

Rudel settled down in his chair.

"Already in mid–1944," he began, "wise heads in Berlin realized that the day would come when many of the most important men of the Third Reich would be forced to go into hiding to escape the vengeance of the Allies—and that such hiding would be impossible within the borders of Germany herself. They realized that refuge, for a while at least, would have to be sought abroad. That was the beginning."

He stood up and began to pace the room slowly, as if the subject matter he was addressing was too explosive to sit still.

"The first step, of course, had to be to provide the men needing assistance with false papers: passports, *Kennkarten*—identity cards, birth certificates, work permits, marriage licenses, that sort of mundane document. These papers were prepared by special, secret organizations set up for that specific purpose by the SS and the Gestapo, one of them *Aktion Birkenbaum*—Operation Birch Tree. Since the papers were actually prepared by the authorities with the real official stamps and signatures, they were really not forgeries as such, you can see. They merely gave false information, and they were therefore as good as foolproof. The selected individuals, future travelers along the escape routes, were ready to exfiltrate Germany in safety long before the war was over."

"Who selected these people?"

"It was more self–selection. Making application. No deserving person was turned down, and they were all worthy individuals."

"*All* of them?"

Rudel gave him a sharp look. "Yes, Herr Brandenburg, *all* of them."

Frank could not help noticing the rebuff. Careful, he thought. "What were these routes like?" he asked. "The escape routes?"

"There were several of them. The three most active and most important were Die Schleuse—the Sluice; Die Spinne—the Spider, for a long time led by Waffen SS-General Paul Hausser. Die Spinne was known as La Arana in Spain and L'Araignée in France. This organization ran the B–B Achse—the B–B Axis—and—"

"The B–B Axis? Why B–B?"

"Because the route began in Bremen in northern Germany and ended in Bari in southern Italy. It was discontinued shortly after the war, but another took over, perhaps the most effective route of them all, ODESSA, which stood for *Organisation der ehemaligen SS*

Angehörigen—Organization of Ex–SS Members. Eichmann used that one to get out."

"How—how exactly did they work?"

"They all operated pretty much along the same organizational lines. Each had a headquarters, a *Verteilungskopf*—Allocation Center—in a major city in Germany. For security reasons they were moved frequently. ODESSA's first centers were in Stuttgart and Augsburg, then in Munich. And they had branches all over Germany and Austria, as well as in South America."

"South America?"

"Of course. The escape route refugees could not just be sent out of Germany, they would have to have somewhere to go. A radio transmitter, Herr Brandenburg, is not much use without radio receivers, not so?"

Frank nodded.

Rudel continued. "Several of the organizations operated more than one route. ODESSA, for example, ran two main routes, one from Bremen to Rome, the other from Bremen to Genoa, with a third one, a northern route through the Flensburg escape hatch, as it was called, to Denmark and on from there."

"They must have been extremely well organized."

"They were. It was to be expected. They had the services of the best brains of Germany's elite. Everything worked like clockwork. Every route had a series of *Anlaufstellen*—stopping places, safe houses, if you will—along the route every thirty or forty kilometers. These stops were manned by one or two trusted Party members, loyal to the cause, who would provide the escapees travelling the route with safe shelter, money, any necessary new papers, and transportation to the next stop. These *Anlaufstellen* operators knew only the next stop on the route; in that way they could not cause the collapse of the network, if something should go wrong."

"It must all have been very costly. How was it financed?"

"The usual way. From accounts and funds hidden in foreign countries, such as Switzerland for instance, in anticipation of the operation, and from several large hoards of money and valuables, uh—contributed by the Jews and secreted away right here in this country."

"How many escape routes were there?"

Rudel shrugged. "Hard to say. A dozen. More." He frowned in

concentration. "There was HIAG—Hilfsorganisation auf Gegenslitigkeit der ehemaligen Angehörigen der Waffen SS—Aid and Mutual Interest League of Ex–Waffen SS Members. There was Stille Hilfe—silent Aid, and von Manteuffel's Bruderschaft—Brotherhood. Many more. In Austria there was Kameradschaft IV and Der Salzburg Zirkel— the Salzburg Circle. And most other European countries with a German presence had escape routes of their own. There was the St. Martin's Fond in Belgium, Holland's HINAC, the Danish Alliance of Front Fighters in Denmark, the Aid Organization for War Wounded in Norway, and so on."

"And your own, Herr Oberst, *nicht wahr?*—not so?"

"And my own," Rudel nodded. "Der Rudel Klub. In Argentina. You have done your homework, I see."

"How many high–ranking officials of the Third Reich would you say escaped the Allies with the help of these organizations?"

Rudel laughed. "I would not even begin to guess, Herr Brandenburg," he said. "But this is certain: many more than the Allies wanted to get away—and not as many as should have reached safety." He nodded. "But—enough."

"And they were your friends in South America."

"Many of them, yes." He stopped pacing and sat down again.

"Did Martin Bormann survive?" Frank asked. "Did he—escape?"

Rudel gave him a quick look. "He did."

"Do you know how *he* got out?"

"The Vatican helped him," Rudel answered, settling back in his chair. "The Vatican helped everyone who was anti–Communist or Catholic. There was a special escape route called Die Vatikanische Hilfslinie—The Vatican Aid Line. They helped persecuted Germans reach South America."

"Why South America?"

"The countries there were sympathetic. And Catholic. The Vatican could exert certain—pressure."

"And that is how the Reichsleiter got out?"

Rudel nodded. "He was taken to Italy. He saw Bishop Hudal there, the Catholic leader of the pro–Nazi Croats in Yugoslavia, Bishop Alois Hudal, a good friend of our cause. They—"

"Bishop Hudal? Was he involved in the escape route operations?" Frank was startled.

"Up to the cross around his neck," Rudel laughed. "He had excellent connections in the International Red Cross. They would provide him with valuable false credentials for the people he wanted to help get away. The papers would be marked *Politisch Verfolgter*—Subject to Political Persecution, it practically guaranteed their safety. And, of course, he had the protection of the Vatican. Hudal was most helpful to us. He saved the skins of a lot of us. Franz Stangl. Eichmann. Many others."

"What happened when Bormann met him?"

"They met in the sanctuary of a monastery near Rome. The Vatican escape route was also known as the Monastery Route or the Papal Aid Line. At that meeting Bormann made his arrangement with Hudal. And with Evita Peron."

"Evita Peron? The Argentine President's wife?"

"Exactly." Rudel smiled. "Certain—financial arrangements were made."

"You mean, the Perons took money from Bormann to let him stay in hiding in Argentina?"

"Draw your own conclusion, Herr Brandenburg."

"How do you know this?" Frank asked. "Did you talk to Martin Bormann? How do you know?" he persisted.

For a moment Rudel contemplated him, as if trying to come to a decision. "There are things known in Germany, *mein lieber Herr Brandenburg*," he said finally, "by the right people. But best not bandied about. I talked to friends and comrades, both here and in South America. New and old. I still do. It is best we do not go into details."

"Then there are really important people from the Third Reich days still living in South America?"

Rudel nodded. He grew serious.

"You seem to be genuinely interested in the old times," he said, watching Frank closely. "We need such interest. We welcome it. You seem to be the kind of young man we would like to know better. Of course," he said pointedly, "your attitude in some things could be a little more—enthusiastic, shall we say, a little stronger in your feelings about us." He leaned forward in his chair. "If, or rather, when I go back to South America, would you like to come with me? For a short stay? Make your own observations? Learn for yourself?"

Frank was startled.

"My—my studies—" he began. "I—"

Rudel waved a hand. "We would make it at a time you could get away. Without inconvenience. And without causing—talk." He smiled at Frank. "I could introduce you to—to some of my friends. I am certain you would be interested in meeting them. Klaus Barbie. Walter Kutschmann, Walter Rauff.* They are all still there. Many others. President Stroessner. It would be a great opportunity to further your research."

Frank cast about for a not–too–obvious way of changing the subject and avoiding a direct answer. The conversation was taking a turn he had not anticipated and did not know how to handle.

"All those people," he said, his voice perhaps a shade too high. "They all got out by using the escape routes you told me about?"

"They did."

"Did you use one of them?"

"No. I did not have to." A little smile tugged at Rudel's mouth. Frank was uncomfortably certain that the man knew what he was trying to do. But Rudel did not press the point.

"Many of the top people, however, did use them," he said. "Adolf Eichmann. Heinrich Müller. And Mengele."

"You know Josef Mengele? The Auschwitz doctor? The one they call the Angel of Death?"

"That ridiculous epithet," Rudel snapped impatiently. "Of course I knew him."

"*Knew?*"

"Yes. Before—"

He suddenly stopped, as if pulling himself up short. He sat for a brief moment in silence, studying Frank, an enigmatic look on his face. He stood up and slowly walked to the picture window. The surface of the lake below was lightly discomfited by the drizzle of rain, the mountains were shrouded in slow–moving, diaphanous clouds.

"I think," he said after a moment. "I think I just told you something I should not have." He turned toward Frank, a drawn smile on his face.

"Why don't we take a nice walk, you and I," he suggested. "We can talk."

* Barbie, ex–Gestapo chief of Lyon, France, was apprehended the following year, 1983, and brought to justice. Rauff, ex–SS colonel blamed for 97,000 deaths, died in Chile in 1984.

"But—it is raining," Frank protested. He had a sudden tight feeling in his chest.

"My mountains are beautiful in the rain."

Frank looked down at his low cut shoes. "I—I do not—"

"Not another word, Herr Brandenburg," Rudel insisted. "I will lend you a pair of my walking boots. You will be quite comfortable, I assure you. And a raincoat, of course."

Resolutely he walked toward the hall closet.

"We will have a nice walk," he said. "And we can have all the privacy we want." It was obvious that he would not be denied.

He returned with a pair of boots. "Try these," he said.

As Frank struggled to put on the borrowed boots, at least one full size too large, Rudel walked over to the picture window.

"You may not be aware of it, Herr Brandenburg," he said calmly, "but my home is being watched. Constantly."

He nodded toward the window.

"Out there—we can be alone."

X

The rain–softened path Rudel had chosen for their walk meandered along a meadow above the lake, clean and fresh with new grass and leading toward a thicket of spruce trees that ran all the way down to the water.

Rudel turned his face up toward the gentle drizzle.

"Nectar of the mountains, Herr Brandenburg," he said almost reverently. "The mist from the Fountain of Youth itself. Ponce de Leon went in the wrong direction in his search for his magic spring. It is right here. No wonder the mountain people live to such ripe old ages, yes?"

He strode on toward the thicket.

Frank marvelled at the ease with which he walked. Only a slight limp betrayed the fact that he had an artificial leg. That, and of course the cane.

The cane with the heavy metal knob.

He looked around apprehensively. Somebody watching? No one was in sight. He wondered who was keeping Rudel's house under observation. No logical answers surfaced. He gave it up.

He was more concerned about himself, and the immediate now.

"You must really give some serious thought to my suggestion," Rudel said. "That you accompany me the next time I go to South America." With his cane he hit a stone, propelling it into the grass. "We could stop off in Spain on the way. Visit an old friend of mine. Leon Degrelle."

"The Nazi governor of Belgium?"

Rudel nodded. "An interesting man," he said. "You will enjoy him."

"I—know only little about him."

"He was very active in Belgium on our behalf. Very loyal to the Führer and his ideals." He hit another stone, sending it flying. "He was head of the Belgian SS and founded the honored SS Division *Wallonie,* serving as its commanding officer. The Belgians sentenced him to death *in absentia*, but they were never able to lay their hands on him to carry out the sentence. He lives in great good comfort on the Costa del Sol, and Spain has refused to extradite him." He laughed. "He has the distinction of being one of the six most wanted 'Nazi war criminals.' As I said, you will enjoy him."

They had reached the thicket.

Frank felt his heart beat faster than usual. It was either because of the brisk walk—or the apprehension he finally admitted to himself. What did Rudel want? What did he intend to do?

He had a sudden impulse to run. Rudel could never catch him. But if they were indeed being watched, the watchers could as easily be neo–Nazis as *polizei*. And he would then definitely have shown himself as being unsympathetic to their cause. And if he were caught...

A few feet along the path that led into the thicket an old moss–covered log lay among the shrubbery. Rudel walked over to it and sat down.

"This will do," he said. "We should be safe from eavesdroppers here."

"Eavesdroppers?" Frank was puzzled. They hadn't seen a soul.

Rudel laughed. "For want of a better word." He grew serious. "You may think me melodramatic, Herr Brandenburg, but I have good reason to believe that the men who watch my house and me do so with strong binoculars, hoping to be able to read on your lips what you are talking about." He placed his cane across his knees. "Here, no one can see us."

He gave Frank a calculating look. "You see, I am about to tell you something that I do not want anyone else to hear. Or see."

"Me?"

"You picked up on my little slip quickly enough," Rudel said. "It could become awkward—damned awkward—if you tried to learn about certain events on your own. If you should begin to ask questions better not asked. So I have decided to take you into our confidence with all the obligations and risks that entails, and with the warning that what you learn should remain strictly confidential."

The tone of Rudel's voice conveyed enough of a warning to render his words superfluous.

"Josef Mengele *is* dead," Rudel said. "As you surmised from my slip of the tongue. He died in 1979, in February. A little more than three years ago. He was only sixty–seven. He was vacationing at Bertioga Beach near Sao Paulo in Brazil when he suffered a stroke while swimming and drowned."

Frank stared at Rudel. That was it? The fact that Mengele was dead? Of course he knew that Mengele was constantly hunted. He had read numerous accounts of the atrocities committed by the ice–blooded doctor from Auschwitz. They said that he personally ordered the death of more than four hundred thousand people. Men, women and children. So—he was dead. Why all the fuss? It was quite unimportant. And he had let his imagination conjure up all kinds of sinister machinations. He felt uncomfortably sheepish.

"I will say nothing about it, Herr Oberst," he said. He frowned. "But—if I may ask—why? Why is it important that Mengele's death be kept a secret?"

Rudel gave a thin smile. "It is important that it *has been* kept secret," he explained. "It is important that it will *continue* to be kept secret. Understand, Herr Brandenburg, the hunt of Mengele goes on as avidly as ever. The more people who waste their time looking for Mengele, the fewer are looking for others in hiding. And we want to keep it that way. We are tying up the enemy forces on a wild goose chase, as it were, and that is an excellent strategy."*

"I will say nothing," Frank repeated. He had no way of knowing that it would be another three years before the world would share the knowledge he had just acquired.

As if to lend emphasis to his vow, a blinding white lightning bolt

---

* Not until three years later, six years after his drowning, did the world learn of Mengele's death and the hunt for him cease.

lanced into the lake from the black clouds overhead, instantaneously followed by a clap of thunder that nearly split their eardrums.

And the heavens opened up.

Back in the house they dried out and warmed themselves in front of a cozy fire, Frank in a borrowed shirt, pants, and socks while his own clothes were drying out. The cloudburst had been so torrential that both men were soaked to the skin despite their raincoats.

Mrs. Rudel, a pleasant, quiet woman in her late forties, joined them and served coffee and cookies. Almost in a twinkle of an eye the atmosphere in the Rudel home had changed from tense and vaguely menacing to comfortable and social.

"Your desire to meet and talk to as many of us old–timers as you can is commendable and an interesting one, *mein lieber Herr Brandenburg*," Rudel said expansively. "And there are many of us around. Not men defeated and disheartened, but men still proud and impassioned. My motto has always been: Only he is lost, who gives up on himself. Many of us have not given up. And never will!"

He stood up. The meeting had come to an end.

"It has been a pleasure meeting you, Herr Oberst," Frank said. He turned to Mrs. Rudel. "*Gnädige Frau.*"

"Are you returning to Hildesheim right away?" Rudel asked.

"I was planning to."

"Could you perhaps postpone your return for a day?"

Frank was at once interested. "I could."

"*Prima!* There is someone I think you should meet. And talk to. He lives in the Allgäu in Bavaria. In Kaufbeuren. The Führer and our fatherland owe him a great deal. His name is Remer. Generalmajor Otto Ernst Remer, Commander of the Panzer–Führer–Begleitdivision— the Führer Tank Escort Division. He can tell you about things I guarantee you have never heard of. If he so chooses."

It was nearly six months before Frank could make his connection with Generalmajor Otto Ernst Remer in Kaufbeuren. This was the officer, Frank had learned, whose personal actions had played a pivotal role in the failure of the July 1944 plot to overthrow Adolf Hitler, and who had been decorated for bravery with the Knight's Cross with Oak Leaves by the Führer personally. Remer had been unavailable when Rudel had first suggested that Frank pay him a visit. Only after persistent letter–writing and telephoning had Remer finally agreed to a meeting.

In the meantime Frank had consolidated his connections with Baur and Wolff, and tended to his studies at Michelsengymnasium, which were, of course, important to him, and which increasingly demanded his time.

His grandfather, the only one of his family ever to do so, had asked him about General Wolff, unable to believe that Frank really knew that erstwhile officer of top importance in the Third Reich. Frank had put him on the telephone with Wolff during one of the calls, and his grandfather had been speechless with astonishment.

In constant pursuit of his journey into the past, Frank had written again to Reichsminister Albert Speer, Hitler's chief architect and munitions minister, at his home on Schloss–Wolfsbrunnenweg in Heidelberg, but Speer had already published three books, which Frank had read, and he doubted that Speer would have anything new to tell him. He had been right, but in a way quite different from what he had expected. Speer, in a brief note, pleaded a workload so great it prohibited him from seeing Frank, or talking to him on the phone, or even answering any questions whatsoever by letter.

He had visited one other person during the six months, a man whose picture he had seen in a photograph taken in Paris, showing Hitler standing at the Eiffel Tower with Speer and a group of Nazi officials. He had recognized him as the renowned sculptor Arno Breker, one of the Führer's favorite artists, whose sculpture called The Party had flanked one of the Reich Chancellery entrances. Breker had been one of the Führer's inner circle.

Frank had made an enlargement of the photograph and sent it to Breker, asking him to sign it. Breker had complied and asked for a copy of the enlargement for himself—and a meeting had been arranged.

In fact, Frank had visited the sculptor more than once at his studio on Niederrheinstrasse in Düsseldorf, a tall, barn–like building situated on a park–like estate adorned with several statues and sculptures, all by Breker himself, including a bronze bust of Richard Wagner. Balding and bespectacled, Breker had worn a long white smock, which to Frank made him look like a chief surgeon at a hospital. The man had been cordial and comfortable to talk to.

Frank had wondered about Breker's association with the Nazis, such a virulent political force, but Breker had said, "Politics cannot stop the development, the impact of culture and art. It may curtail it, impede it, but it cannot obliterate it."

And Breker had told him about Pablo Picasso. Because his work was considered decadent by the Nazis, Picasso was forbidden to exhibit his paintings anywhere after the occupation of Paris. He fell on inhospitable days and sank into despair. In rebellion, he became involved with the anti–Nazi underground. But he was caught and imprisoned. Breker found out, and he told Frank that he had gone to Gestapo Chief Heinrich Müller and demanded that Picasso be set free. Müller had refused—and Breker, who had Hitler's ear, had threatened to go directly to the Führer.

Picasso had been released.

And shortly after the liberation of Paris in August of 1944, Picasso joined the Communist Party.

Frank, who had gone to see Breker to gain an understanding of how Hitler could have shown such an interest in the beauty of art at the same time as he was dragging his country and his people down into ugly horror, had been startled by what the artist had told him during their last meeting, when the talk had turned to Rudolf Hess, the Old Man of Spandau.

Contrary to accepted historical opinion, Breker had insisted, Adolf Hitler not only knew of Hess's flight to England, but had been part of its orchestration. He, Breker, had been told so in confidence by one of the Führer's closest intimates. He refused to divulge the informer's name, but swore that his information was correct. "The history books are wrong," he had declared, "as they are about so many things." Frank had been intrigued, and he had promised himself to make finding out about Hess and his flight another subject of his quest.

Breker had been a veritable cornucopia of new contacts, his friends from the old days, many of whom he still saw. He had told Frank where to find SS Sturmbannführer Otto Günsche, Hitler's SS adjutant; SS Obersturmbannführer Richard Schulze–Kossens, the last surviving German officer present at the negotiation and signing of the notorious Hitler–Stalin Pact; Gerda Christian, one of the Führer's four permanent women secretaries, who was with her boss in the Bunker to the last, and Prof. Hermann Giesler, Hitler's Munich architect. Frank had thought him long since dead, but Breker told him the man lived in Düsseldorf, as did Frau Christian. All that information had been given

Frank in a quite recent meeting, and he had had no opportunity to act on it yet.

And Breker had been a treasure trove in quite another way—contributing to the financing of Frank's by now quite expensive undertaking.

His needs for funds had quickly exceeded his earlier sources, his allowance and his wages from working in the little flower stand in the Hildesheim town hall square, and he soon found out that there were not enough hours in the day to study, go to school, do his research, travel to see his subjects, and also attend the flower stand. And the cost of his quest had kept on rising the more involved he got. Something had to be done.

In a magazine Frank saw that there were collectors who would spend real money to buy autographs of famous, or infamous, people and dealers who handled the material. He already had been given several autographs by the people he had been visiting, and he had begun to ask tactfully for more, for friends. He then wrote to an auction house in Düsseldorf called Felzmann Stamps & Autographs, and asked if they would be interested in handling his collection.

They were, and it was the beginning of an arrangement by which Frank, unbeknownst to his subjects, had them themselves pay for his expenses in hunting them down and traveling to see them, by giving him autographed pictures and cards. In the beginning all transactions with the autograph dealer had to be carried out by mail, because Frank was still under age and could not legally enter into business deals.

But his "arrangement" flourished, and Arno Breker had contributed handsomely.

And now Frank stood on the third floor landing of an apartment house in Kaufbeuren in Bavaria, before the door to Generalmajor Otto Ernst Remer's apartment, tightly clutching a bouquet of flowers he had brought for the general's wife.

Somehow he felt nervous at the prospect of meeting the general. He wondered why.

He stared at the name plate on the door. REMER, it said. That was all. REMER. He rang the bell.

He started when a voice rasped, *"Wer ist da?*—Who is there?"

It was a woman's voice. He saw a small security intercom box on the wall next to the door. Feeling foolish, he addressed the box and identified himself.

The door was opened and a woman peered out. She gave a quick look past Frank out at the empty landing beyond. Then she returned her attention to Frank. She opened the door wide.

"I am Frau Remer," she said. "Please come in." She led the way through a small hallway into a living room.

Across the room stood a tall, slender man, legs slightly apart, hands behind his back, and chin held high. With his receding grey hair and large horn–rimmed glasses, and clad in a grey suit and open–neck white shirt, he carried his seventy years well and still conveyed the ramrod–straight bearing of a German officer. Behind him, displayed on a shelf of a bookcase filled with books pertaining to the Third Reich and World War II, was a board with medals and decorations and a gleaming grey *Stahlhelm*—steel helmet—with the black–white–red insignia of the Wehrmacht.

"Brandenburg, I trust you have not brought those flowers for me," he barked, as if he were addressing a barracks full of recruits. He pointed a stiff finger at the bouquet of flowers Frank still clutched in his hand.

"Oh, no, Herr General!" Frank exclaimed, flustered. "I—they—they are for Frau Remer." He turned to the woman and with a little bow presented the flowers to her. "*Bitte, gnädige Frau*," he said.

The woman took the flowers. "Thank you," she said. "I shall put them in water." She left the room.

Remer pointed to a straight–backed chair. "Sit down," he ordered. Frank sat. Remer remained standing, towering over Frank. He lit a cigarette.

"Why are you here?" he demanded to know.

"I wanted—I know that—Colonel Rudel suggested that I talk with you."

"Why?" The question was shot at him.

"I—I am doing research on the Third Reich, Herr General, and I—"

"Why?" Remer barked at him again.

"Why am I doing research? It was a time of—of much interest. I want to know exactly what it was like. I—"

"Why?" Again the staccato delivery.

Frank was catching on to the man's drill sergeant delivery. "So much has been said about that time," he explained. "So much written about it. I want to know what is true, and what is not."

"Such as?"

"Such as? Well—they talk about the Holocaust, and—"

"*Unsinn!*" Remer barked. "Nonsense!" He jabbed his cigarette at Frank. "Absurd exaggeration. What else?"

Frank decided to plough right in. Remer was obviously a man who believed in coming straight to the point. "The plot to assassinate the Führer," he said. "The July 1944 bombing at the Führer Headquarters at Rastenburg."

Frau Remer returned carrying a white–and–blue vase with the flowers Frank had brought. She put it on a side table and sat down.

"So," Remer said. "You want to know about 'Operation *Walküre*'—the Führer murder plot." It was a statement, not a question.

"I do. I have been told you were personally involved, Herr General, in the outcome, that is. I would—"

"I was at the time commanding officer of the Wachbataillon—the Guard Battalion—in Berlin," Remer said in his clipped manner of speaking. "It was July 20, 1944. My superiors informed me that a bomb had exploded in the Führer's headquarters at Rastenburg, placed there by Claus Schenk Count von Stauffenberg, member of a group of officer conspirators who planned to kill the Führer, take over the leadership of the Reich, and take control of the war. I was told the Führer was dead, and ordered to place Dr. Joseph Goebbels under arrest."

"What did you do?"

"It was 1900 hours. I went to the house of Dr. Goebbels."

"You went with your men?"

"I went alone."

"Alone? To arrest Dr. Goebbels?"

A thin smile stretched Remer's lips. "To warn him," he said. His eyes flashed angrily behind his glasses. "Those Stauffenberg conspirators were traitors. All of them. They would knife the German soldier, the German people in the back." He stabbed a finger at Frank. "I repeat," he snapped. "They were traitors. Traitors!"

Frank stared at the man. He fervently hoped his astonishment did not show on his face. In all the references he had been able to find to Remer in books and periodicals, there was little doubt that Remer had known all about the conspiracy he now so vehemently condemned, had in fact been part of it, and had at one time been under serious suspicion by the SS officers investigating the plot. And that he had made a complete about–face only when he learned Hitler was alive, when he had promptly betrayed all his coconspirators. That had been the reason for his quick success in rounding them up. He had known.

Remer was obviously telling him a very much doctored version of the events. Frank suddenly wondered if any of the others with whom he had talked had done the same. Probably, he thought. To some extent at least. It was the extent of *that* extent he had to find out....

Aloud he asked, "What happened?"

"Dr. Goebbels informed me the Führer was still alive. Only slightly injured. He placed a call to Rastenburg, and I, myself, talked to the Führer."

"What did he say?"

"He gave me his orders. He promoted me to full colonel on the spot. He placed me in charge until Reichsführer Himmler arrived. He instructed me to report directly to him."

"In charge of what? What orders did the Führer give you?"

"He charged me with rounding up as many of the Stauffenberg gang as I could unearth."

"And did you?"

"I did."

"What happened to Stauffenberg?"

"He was at once court–martialed and sentenced to be executed immediately." Remer gave Frank one of his thin, mirthless smiles. "He was shot," he said matter–of–factly. "In the courtyard of the War Ministry. My men. Ten riflemen. One officer— a lieutenant who could be relied upon to keep his trousers dry. There were, of course, several more executions. It was done quickly and efficiently. The abortive coup d'etat came to an abrupt and most satisfactory end."

"Did you talk to the Führer about all this? Later?"

"I did."

"What did he say?"

"I must tell you, Brandenburg," Remer said, "the Führer was most generous in his remarks about my role in the events." He drew himself up. "I remember his words to me with great pride. I repeat, great pride. 'If I had a few more fine, clear–thinking officers like you,' he said, 'I would not have to worry about the future.' I was promoted to Generalmajor and given command of a division."

"And that was the end of the takeover attempt," Frank observed.

"There were several more executions, of course, as more of the traitors were rounded up. A few were allowed to take their own lives. And when the Führer returned to Berlin, he ordered the body of Stauffenberg exhumed, so he could verify for himself that the would–be assassin had in fact been executed."

"You mean, the Führer did not trust you? After all you had done?"

"I mean, Brandenburg, that the Führer left no detail unchecked," Remer said sharply. "I repeat—no detail."

He lit another cigarette using the glowing butt of his last one. Coldly he contemplated Frank.

"You come here, Brandenburg," he said, "presenting yourself as a serious researcher. But you ask only frivolous, banal questions. About the anti–Nazi traitors. They were nothing but an abominable stain on the shield of the honorable German officer corps." Again he stabbed a finger at Frank. "I repeat, a disgraceful stain. We can go on like that. I can tell you more platitudes. I can tell you that Germany should get out of that insidious NATO organization. I can tell you that I elected to remain in Germany rather than join my friends in South America, because I *am* and *feel* German. I can tell you that I advocate a strong army of Arabs and their German friends to fight and destroy the oppressive international Jewry, and to put an end to the inhuman atrocities committed by the Jews in the Middle East." Once more he stabbed a finger at Frank. "I can tell you all that—and more. Platitudes. Banalities. I repeat—I can tell you all that, but that is not why you are here, is it, Brandenburg?"

To Frank's relief he did not wait for an answer, but, like a lecturer warming to his subject, he went right on. "I am certain you know that after the war I founded the SRP, the Socialist Reich Party. They called it neo–Nazi. It was not. It was Nazi. I repeat—Nazi! So it was outlawed. And I am also certain that you know that I am now the leader of Der Bismarck–Deutsche, the club for right–thinking people who, like Bismarck himself, fight for our right to exist, for the security and freedom of a united Germany. People like me, Brandenburg. And like you, right? *That* is the reason you are here, *nicht wahr?*—not so? To learn what you can about us? to join us? That is why Rudel sent you to me. Am I right, Brandenburg? Am I right?"

The way he drummed the questions made it clear that there was not the slightest doubt in his mind that he was right.

"Ours is the fight for German liberty," he went on. "Germany must be strong, as it was under Bismarck. That is why our club carries his name. Since the war a fight has raged, a fight for justice, for truth, and for freedom for the German people, and we of Der Bismarck –Deutsche stand in the forefront of that fight. And you, Brandenburg, want to stand with us. Right?"

Frank had been listening to Remer's finger–stabbing lecture with growing apprehension. He did not want to be recruited into a neo–Nazi organization. But if he flatly refused—what then? Certainly he would learn nothing further from Remer. How could he say yes and no at the same time?

"You are right, Herr General," he conceded. "I am interested in learning more about Der Bismarck–Deutsche, and I—"

"*Gut!* I shall get you some literature on us. You will be interested."

"Who are your members, Herr General? Where do they come from?"

"From all walks of life, Brandenburg, all walks. But we all have one thing in common. Our love for our fatherland—and what our Führer wanted the German people to be. Nationalism is not confined to one group. We are old; we are young. We are especially interested in young people. People such as you." He poked a finger at Frank. "I repeat, young people. The right kind of young people. To carry on our work. And as such, you are welcome."

"What about fees? Dues?"

"They are minimal. Mere tokens."

"But it must be a costly operation. How do you manage? Financially, I mean?"

Remer frowned at him. "You are touching a delicate point, Brandenburg," he warned. "I can tell you nothing about that. Now." He pointed a stiff finger at Frank. "In fact, I caution you to—to be careful."

Frau Remer suddenly spoke up.

"We are still being bothered, Herr Brandenburg," she said plaintively. "By the authorities. The *Verfassungsschutz*. They even photograph our visitors. It is most bothersome. As my husband said, you must be careful."

She stood up, suddenly cheery. "I think it is about time we had a nice cup of coffee. And perhaps some nice crackers. You do like crackers, Herr Brandenburg?"

Frank nodded. "*Bitte.*"

Frau Remer started for the door. As she passed the flowers she turned back to Frank.

"So lovely, the flowers, so lovely."

And she left.

Frank watched her leave, concerned. Photographed? Damn! He did not want to end up in some police file as a neo–Nazi, as someone to be watched. He'd be careful, all right. Damned careful!

"I shall get you a membership application, Brandenburg," Remer said. "Look it over and fill it out."

He walked to the bookcase and took a piece of paper from a stack of forms. He pointed to a medal on the display board.

"That, Brandenburg, is the decoration given me by the Führer personally. The Knights Cross with Oak Leaves. I am proud of it. I repeat, proud. Justifiably so, yes?"

"An honor only few achieved," Frank agreed. He looked at Remer. "Herr General," he said. "You spoke of your friends in South America. Are you still in touch with them?"

"Of course."

"Colonel Rudel mentioned some of his friends to me, such as Klaus Barbie, Walter Rauff, and Walter Kutschmann. I suppose you know them, too?"

"I do."

"And—Martin Bormann? Are you in touch with him as well?"

Remer gave him a quick look. He reached over and slapped the application form in Frank's hand.

"Fill it out," he said curtly. "Send it in. And wait with your questions."

Frau Remer returned, and they sat down to enjoy her coffee and crackers. Remer took his coffee black. Comfortably he leaned back in his chair and looked at Frank.

"You will find," he said, "that we Bismarck–Deutsche have a favorable, positive, and optimistic view of the Germany yet to come. A Germany for Germans." He reached for a cracker. "The world is too busy laying a continuous burden of guilt across our shoulders. A perpetual, collective guilt. Too busy to see where the future must lead." He gave Frank a quick glance. "Of course," he said, "we *are* guilty."

Frank was startled at the apparent about–face.

"Guilty, Herr General?"

"Yes. I repeat—guilty. Guilty of having lost the war. Guilty of having destroyed the Führer's plans for our fatherland and our people." He pointed the ubiquitous finger at Frank. "Mark my words, Brandenburg, *we* lost the war. We were not defeated by our enemies, we were betrayed from within." His voice took on a bitter tinge. "The Führer was betrayed. The German people were betrayed. We defeated ourselves."

"You mean, by not fighting hard enough? By not being willing to accept enough sacrifices? Is that what you mean?"

"I mean betrayed, Brandenburg. I repeat, betrayed. As in traitors."

"I—do not understand?"

Remer pursed his lips and looked at Frank speculatively. He put down his cup, and leaned forward.

"Have you ever heard of *Die Tonne?*" he asked.

Frank shook his head. "I have not, Herr General. What is it?"

"*Was*, Brandenburg," Remer said flatly. "Was. It was the most sophisticated, the most effective of the new weapons the Führer gave us. It was a weapon which would have assured us victory. I repeat, undisputed victory." He looked hard at Frank. "But the victory was denied us by the actions of one man, a traitor, who disgraced the general's uniform he wore and befouled his birthright as a German. *Die Tonne* was a weapon far ahead of its time, developed through the farsightedness of the Führer. It was code–named *Die Tonne*—The Tub—a name as far from reality as it could possibly be." He paused.

"I shall tell you about *Die Tonne*, Brandenburg," he said. "It is a sad and infamous chapter in the history of the Third Reich."

He nodded his head almost imperceptibly in disturbed remembrance.

"A discordant swan song..."

XI

*D*ie Tonne was ingenious, Brandenburg. I repeat, ingenious. The Führer's experts employed the newest inventions, the newest technologies in the creation of the device." He paused to munch a cracker.

Frank was intrigued. "What exactly was this—this tub, Herr General?" he asked.

Remer smiled, a smile of satisfaction. "I thought you would be interested, Brandenburg," he said. "I thought so." He settled back.

"*Die Tonne* was a large, powerful rocket projectile which held a warhead of high explosives," he began. "But like no other projectile you have ever heard of. I guarantee it. It was carried close to an important target mounted under a medium bomber. It was locked on to the target and released, headed for the objective."

He paused. Frank was puzzled. It did not seem that special a weapon. But Remer continued.

"The extraordinary, totally new feature of *Die Tonne* was its steering mechanism. In the nose of the rocket was mounted a small television transmitter, a quite new invention for the time, Brandenburg, I repeat, quite new. The picture transmitted by this television camera was received on two monitoring screens, one in the plane itself and the other at the home base. The rocket also included a remote–control steering mechanism. So from either the plane, in the air at a safe distance from the target to be destroyed, or from the home station, the rocket could be instantly and accurately steered in its flight. Steered to avoid interference. Steered to correct any flight deviation. Steered to hit the designated target with the greatest accuracy!"

He pointed a finger at Frank. "Think, Brandenburg," he said. "Every rocket projectile would hit its target exactly. It would be like a swarm of thousands of the Japanese *kamikaze* bombers unleashed against the enemy—without the loss of the valuable pilot. And there would be only minimal defense possible. That, Brandenburg, was *Die Tonne!*"

Frank stared at him. His first thought was that the general's description of the rocket sounded like something out of that big American science fiction film *Star Wars*. He was aware of some extraordinary developments in weaponry, proximity fuzes, variable–type fuzes, heat–seeking rockets, that sort of thing, invented after 1945. But *Die Tonne* seemed incredible for its time. But then he remembered—Hitler *had* delivered some extraordinary weapons. The jet plane, for instance. Who at that time would have envisioned a plane without propellers? And the *Vergeltungswaffe 1*—the Reprisal Weapon 1, or V–1, the flying bomb that wreaked such terrible damage on London. The V–2 rocket that would reach Earth's stratosphere before coming crashing down on the enemy. And the *Tausendfüssler*—the Millipede, that astounding gun with a barrel one hundred and fifty meters long, as long as five tennis courts laid end to end and capable of shooting a projectile over one hundred and fifty kilometers. All incredible weapons. And all real.

But each one of them could hit only indiscriminate or general targets. None of them could have streaked directly at a specific enemy target such as the weapon Remer had described. Such as *Die Tonne*.

"What—what happened, Herr General?" he asked. "Why was *Die Tonne* never used?"

Gravely Remer regarded him. "That, Brandenburg," he said soberly. "That is our shame. Our betrayal."

"Is that why *Die Tonne* never saw action? Because of betrayal?"

"Precisely. Completion of the project, which might well have meant the difference between victory and defeat, was sabotaged, stopped dead by one of us."

"By whom?"

"General Erich Fellgiebel, Brandenburg, Erich Fellgiebel, General der Signaltruppen—the Chief Army Signal Officer in charge of all communications."

"I—I am not familiar with General Fellgiebel. How did he sabotage *Die Tonne?*"

"Everything was ready for the production of the special weapon, Brandenburg. Everything. At plants in Karlshagen. In Neu–Mecklenburg and Roechlin. In the spring of '44. Only a *Spezialmehrfachstecker*— a special electronic plug mechanism—had yet to be installed. These devices were available in Berlin. More than a thousand of them. But they could not be released for installation without the signature of General Fellgiebel, who had jurisdiction over the television equipment. He, however, deliberately withheld his authorization until it was too late. The devices were shipped to a storage facility in Klein –Machnow." He grunted angrily. "Fellgiebel's actions were, of course, in character, as we discovered. Too late."

"What do you mean?"

"We found out that Fellgiebel had sabotaged the war effort and the Führer in many other ways, Brandenburg. I repeat, in many other ways. As general of the army signal organization he was able to betray our secrets to the enemy. The Führer was convinced he had done so. And it would, of course, explain the disastrous accuracy of the enemy's knowledge of our plans, our moves. Such as the uncanny precision of the *Soldatensender Calais*. And the Führer was certain Fellgiebel had had a direct, clandestine line to Switzerland. Had fed all his plans to the Russians. That was why his campaign on the eastern front failed, Brandenburg. That was why."

He regarded Frank with his cold eyes. "Fellgiebel, who was *Army* Signal, had been fighting vigorously to combine all the signal organizations into one: Army, Navy, Luftwaffe. One organization, Brandenburg. Under him. Citing the waste of duplication. The squandering of men and material. The difficulties in intercommunication. Wisely the Führer rejected his proposition. And the reason became obvious. Controlling all, Fellgiebel would better be able to betray his Fatherland, and his Führer, to the enemy." Remer's anger at remembering made his staccato way of speaking even more pronounced.

"But why? What do you think made him do it? What—what kind of man was the general?"

"Fellgiebel? What kind of man?" Remer sounded acidly bitter. "He was one of the traitorous generals in the forefront of the plot to assassinate the Führer. To deliver the Reich into enemy hands, Brandenburg. That was the kind of *Schweinehund* he was. He was present at Rastenburg at the Wolfsschanze on that day of infamy— albeit uninvited. And he kept himself at a respectable distance from where the bomb exploded, I might add. It was his responsibility to inform his fellow conspirators sitting back at Wehrmacht Headquarters on Bendlerstrasse in Berlin, once the deed was done, and then to isolate the Führer Headquarters."

Remer's face stretched into a contemptuous sneer. "He failed to do so—not even man enough to act with determination and vigor in a crisis, when the bomb failed to kill the Führer."

He paused, glowering at Frank. "It was little consolation that the man was executed," he said. "The damage had been done. The Reich had been betrayed. He was offered a pistol before he was formally arrested. He rejected it. A coward without honor in all things." His eyes seemed to freeze into Frank. "He may have regretted that choice, Brandenburg," he said tonelessly. "I repeat—he may have regretted it. I remember the Führer's rage, when he was told of Fellgiebel's complicity in the assassination plot. 'He must be made to confess,' the Führer insisted. 'Everything he had done. Even if you have to skin him alive!'"

There was a moment's silence. An uncomfortable silence. Then Remer spoke.

"Would you like to know the ignominious end to the story of *Die Tonne?*" he asked.

Frank nodded.

"The all–important electronic devices that had been stored in Klein–Machnow were discovered by the Russian barbarians when they overran the place. They thought they were some kind of compact new radios. When they could get no music out of them, they poured gasoline over them and burned them."

The clickety–clack of the railroad car wheels lulled Frank into dozing relaxation. He snuggled into the corner of the window seat and closed his eyes. Already it was dark outside.

He sighed. The stayover and his visit with Generalmajor Remer had definitely been worthwhile. He touched his inside jacket pocket. Half a dozen signed photographs showing Remer as a cocky young officer nestled there.

He took stock. He suddenly realized that his original search for the truth about the Holocaust had changed and grown drastically. He was quite certain now that the accounts of the death camps and the systematic annihilation of the Jews were indeed fact, despite the categorical denials of some of the people he had talked to. Even those denials, he realized, and the way they had been offered, had helped convince him of that fact. But in the process of asking his questions, new and even more intriguing questions had presented themselves, all to become part of his quest. And he had learned a great deal more than he had thought possible, about intrigues and events, from the people who had lived them. He was actually astounded at the way almost everyone had opened up to him. Except on one thing.

The question of Martin Bormann.

What was it about the Bormann question which seemed to evoke such definite but diverse reactions? often causing the individual to whom he talked to clam up completely? He had been given absolutely definite statements that Bormann died in Berlin, and equally definite statements that he survived. Or, like Remer, the individual he was talking to would simply refuse to say anything at all. Remer had been extremely open about everything except Martin Bormann. Why? Was Bormann killed? Or did he survive? It had to be one or the other. There was no middle ground.

The wheels of the railroad car clacked rhythmically: Sur–vived–or–killed—sur–vived–or–killed—sur–vived–or–killed—

Herta, he thought. He suddenly longed for her. He had left her alone once again. He would have to make it up to her—make it up to her—

He fell asleep.

"What has gotten into you?" Karl–Peter Brandenburg looked at his son. Not with anger. Not with disgust. But with honest puzzlement. "These—these men are all criminals. And you—consort with them."

"It is not like that, Papa," Frank said.

"What is it then? They have blood on their hands, all those men. Why is it you seek them out? What is it you want from them, Frank? I cannot understand you."

Karl–Peter was genuinely dismayed. He did not understand his son's fascination with the past. A repugnant past, best forgotten. He was disturbed by the mail that was arriving for Frank at the Brandenburg home. Mail marked Confidential and Personal. Most of it from men whose names evoked uncomfortable memories. And the telephone calls. From people who declined to give their names when Frank was not at home, but asked strangely intrusive questions about him. It disturbed Karl–Peter. It was the kind of happening that made him feel uneasy.

"It is a matter of knowledge, Papa," Frank explained. "There is nothing wrong with wanting to learn the truth, however unsavory it may be."

"But, Frank—"

"Look, Papa. Every German, your age and mine, has at some time wondered what really did happen in our country fifty years ago. And when they began to find out, they felt shame. Shame at what they learned happened, and they wished it had not happened. But it did. So—they suppressed it. They acted as if it never happened." He looked earnestly at his father. "I—I cannot do that, Papa. I have to know the truth. All of it. And the ones from whom I can learn that truth, they are the ones you say have blood on their hands."

Karl–Peter shook his head. "You are your own master, Frank," he sighed. "You must do as you feel you must do. But do not make your family part of it." He began to walk away. He turned back.

"And Frank," he said quietly. "Be careful."

Frank looked after his father. Then at the letter in his hand. The letter that had started it all. It wasn't even a letter from one of his old Nazi correspondents, such as Baur or Wolff. It was from Arno Breker. But it was marked Confidential.

"Listen to Papa, Frank."

It was Ulrike, his younger sister, who had witnessed the confrontation. "Don't get too involved with all that Nazi stuff."

"It's history, Ulrike. And history is to be studied." He grinned at her. "You know what they say happens if you don't," he added.

"But you—you are getting caught up in it, like in a spider's web. Just be careful that you can get free again. It's dumb what you are doing."

"That is not what you said to Herta," Frank chided her.

"What do you mean?" Ulrike bridled.

"Herta told me that you were quite proud of your big brother," he said. "The way he could get to just about anyone he wanted to. And find out things."

"Herta says a lot of things," Ulrike dismissed it.

But it was true. She did have mixed emotions about her brother's "old Nazi" activities. She was afraid for him. It seemed such a dangerous thing to be involved with. But she was also proud of the way he was able to make things go his way.

Frank regarded his sister with affection. They weren't just brother and sister. They liked each other. Ulrike's reactions to his doings were not that different from those of his friends in school. At first, when he had told them a little about his experiences, there had been general skepticism. An unwillingness to believe that what he told them he had found out was really true. And there was disbelief that he had actually been with the people he said he had.

Some of his close friends became concerned for his safety, as he had gotten deeper and deeper into his project, and had met more and more controversial people; afraid that their friend was playing with fire. Fire that could do more than burn him, as one of them had said.

Others flat out chose not to believe him at all. He knew that they would ridicule him behind his back. "Frank is a great one for telling stories," they would scoff. "The taller the better!" And when he had shown one of the more outspoken skeptics a picture of himself and Generaloberst Karl Wolff, the disbeliever had accused him to his face of doctoring the photograph.

Mentally he shrugged. After all, he wasn't doing it for them.

But he couldn't quite keep it from bothering him.

A little.

He opened the letter. It was a brief note with the telephone number in Düsseldorf of Gerda Christian, one of Adolf Hitler's four personal secretaries....

The woman's voice that answered the telephone was pleasant, controlled, and surprised, as Frank stated his name and explained his reason for calling.

"I understand from Herr Breker that you might grant me a few minutes of your time, Frau Christian," he said.

There was a pause. "Of course I know Arno Breker." The voice was guarded. "He is my neighbor. His studio is just around the corner. But—"

"It would mean a lot to me, Frau Christian," Frank pressed. "I very much want to talk to someone who was with the Führer during his last days, his last hours in the Berlin Bunker."

"It is not that I do not wish to see you, Herr Brandenburg," Gerda Christian said. "But I fear there is little I can tell you that you do not already know." There was a slight pause. "However, I do have another thought, if you are interested."

"Of course."

"There are three others of the Führer's secretaries. I know them. I can send you their addresses, if you wish. Perhaps they can be of help to you."

"That would be most kind of you."

Frank was disappointed. Gerda Christian, as well as being Hitler's personal secretary, had been engaged to SS Col. Erich Kempka, the Führer's personal chauffeur, and later married Luftwaffe Maj. Gen. Eckard Christian. No ordinary secretary. He had hoped she would be a treasure trove of intimate information. Perhaps she was, but she was obviously not willing to let go of her treasures.

"As a matter of fact, Herr Brandenburg," the woman continued, "I do have a suggestion." There was a curious hesitation in her voice.

"Yes, Frau Christian?"

"I—I think you should talk to Schroeder. Fräulein Christa Schroeder. She was one of us. Our speed typist. I—I can give you her number. She lives in Munich. I think she can tell you some—some most interesting things." Again the slight, hesitant pause.

"If you can get her to talk to you."

XII

He had decided to bring flowers.

It was such a beautiful summer day, and even though he had meant to buy a box of chocolates, the cheerful colors of the bouquets on a flower cart had won out. Summer vacation from school was beginning, which meant that he had more time to spend on his project, such as time to go to Munich to visit Christa Schroeder.

As he mounted the stairs to her walkup in the modest apartment house on Belgraderstrasse, the sparse information he had been able to dig up about the woman ran through his mind.

Christa Schroeder had been one of Hitler's personal secretaries for twelve years, working closely with him, travelling with him wherever he went, ever since the Führer had noticed her when she was working for Martin Bormann and had requested her services. She had had a reputation for being efficient, as well as for being the most sharp–tongued, querulous, and critical of the women, often dangerously outspoken. Her total involvement with the Führer had become her life, and although she was only twenty–five when she first began to work for him she had never married. He was curious to see what kind of woman Christa Schroeder was.

Plump, he thought, as he stared at the elderly woman who opened the door. A short, plump body, a plump face with a perpetual little frown under grey hair gathered into a plump bun. Plump.

"Would you like a cup of coffee, Herr Brandenburg?" she asked as soon as they entered the small, sparsely furnished sitting room of the apartment where Christa Schroeder lived alone.

"*Bitte sehr*—thank you very much."

As they sat sipping their hot black coffee Frank looked around. The room was totally without individual character, he thought, totally uninteresting. A textbook case of genteel poverty. He felt slightly ill at ease.

Christa Schroeder regarded him seriously. "Dara—Frau Christian—she did not see you, Herr Brandenburg, *ja?* She did not talk to you? Give you any information?"

"No, Fräulein Schroeder," Frank said honestly. "She did not."

Christa Schroeder nodded gravely. "I did not think she had," she said.

"Why not?"

"Gerda does not like to talk about the—the old days."

"Why not?"

The woman looked at him curiously. "You do not know about Dara, *Ja?*"

"No. Not very much."

"She chose to stay in the Bunker. In Berlin. To the very end. When—when it was all over, and she left during the final breakout, she was caught by Russian soldiers." She peered at Frank over her cup. "She had some very disagreeable experiences." She shook her head slowly. "Dara does not like to talk about—the old days." She fell silent.

"You yourself had left the Bunker before the final breakout, hadn't you?" Frank asked after a while.

Christa nodded solemnly. "At the Führer's orders. I wanted to stay. One of the younger secretaries had a mother in Munich. I wanted her to go. But the Führer said to me, 'You must go, Christa. I am starting a resistance movement in Bavaria, and I need you there for that. You mean the most to me.' I cried, Herr Brandenburg, I cried. And the Führer tried to comfort me. 'We shall see each other soon again,' he promised me. 'I shall be coming down there myself in a few days.'" Solemnly she regarded Frank. "He never did."

"But you left when he asked you to."

She nodded. "As part of General Baur's evacuation operation. By air. Late in the evening of April 22nd. There were ten planes that left Berlin." She sighed. "I was told that the last plane to leave, the one that carried Willi Arndt, the Führer's favorite servant, and all the documents, I was told it was shot down."

"What documents, Fräulein Schroeder?"

The woman shook her head. "I do not know. All I know is that they were supposed to be very important. And secret. There were many cases of them."

"What happened to the plane? Do you know? and to the documents?"

"No one knows." Again she shook her head. "No one knows, Herr Brandenburg. The plane, everyone and everything in it, it was all lost." Again she sighed. "And it had such a lovely name, that operation. Most of them had such—such mundane names. But this one— *Geheimoperation Serail*—Secret Operation Seraglio."

"It was General Baur's operation?"

"Yes. Operation Seraglio." She got a dreamy expression on her unsmiling face. "Seraglio," she said softly. "It was such a romantic name. A sultan's harem. It brought us visions of wafting palm fronds and the fragrance of jasmine. And protection. Not at all like the columns of black smoke and the stench of a burning Berlin, overrun with Russian barbarians." She looked almost pleadingly at Frank. "You see, *ja?* The Führer wanted to spare us all that. He wanted us safe— while he, himself, made the ultimate sacrifice for his people."

"I am glad you got out," Frank said.

"The Führer was always so considerate of others," Christa went on. "I remember once. It was my birthday, and I was sick in the hospital. It was in March of 1944. The Führer sent Dara to me with beautiful flowers and champagne. And a note asking me to get well, written in his own hand."

"That certainly was considerate of him."

Sternly Christa peered at him. "It was more than that, Herr Brandenburg," she intoned gravely. "Much more than that. It was a singular honor!"

"An honor?"

"Yes. An honor. When Schaub—"

Frank frowned his question at her.

"Obergruppenführer—Major General—Julius Schaub, one of the Führer's two personal adjutants—when Schaub reminded him of someone's birthday, or anniversary, or loss, the Führer made strict distinctions about how his congratulations or concern should be handled. A brief note bearing only his signature, with the flowers chosen by the adjutant, was a mere step above a simple, printed card. But if it were a special person, the Führer himself would write the note and select what flowers to send. So you see, his solicitude for me had a category all its own. A real honor, *ja?*"

"I agree with you, Fräulein Schroeder."

For the first time a hint of a smile tugged at this serious woman's lips. It quickly disappeared.

"The Führer always thought of others," the woman said. "One of his last concerns was for his friends. That is why he took such extreme steps to protect them. That is why, even when all was lost and the world must have weighed heavily on his shoulders, he found time to make certain they would continue to be protected."

Frank picked up at once. "What steps, Fräulein Schroeder?" he asked.

For a moment she peered at him solemnly. "I shall tell you," she said. "People should know. I am certain the story has been told before. But not the full story, Herr Brandenburg. Not the full story. No. I do not think the full story of the Führer's consideration for others has been told. If it has," she added, "it has quickly been forgotten."

"I should be most interested."

"I worked for the Führer for many years, Herr Brandenburg, so I know," Christa Schroeder began. "It was not always pleasant. During the war many of the places we had to work in and live in were cold and dank, or intensely hot and stuffy, like the awful train we lived and worked in for days and days while the Führer inspected the situation in Poland. Or the clamminess and chill of Felsennest—the Nest of Rocks—in the Eifel Mountains in the west. That was the Führer's first field headquarters bunker, and it was barely livable. There were many others, one more uncomfortable than the other. Even the Führerbunker in Berlin was awful, and the Führer's own study was small and cold and thoroughly unpleasant. We were always isolated, Herr Brandenburg. Confined. Cut off from the world. In the Berghof. In Berlin. Everywhere."

Frank listened impatiently. What *was* that act of extreme consideration on part of the Führer? When would the woman come to the point? He did not dare interrupt her, lest she should decide not to open up after all. So he let her ramble on.

"Schaub had been with the Führer forever," she continued. "Twenty years at least. Since the very early days. His Party number was 71 and his SS number was 7," she added with typical secretarial recall, a hint of awe in her voice. "I remember him well. He was a hard–drinking man with a moon–like face. And he was the one the Führer chose to help him. He kept Schaub in Berlin to the very last moment, before he sent him on his way." She leaned forward conspiratorially. "You see, Herr Brandenburg, the Führer had an armored safe. Only he himself had the key to it. It had been up in the Chancellery, now it was in the Bunker. And he had another one at Berchtesgaden. And one in the bedroom of his apartment in Munich. Three armored safes. With highly secret papers and documents. And just before the end, the Führer and Schaub spent hours sorting through the records in the Bunker safe. And then the Führer ordered Schaub to burn them."

"All of them?"

"I do not know. I think so."

"If any of them had been saved, what would have happened to them? Where would they be now?"

Christa shrugged. "I do not know. All I know is that Schaub flew to Munich and to Berchtesgaden to burn all the papers in the safes there."

"But why, Fräulein Schroeder? What were those papers?"

"All the records of the Führer's personal intelligence network," Christa said solemnly.

Frank stared at her. "Personal—intelligence—network?"

"They were the most important, the most secret, the most sensitive documents pertaining to the Führer personally, and to the Third Reich, Herr Brandenburg. And they dated back all the way to the Führer's early years. You see, the Führer did not trust the military intelligence networks, nor his political intelligence networks. And he was right, as usual. Had he done so, the secrets he wanted kept secret forever would have become common knowledge, as is everything else these networks handled."

Frank was puzzled. "But—what kind of intelligence? What were these documents the Führer so desperately wanted safeguarded? And what did their destruction have to do with protecting the Führer's friends? I do not understand."

"Then you must listen," Christa said primly. "The Führer had a far–flung network of informants, advisors, and confidants. And supporters. All over the world, and through a period of many years.

Oh, it was not an ordinary network, mind you. Many of its members did not even know they were part of it."

"Did not know? How—"

"Hear me out, Herr Brandenburg. Throughout the Führer's rise to power he was in contact with many of the world's top political leaders as well as many powerful and influential men in other areas of life. Big business. Scientists. Many important industrialists. He corresponded with them. He solicited their confidential advice and opinions—and he got them. He exchanged confidences and plans with them. And he kept all the papers and documents in those three safes. The correspondence. The notes of conversations and conferences. Everything." She peered closely at Frank. "After all, the Führer could not have built and reached the level of his power without the help, conscious or not, of such people, could he?"

She shook her head, answering herself. "But had all those papers, all those records fallen into the wrong hands, the lives and reputations of many great names would have been destroyed. History would have been rewritten. I know, Herr Brandenburg, I typed many of those documents. The Führer was aware of that possibility, and he took his drastic measures to keep it from happening. Because he honored his friends and was loyal to them, even though some of them had since abandoned him."

"Who were these friends, Fräulein Schroeder? Can you mention names?"

"Certainly."

He waited.

"The Führer used his own secret weapon to succeed. Knowledge. Knowledge which no one suspected him of having. Knowledge that could help him make bold and unexpected moves, which the world often would regard as inspired foolhardiness, when in reality everything was quite logical—in the light of the knowledge his friends, wittingly or unwittingly, had given him."

"The names," Frank reminded her. "You were going to give me some names."

Soberly Christa eyed him.

"The ones you would expect, of course. Mussolini. Admiral Horthy. King Boris of Bulgaria. But also such prominent *Engländer* as Lord Londonderry and Lord Rothermere, the British newspaper king. The Führer had written articles for his papers under a pen name. And

Amerikaner such as Joseph Kennedy and Charles Lindbergh. There were Indian maharajas and Chinese generals. Kings of Siam and Egypt, including Farouk, to whom the Führer gave a beautiful Mercedes as a gift. And the Shah of Persia, Reza Pahlavi, who also was presented with a Mercedes. There was the Imam of Yemen, Yahya, and the Agha Khan, who—to the delight of the Führer—knew whole passages from *Mein Kampf* by heart."

She paused for breath. "And there were transcripts of notes on meetings and conversations with such foreign statesmen as Lloyd George, Lord Vansittart, the undersecretary of state for foreign affairs, Chamberlain, and the Duke of Windsor. Molotov and Franco. And Petain. The Führer admired Marshal Petain. And many, many more powerful and knowledgeable men."

She looked gravely at Frank. "The Führer was a thorough man, Herr Brandenburg. A very thorough man."

"And you typed some of those memos?"

Christa nodded. "I did."

"Do you remember anything that was in them?"

Christa frowned at him. "It was my duty to take notes, Herr Brandenburg. To type them up. *Not* to remember them."

She got a distant look on her face. "The Führer trusted us. All of us. He was wonderful to work for. Always kind. Always considerate. And always a perfect gentleman, even though we often spent much time in close and intimate quarters. Only once—"

She stopped.

"Only once?" Frank prompted.

"It was not his fault," Christa said defensively. "It was—because of Dr. Morell."

"Dr. Morell? Dr. Theodor Morell, the Führer's personal doctor? What do you mean?"

"It was—it was because of something he had given the Führer," Christa said stiffly. "I am certain of it. Or it would never have happened."

"What, Fräulein? What happened?"

Christa bit her lip. "The Führer was always perfectly correct," she said. "But once—once, it was in the autumn of '44, when we were having tea with the Führer, Dara and I, he—suddenly looked at me, like he had never looked at me before. And he—he began to talk about love. He acted like he had never acted before. Virtually without—

without inhibitions. He said how wonderful it would be for two people to—to love one another. And he looked straight at me. We had never heard him speak like that before. Never."

"But what has that to do with Dr. Morell?"

"Oh. We found out later that Dr. Morell had given the Führer an injection. To make him stronger."

Frank looked blank.

"You see, Herr Brandenburg," Christa explained. "The injection was made from the testicles of young bulls."

There was a moment's silence. Frank didn't know what to say. He was relieved when Christa Schroeder went on.

"The Führer was always so careful with what he drank. And ate. You know he was a vegetarian."

Frank nodded. "I know."

"But not always. Only after—after his favorite niece, Geli, Geli Raubal, shot herself. After a quarrel with the Führer. It was, of course, a terrible shock to him. He had been very fond of her. And then— then he saw her lying there. Dead. Dead and bloody. And he thought of—dead meat. In a butcher's shop. And he never ate meat again."

Frank gaped openly at her. What on earth was she telling him?

"That is when Eva Braun saw her chance," Christa went on tartly. "As long as Geli had been the Führer's favorite, Eva had had to stay in the shadows. But after Geli's death—she made her move. Of course, to their dying days, the Führer never *knew* the girl."

"What do you mean—*knew?*"

"I mean, Herr Brandenburg, they were never in bed together. They never had sexual intercourse, that is what I mean. I know that for a fact," she added earnestly.

"How?"

"Eva's own hairdresser told me."

Frank stared at the woman, not sure how to react to her astounding assertions.

"Anyway," Christa continued. "Eva was never really in love with the Führer."

"I thought—"

Christa went right on. "She was in love with her sister's husband, with Gretl's husband, SS Lt. Gen. Hermann Fegelein. He was Himmler's liaison officer. You know that she influenced the Führer to keep her precious Fegelein in the bunker with her, while her pregnant sister stayed down in Bavaria."

She leaned forward, her tone of voice becoming a conspiratorial whisper. "So he could be close to her, *ja?* And then, when Fegelein had left the Bunker without permission, and they could not find him, and they sent out a patrol to locate him, and it was discovered that he had a mistress in Berlin on Bleibtreustrasse—" She peered at Frank, more animated than ever. "Such an ironic name, *ja? Bleibtreustrasse—* Stay True Street. Ironic, *ja?* And they found him there, in civilian clothes. He had taken off his SS general's uniform, ready to desert. With his mistress. And they brought him back. But not before he had been brazen enough to call Eva on the telephone and suggest that they run away together! *Unverschämt*—shameless, *ja?* Of course, she could only decline. And they took him back to the Bunker, along with a little valise he had been packing. And they found it was filled with money and gold and jewelry, including a gold watch Eva, herself, had given him for repair. Eva was furious. Over the mistress, and the watch, and everything. So she did not lift a finger to stop the Führer from having Fegelein shot—just hours before she was married." She wagged a finger at Frank. "I tell you, Herr Brandenburg, it was a classic case of hell having no fury like a woman scorned!"

Frank stared at the woman. He was speechless. But not Christa. It was as if a verbal floodgate had been opened up.

"What I cannot understand, Herr Brandenburg," she said confidentially, "is why the Führer did not know. About Eva, I mean. He was always so—intuitive. I remember, on the day of the attempt on his life. At Rastenburg. He said to me, 'There is something in the air.' He knew something was about to happen." She looked earnestly at Frank. "Did you know, Herr Brandenburg, that I was asked to have lunch with the Führer, right after the attempt to murder him? I was. He looked just fine, almost invigorated, full of spirit and resolve. He told me he was certain that this was the turning point for Germany. For the war. For him. From now on all would be well. His miraculous escape was a sign. An omen. 'I am happy the *Schweinehunde* have unmasked themselves!' he said. Those were his very words, and that is exactly what I told all those Allied interrogators who hounded me after the war."

For a brief moment she was silent, remembering.

"But, toward the end," she said, her voice subdued, "he was so— different. So tired and listless, his color so bad. It was so sad, when I saw him for the last time."

"Before you left the Bunker."

Christa nodded.

"Dara and I had lunch with him. In his desperately depressing little study, where he had taken all his meals for some time." She sighed. "That is when he told us we had to leave the Bunker. We were supposed to drive by car through Bohemia down to Bavaria. But as I was packing the few things I would need, the Führer called me on the intercom telephone. 'We have been cut off,' he said to me. His once–vigorous voice was now flat and dead. 'Your car cannot get through,' he said. And he told me we would have to fly out. At dawn. As soon as the all–clear sounded."

She stopped. She swallowed. Hard.

"I had never heard the Führer sound so sad, so dull," she said softly. "And he stopped speaking in mid–sentence. And when I said something to him, he never answered."

Her eyes growing moist, she looked straight at Frank.

"I never heard his voice again."

As Frank walked down the narrow staircase from Christa Schroeder's walk–up apartment, he felt as if he were returning from a trip through Alice's looking glass. It was difficult for him to skim off the hard facts from what appeared to be a pool of rumors and gossip. And yet, gossip often did flow from fact.

He suddenly realized that he had been so mesmerized by Christa's tales that he had forgotten to ask her what she knew about Martin Bormann. He slowed his steps. Should he turn back? He decided he would have to write.

But Christa had told him some fascinating things. What did happen to those secret papers of Hitler's, for instance? Were they all burned? He made up his mind not to dismiss any of it summarily, before he had had a chance to check it out with Baur, when next he had an opportunity to see the general who played such an important role in Christa's account. (Christa Schroeder died in Munich in June 1984.)

Meanwhile he was anxious to get back home and write everything down in detail, while it was still fresh in his mind.

The air was permeated with it.

Someone had just mowed one of the lawns, and the sweet, fresh smell of newly–cut grass filled his nostrils. It was one of his favorite smells.

He was walking briskly from the house to one of the greenhouses, where his father was working. It was a crisp and clear spring day, but a few clouds were gathering on the horizon.

It had been a busy year for him. He had made a second trip to Munich, this time to see Henriette von Schirach, the former wife of Hitler Youth leader Baldur von Schirach, about whom Ministerialdirigent Heinrich Heim had told him. She had divorced her husband while he was serving a twenty–year sentence in Spandau Prison, convicted of war crimes at the Nürnberg Trials.

Baldur von Schirach was the son of a German aristocrat and his American wife, whose ancestors included two signatories of the Declaration of Independence. Baldur joined the Party in 1924. He became an avid anti–Semite after reading *The International Jew*, by Henry Ford. He worshipped the Führer, and in 1931 he was appointed Reich Youth Leader of the NSDAP. Two years later, at the age of twenty–six, he was made Leader of the Youth of the German Reich, an organization which by 1936 had over six million members.

He married Henriette Hoffmann, daughter of Adolf Hitler's official photographer, Heinrich Hoffmann. Toward the outbreak of World War II he incurred the animosity of Martin Bormann because of his rising popularity and favor with the Führer. Rumors and snide allegations of "feminine behavior" and stories of his white bedroom furnished in a girlish manner began to make the rounds in Nazi circles. To offset this unflattering image of the leader of the Nazi youth, Baldur enlisted in the army in 1940. He served briefly as an infantry officer in France and earned the Iron Cross, Second Class. After only a few months active service he was, however, called home, relieved of his position as Youth Leader, as being too old for the post, and appointed Gauleiter— Governor and Defense Commissioner of Vienna.

But Bormann's attempts to discredit him were too strong, and Baldur by then had no real power or influence.

Although he had advocated a more humane treatment of the Jews, Baldur was still on record with his recommendation of deporting the Jews for the good of the German Reich, and during his tenure as Gauleiter of Vienna close to 180,000 Jews were deported to camps in Poland. It was this record that earned him his conviction at the Nürnberg Trials, even though at that time he denied all knowledge of the extermination of the Jews and called Hitler a "millionfold murderer."

After his release in 1966, Baldur von Schirach lived in seclusion, and died in his sleep in 1974.

The meeting with Henriette von Schirach had been pleasant enough; the woman was obviously intelligent, although Frank had had the impression that she was a tippler who had overfortified herself for the meeting, occasionally becoming slightly confused.

Their meeting had taken place in her one–room, third–floor apartment on Schönfelderstrasse in Munich, where Henriette von Schirach lived alone. The apartment had a tiny balcony ringed with planter boxes overhung with knotgrass. To Frank it had looked a little like an oversized bird's nest, and when the woman had shown it to him, standing waist–deep among the plants, she had looked like an exotic stork in her lilac pullover, black pants, and black boots.

It had been interesting meeting her, but what she had had to say had been only marginally important. She believed Hitler knew about Hess's flight to England and its purpose, although she could offer no proof. She refused to discuss Martin Bormann, but she was certain that the Führer knew all about the concentration camps, telling Frank in her Bavarian accent in detail about one of her own experiences, when she was visiting friends in Amsterdam in the spring of 1943.

One night, in her hotel, she had been aroused from her sleep by the screams and cries of women coming from the street. She had looked out the window. Below, a large group of women of all ages were being brutally herded into waiting trucks by German soldiers. The next morning no one in the hotel would discuss the occurrence at all, but her Dutch friends told her that the women had been Jewesses who were being rounded up for transportation to internment camps abroad. She had been shaken. The women had obviously been mistreated, and she vowed to tell the Führer about it at the first opportunity.

Shortly thereafter her husband and she were invited to the Berghof in Berchtesgaden, and after dinner she told Hitler about her experience in Holland.

There had been an uneasy silence. No one had spoken a word. Hitler himself had been visibly embarrassed. Finally he had turned on her and brusquely asked, "What concern of yours are the Jewesses in Holland?"

And she had quoted to Frank the impassioned speech the Führer had delivered to her.

"Do you not understand?" he had said. "Every day ten thousand of my most valuable men die, men who are irreplaceable. The best. The balance, then, no longer adds up. The parity of strength in Europe will no longer exist, when the *others* do not cease to be. They would live, those in the camps, those inferiors, and how will it then be in Europe in a hundred years? In a thousand? I am accountable to my people. To no one else. If I am branded a bloodhound in the eyes of the world, so be it. I care nothing about posthumous fame." And he had fixed her with his burning, angry eyes. "You must learn to hate!" he had blazed. "*I* had to."

The Schirachs had been asked to leave the Berghof the next day. They were never asked back.

While in Munich, Frank had taken the opportunity to visit Dachau, one of the most infamous of the Nazi concentration camps.

It had been a sobering experience, although somehow the antiseptic museum atmosphere of the place, with its dispassionate printed *Wegweiser*—guidebook: "l. *Lagerstrasse*—Camp Street...7. *Totenkammer*—Room of the Dead, continually filled with corpses...17. *SS Schiessplatz*—SS Shooting Range, some 6,000 Russian prisoners of war were shot here," and so on, failed to generate any real feeling of the camp as it must have been. The impersonal treatment of it all tended to desensitize rather than stimulate the emotions.

In "12. *Lagergärtnerei*—Camp Nursery," of special interest to Frank, he had picked up a piece of broken brick. It had found its place in his bunker at home along with some photographs and a book given to him by Henriette von Schirach, a personal Christmas gift from Hitler to her mother, as well as the Schaub documents he had obtained from Christa Schroeder.

His collection of Nazi memorabilia had been growing steadily. The macabre aspect of it never occurred to Frank. In that room, steeped in Nazi relics, he would transcribe his notes, do his research, and organize his material, including the photographs that were taken of him and his subjects at each meeting. To him the bunker was a "tool of his trade." But the family shunned the place. Only Gritti, his little dachshund, would happily join him there.

Frank would sit in his bunker and submerge himself in the ghostly atmosphere of an unsavory forty–year–old past, putting himself in the proper frame of mind to meet and relate to the living relics of that musty past.

And during his vacation he had finally been successful in meeting one more of his targeted subjects, Col. Nicolaus von Below. After copious correspondence and on–again–off–again appointments, von Below had consented to talk to him in person.

Frank had visited him in his duplex apartment building on Joseph Haydn-Weg in Detmold, Westphalia, where von Below and his wife occupied the upstairs apartment. The place had been beautifully furnished and carpeted. A bookcase held many books about the Reich and the war as well as biographies of several prominent Nazi personalities, and on the wall were silhouette clippings of von Below and his wife. In the foyer hung a large rendering of the New Chancellery that had been given to von Below by Albert Speer.

At seventy–four the former Luftwaffe adjutant to the Führer had an impressive and elegant appearance, Frank had thought. Tall, well built, with greying hair, he had worn an open white shirt and white pants with a black belt and a bright red sweater. Polite and dignified, he had seemed to Frank more like a bank director relaxing at home than a former high–ranking Nazi officer.

But Frank's high expectations had been deflated; the interview had been disappointing.

Von Below had stated the "facts" as he saw them in a strictly noncommittal way without any self–involvement.

Regarding the fate of Martin Bormann, he was of the opinion that the Reichsleiter died in Berlin, although he stressed that this opinion was not based on personal knowledge, but strictly on hearsay. And he had no involvement, nor indeed knowledge, of any current Bormann organization.

Adolf Hitler was neither a madman nor a "rug–chewer," as had been reported so often. The Führer knew exactly what he was doing. At all times. But, the adjutant told Frank, even though he, himself, worked closely with the Führer, he had never heard about the extermination camps or the concentration camps. Only after the war did he learn of their existence. Now, however, he was convinced that they did exist. And also that the annihilation of Jews had been carried out on direct orders from Hitler, certainly with his full knowledge, even though there was no written documentation to support that view. But, he felt, it would have been impossible even for Göring or Himmler to have carried out the—the final solution without the Führer's knowledge.

Nothing new.

He had talked on the phone and corresponded with Frau Luise Jodl, the widow of Generaloberst Alfred Jodl, hanged at Nürnberg, but he had not been able to see her. Frau Jodl had simply referred him to the books written about her husband, and had asked for proof that Frank was not a neo–Nazi. He had let it go. It had not seemed important enough to pursue. But he had taken the time to visit both Baur and Wolff again.

Frank was just about to enter the greenhouse when he heard Ulrike call his name.

He turned to look toward the house.

His sister was gesturing to him, holding up one hand to her ear as if grasping a telephone receiver.

"What is it?" he called to her.

"Telephone!" she shouted back.

"Who?"

Ulrike took her hand from her ear.

"He says," she called to her brother. "He says his name is Karl Wolff!"

XIII

He hung up.

For a moment he sat staring at the telephone, a frown clouding his face.

Had he done the right thing?

Do not involve your family, his father had warned him. But his parents were about to leave on a trip and would be gone for two weeks, and Ulrike would be away too. Only his grandparents would be home. It might be all right, but his father would skin him alive when he found out. And find out he would.

But what the hell else could he have done?

On the phone General Wolff had told Frank that he was going to Hamburg and would like to stop off in Hildesheim on the way and pay Frank a visit.

Frank had said yes.

He had had no other choice. Had he said no, he likely as not would have lost Wolff, and the general was much too valuable a contact to risk losing.

So, in two days SS-Generaloberst Karl Wolff, intimate of Himmler,

Hitler, and the entire Nazi hierarchy, affectionately called "Wölffchen"—
little wolf—by Hitler, would be a guest in the Brandenburg home.

Karl Wolff had tears in his eyes.

He stood just inside the door to Frank's bunker. Slowly he looked
all around the room. The photographs on the bare cement walls, the
swastika–adorned "people's radio," the Berghof letter folder once
owned by Hitler, and the portrait of the Führer himself; all the Third
Reich mementos.

"*Ach, du lieber Gott*—Oh, my dear God," he whispered slowly.
"This is just like stepping into yesterday. Into the glorious past." He
turned to Frank. "I—I almost expect the Führer to join us any moment."

He returned his attention to the room. Slowly he walked through
it, reverently examining each object, each memento.

"*Mein lieber Frank*," he said. "My dear Frank. You have created
a small piece of history. A haven for memories."

He walked over to the crammed bookcase. He took out a book. It
was Adolf Hitler's *Mein Kampf.*

"I have not seen a copy of this for many years, my boy." Without
opening the book he quoted: "'Just as the State of the People must
devote the greatest attention to the training of the will and the strength
of decision, it must, from an early age, implant the joy of responsibility
and the courage of acceptance—'" he looked straight at Frank, "'—
in the hearts of youth!' Those were the words of the Führer."

He placed the book back on the shelf and took out another, *The
Bormann Brotherhood*, by the prominent British journalist, William
Stevenson. He looked at it, a sardonic little smile on his lips.

"You read everything, it appears," he commented.

Frank saw his chance. "I once asked you, Herr General," he ventured,
"if you knew whether Martin Bormann died in Berlin or survived to
escape. I—I had the impression you would tell me at a later date."
He paused. "Did he survive?"

Wolff turned the book over in his hands. He seemed to be delib-
erating with himself. "The remains found in Berlin in 1973 were
authenticated as those of Martin Bormann," he said finally. "By an
expert, Frank. Dr. Hans Jürgen Spengler of the West Berlin Forensic
Institute."

"The remains of Eva Braun were also authenticated, Herr General,"

Frank countered. "By experts. Yet one of those experts, the dental expert, Professor Sognnaes, from UCLA in America—only last year he declared that authentication wrong. It was not Eva Braun after all. Is it not possible that the authentication of the Bormann remains could be wrong as well?"

Wolff gave him an amused little smile. "If you keep digging deep enough, my boy, you might unearth his bones. Or his ghost."

Frank would not let it go. "Is he really a ghost, Herr General? Or did he survive?"

Wolff put the book back on the shelf with an impatient shove. "Of course he survived," he said testily. "Of course he escaped." He turned to Frank and looked him gravely in the eyes. "I did not tell you that when you came to me for the first time. Edeltraut—does not want me to talk about it. To anyone."

Frank nodded. He remembered the woman's outburst when the subject of Bormann had come up in Wolff's home. "Why not?" he asked.

"It could have—unpleasant consequences."

"What do you mean, Herr General, unpleasant consequences?"

Wolff turned back to the bookcase. "We will not discuss this any further," he said. It was suddenly evident that he had once been used to total obedience. "There are some things which could too easily become dangerous for you to know, and to talk about," he finished. The matter was closed.

Wolff pulled out another book from a shelf on the bookcase. It was titled *Verrat auf Deutsch—Betrayal in German*, written by Erich Kuby. His mouth grew tight.

Frank knew why. Wolff had told him. While writing the book, Kuby had solicited Wolff's help in researching the general's involvement in what was known as *Unternehmen Sunrise*—Operation Sunrise, the secret negotiations carried out between Allen Dulles of the United States OSS and Generaloberst Wolff without Hitler's knowledge, to effect the surrender of the German armed forces in Italy only days before VE–Day. Wolff had supplied Kuby with much information and many personal observations, and he felt the author had betrayed him, when instead of telling the story as Wolff himself had seen it and told it, he had portrayed the general in a far from flattering light. Just as had Stevenson in his book *The Bormann Brotherhood*, when he wrote that General Wolff had "sold out" for assurances by Allen Dulles that he himself would not be tried for any war crimes. Something Wolff bitterly denied.

Wolff was about to replace the book in the bookcase when Frank stopped him.

"Please, Herr General," he said. "Would you write in it for me? I should appreciate it very much."

Wolff gave him a quick look, his eyes angry. Without a word he strode to Frank's desk, sat down and placed the book on top of the Hitler letter folder. He opened it to the flyleaf and began to write.

Finished, he slammed the book shut and handed it to Frank.

"Here," he said curtly.

Frank took the book.

"Thank you," he said. He opened it and read:

I herewith inscribe this frivolous and maliciously falsified book, which in the most vicious manner defiles the German honor and the German aerie, to

Frank Brandenburg
(signed) Karl Wolff
Colonel General of the Waffen SS, Ret.
Prien am Chiemsee

"Thank you, Herr General." Frank put the book away. He turned back to Wolff.

"I have some nice wine," he said. "Perhaps you would like a glass? We could listen to some music. I have some wonderful Wagner tapes."

"Ah, Wagner," Wolff said appreciatively. He relaxed. "He was the Führer's favorite composer. By all means, Wagner."

As they sat and sipped their wine, listening to the stirring music, Wolff behind the desk beneath the portrait of the Führer and Frank in one of the chairs pulled away from the table, Frank felt himself transported back in time. He felt part of the past, as he and Wolff exchanged small talk about the days of long ago when Hitler's Reich was strong and powerful. Wolff was a charming and fascinating conversationalist and Frank felt himself drawn to the older man.

As Frank was changing a tape, his grandfather suddenly appeared in the door.

Wolff stood up, and Frank introduced the two men to each other.

As he stood watching them making polite conversation—two dignified elderly men, one who years ago would never have had the opportunity of being in the other's presence, let alone conversing with him as an equal—the spell in which he had allowed himself to be caught cleared away. A little frightened, he realized the danger he was courting, the ease with which reality could be replaced with induced nostalgia.

He resolved once again to be careful. Extra careful.

For perhaps another half hour the men talked and listened to the music of Richard Wagner. Wolff proudly showed them a ring, the signet ring of Hermann Göring, given to Wolff by Göring's daughter Edda. "I, too, have a few mementos," he said. "Although not in a—a memory–stirring place such as this." Then the general had taken his leave, his visit to Hildesheim and Frank's bunker at an end.

Gen. Wolff had told Frank that Lina Heydrich, the aging widow of Reinhard Heydrich, lived on the small island of Fehmarn in the Baltic Sea north of Lübeck, and when Frank returned to Travemünde, where he now lived while he pursued his studies at Gartenbaubetrieb Wulf in Lübeck, he decided to try to find the woman and pay her a visit. He had heard that she had returned to her maiden name, Lina von Osten.

The day was raw and overcast when he set out on the sixty–odd–mile car trip from Travemünde to Fehmarn. He crossed over to the island on the bridge to Puttgarden and headed for Burg, the main town. Although he had no address or telephone number, he anticipated no trouble in finding Frau von Osten; it was not a common name, and Burg had less than seven thousand inhabitants, the whole island less than thirteen thousand.

The island of Fehmarn has an area of a mere one hundred and twenty square miles. It is part of the Prussian province of Schleswig–Holstein and lies between the Kieler bay and the Mecklenburger bay, separated from Holstein on the mainland by the Fehmarn–Sund. The island is flat, with no forests but with excellent grazing land for the large herds of cattle.

Frank had long since learned that the obvious often pays off, so when he arrived in Burg the first thing he did was to look in the local telephone book, and there she was: Lina von Osten.

He called the number listed. A woman answered.

"Bitte?"

"Frau von Osten?"

"This is Frau von Osten speaking."

"Frau von Osten. My name is Frank Brandenburg. General Wolff told me that you live here and suggested that I call you, and perhaps meet with you."

There was a slight pause, then: "General—Wolff?"

"Yes. Generaloberst Karl Wolff. Your husband knew him quite well."

"I—see."

"I wonder if it would be convenient if I came over to see you for a few moments. I am doing some historical research—"

"Historical research?"

"Yes. And I should very much like to ask you a few questions."

"Me?"

"Yes, Frau von Osten. Some questions pertaining to your husband and his work."

"My husband is dead, Herr Brandenburg. Many years." The woman's voice was flat.

"I know. But I should very much like to talk to you."

Again there was a pause. The woman sounded hesitant when she said: "Well—if I can help you in any way, I—" she let the sentence die.

"Thank you, Frau von Osten," Frank said. "May I come and see you then? I am in Burg."

"Well—yes. If I can be of help to you."

"I'm sure you can, Frau von Osten."

"Very well then."

"May I have your address? And perhaps directions?"

The woman told Frank where she lived and how to get there. It was a little village called Niendorf only a couple of kilometers north of Burg, and Frank at once got in his car and headed for the von Osten home.

As he was driving through town, bound for the little village where Lina von Osten lived, he wondered what she would be like. The widow of one of the most sinister Nazis, the man who was known as "The Blond Beast" or "*Der Henker*—the Hangman." On the phone she'd sounded a little uncertain. Even vague. But then, Wolff had said she was aging. What would she really be like? Was she mentally alert? He knew nothing about Lina Heydrich, although he knew a great deal about her late husband.

The rise of Reinhard Tristan Eugen Heydrich to power and position in Adolf Hitler's Germany had been nothing short of meteoric and paralleled the rise of the Third Reich itself.

Born in 1904 in Halle in the Prussian state of Saxony, young Reinhard at fifteen years of age joined the Maercker Freikorps, one of the paramilitary organizations designed to prevent Poland from encroaching on the Fatherland and to keep Germany safe from Bolshevism. He also became a member of the Deutsche Schutz und Trutzbund—the German Offensive and Defensive Alliance—a violently anti–Semitic organization. He did this to quiet unfounded rumors that there was Jewish blood in the Heydrich family. After all, if young Reinhard belonged to *that* organization there certainly could be no truth in those rumors. However, the rumors persisted and haunted Heydrich throughout his life, and as a young man he smarted at the hated invective, *Isidor!* sometimes hurled at him.

In March 1922 Reinhard joined the Kriegsmarine, the German Navy. When he had been six years old his parents had taken him to Swinemünde on the Baltic coast to watch the Kaiser's Baltic fleet on maneuvers. He had been entranced and had never forgotten the experience. He became a cadet, and in 1925, while serving on the *Braunschweig*, Reinhard Heydrich received his commission as Leutnant–zur–See. Three years later he was promoted to Oberleutnant–zur–See, serving for a time in Navy Intelligence under Wilhelm Canaris, who later, as admiral, would be head of the Abwehr, the Intelligence Service of the High Command of the Armed Forces, and a rival of Reinhard Heydrich.

While stationed in Kiel in July 1930 Reinhard went to a dance, where he met a nineteen–year–old girl named Lina von Osten, who was attending the Technical High School in Kiel, studying to become a teacher. Reinhard was at once enthralled by her, and in only a few days proposed to her. Lina and Reinhard were married in December 1931, but before that, disaster struck Reinhard.

Never tactful nor considerate of others, he had gotten himself into an awkward situation with another girl, a shipyard director's daughter. Although theories abound as to the nature of this indelicate matter, the facts have never come to light and the court records have disappeared. The only fact that remains is that, by order of Admiral Raeder, Heydrich was tried by a Navy *Ehrengericht*—an Honor Court—and was forced to resign from the Navy for "conduct unworthy of an officer." In a way it was the beginning of Reinhard Heydrich's rise to terrible power.

In July that same year he had joined the NSDAP—the Nazi Party—and shortly thereafter the SS, the black–uniformed Elite Corps. Adolf Hitler had expressed his desire to create a new kind of pure Aryan officer corps. These leaders would be young, self–assured, unhampered by past traditions, and so ruthless and brutal that the world would recoil from them in horror. They would be as merciless and ferocious as vicious dogs, beyond good and evil. And shining in the eyes of these new, young leaders would be "the gleam of pride and the unrestraint of the wild beast of prey." They would rule by terror, and by terror alone.

Reinhard Heydrich fit that description in every way.

Tall, slender, with an arrogant military bearing, a hard, sharp–featured face with ice–cold, steel–blue eyes, a tight–lipped, cruel mouth, and straight blond hair, he was the personification of Adolf Hitler's professed ideal. He was an expert horseman, an excellent fencer, and an accomplished pilot. He was totally ruthless and calculating, and would not shrink from carrying out the most inhuman tasks.

He was exactly the kind of man Adolf Hitler sought, and he quickly attracted the attention of Reichsführer SS Heinrich Himmler, his boss.

Already on December 25, 1931, in the month he was married, Heydrich was promoted to SS-Sturmbannführer—SS major—and in July the following year to SS-Standartenführer—SS colonel—and to the post of chief of the Sicherheitsdienst, the elite SS security service of the RSHA, the Reich Main Security Office. The next year he became SS-Brigadeführer—SS major general—and in July of 1934 he attained the rank of SS-Gruppenführer—SS lieutenant general. A phenomenal rise from lowly lieutenant to lieutenant general in only three years! Reinhard had served his Führer and the Third Reich well, and he had made himself all but indispensable.

He had earned the respect of his superiors for his actions during the bloodbath that took place the night of June 30, 1934, which was to become known as the "Night of the Long Knives," during which the top leaders of the Sturmabteilung, the SA—the Stormtroopers—under SA Chief of Staff Ernst Röhm, Germany's most notorious homosexual, were murdered execution style by Hitler and the SS because the SA had become too independently powerful and Röhm too much of a rival to suit the Führer. Seventy–seven high–ranking SA officials were killed, along with at least a hundred others. Heydrich had commanded one of the execution squads and personally administered the coup de grace to Gregor Strasser, who had been one of Hitler's most dangerous rivals during the early days of the Nazi movement.

As one of the instigators, he had been deeply involved in the pogrom of November 9, 1938, known as *Kristallnacht*—Crystal Night—because of the glittering mounds of glass shards from the shattered windows of vandalized Jewish shops and homes destroyed by marauding Nazi hoodlums; an event that signalled the open season of atrocities against the Jews.

And he had become a master of deceit and trickery to further the Nazi cause. Thus he fabricated scandalous but totally unfounded attacks on the integrity of the last two remaining high–ranking officers of the traditional, pre–Nazi armed forces, Field Marshal von Blomberg and Chief of the High Command von Fritsch, who were both professional soldiers of the old Reichswehr school and aroused suspicions of being slow to embrace the new Nazi views. Their careers were ruined. He was also the mastermind behind the staged attack on the German radio transmitter located at the small border town of Gleiwitz. He made it look like an act of Polish military provocation by having a group of concentration camp inmates, clad in Polish army uniforms, hauled to the station and shot on the spot, to make it look as if they had been killed by the brave defenders of the radio transmitter. In this way he provided Hitler with an excuse to invade Poland in force—and start World War II.

In 1939 Heydrich was appointed Chief of the Reich Main Security Office, which included the Criminal Police, the Sicherheitsdienst, and the dreaded Gestapo. And two years later he was again promoted, this time to SS-Obergruppenführer—full general in the SS, and was made General der Polizei—General of the Police—and given the post of Acting Reichsprotector of the Czech regions of Bohemia and Moravia, occupied by the Nazis.

On September 27th Reichsprotector Heydrich entered Prague. His first act of protection was to proclaim a state of emergency. Everyone already under arrest and suspected of treasonable acts was automatically executed, and Heydrich condemned to death six generals and ten colonels of the Czech army, with the number of executions rising to four hundred during the state of emergency. By November over five thousand suspected members of resistance groups had been arrested.

But Heydrich had other, even more important duties to carry out. He had been charged with formulating "the final solution to the Jewish problem." He did, and to coordinate the efforts of all the government departments and agencies involved in the task Heydrich, on January 20, 1942, convened a meeting in the office of the International Criminal Police Commission in Wannsee, a suburb of Berlin. This was to become known as the Wannsee Conference. Present were several high–ranking Nazi officials, including Heinrich Müller, head of the Gestapo, Adolf Eichmann, who had worked closely with Heydrich, and State Secretary Ernst Freiherr von Weizsäcker. Appropriately enough, the operation to handle the extermination of Polish Jews was named Operation Reinhard.

By now Heydrich saw himself as the logical successor to the Führer himself, and in that view he was joined by many others. But he was feared, not respected, and he frightened everyone, including his immediate superior, Reichsführer SS Heinrich Himmler. Perhaps even Hitler himself.

Then, on the morning of May 27, 1942, as Heydrich traversed the Prague suburb of Holeschowitz along the route he customarily took from his estate, Jungfern–Breschau, twenty minutes by car outside Prague, to his office in the Hradcany Castle, two Free Czech agents trained in England, Jan Kubis and Josef Gabcik, ambushed his open green Mercedes as it slowed down at a hairpin turn in the road before coming to the Troja Bridge over the Vltava River, and lobbed a hand grenade into his car. Heydrich was badly but not mortally wounded, and lying in the back of a hastily commandeered baker's van like a dusty sack of flour, he was rushed to the nearest hospital, the Libovka Clinic. Here he died of complications nine days later, on June 4th. The British–mounted Operation Anthropoid had been concluded successfully.

At his funeral Hitler himself eulogized Reinhard Heydrich, calling him "the man with the iron heart, whose name will resound in history with the greatest heroes." And posthumously he awarded him the Nazi Reich's greatest honor, the German Order, highest grade. Only one man had ever received this honor before: the engineering genius of the Reich, Fritz Todt. And Hitler offered one million Reichsmarks as a reward for the capture of the assassins.

Kubis and Gabcik were found hiding in the crypt of the St. Cyrillus and Methodius Church in Prague with several other resistance fighters. All were massacred by the SS. They had been betrayed by a man who broke under Gestapo torture. But the full reprisals for the assassination were truly terrifying in their savagery. Hitler ordered the randomly selected Czech village of Lidice razed to the ground and all its inhabitants annihilated. Every man sixteen years of age and over, 173 of them, was summarily shot. One hundred eighty four women were deported to the notorious Ravensbrück concentration camp, and 98 children were taken away to unknown fates. Elsewhere, over 1,000 other Czechs were condemned to death, a "special action" in Berlin killed an additional 152 Jews, and more than 3,000 others were taken from the Theresienstadt ghetto and exterminated. In all close to 5,000 lives paid for the life of Reinhard Heydrich, and Lidice was left a dead and barren wasteland to the memory of his name.

The clouds were turning the sky leaden as Frank drove his car toward the address Frau von Osten had given him. It was beginning to rain when Frank pulled up in front of the von Osten house, a small, modest–looking one–story structure. A couple of workmen who obviously had been working on the roof were packing up their tools. Frank walked up to the front entrance. A distant thunderclap echoed his knock on the door.

A woman somewhere in her late sixties or early seventies opened the door. Neat, nice looking, Frank thought. Behind her stood another woman. Younger. In her forties. Fifty perhaps. One of Heydrich's two daughters, Frank surmised. Silke? Or Marte?

"Frau von Osten?" he asked.

The woman nodded. "Herr Brandenburg," she said. She looked him over with ill–concealed curiosity. She stood aside. "Please," she said. "Please come in."

She led the way to a small, simply furnished living room.

"May I offer you a cup of coffee? perhaps a cookie?" She nodded at the younger woman, who left the room. "My daughter," she said.

She indicated a chair. "Please," she said. "Make yourself comfortable."

Frank sat down, as the Heydrich daughter returned with a tray holding a coffee pot, three cups, and a plate of cookies. Frau von Osten poured.

As they sat sipping their coffee a few pleasantries were exchanged, as both hostess and guest tried their best to size each other up. Then the von Osten woman said, "Now, Herr Brandenburg. How can I be of help?"

"As I told you on the phone," Frank said, "I'd like to ask you a few questions about your husband. But first—first I'd like to give you a couple of photographs. As a little gift."

"Photographs?" The woman sounded puzzled.

As was his wont when visiting people he wanted to interview, Frank had found and brought along a couple of old photos showing his subject. It seemed to flatter them and put them in a good mood. From his briefcase he pulled out two black–and–white enlargements. One was a group shot with Generaloberst Wolff, Reichsführer SS Himmler, SS-Gruppenführer Best, SS-Gruppenführer Heydrich, and other high–ranking Nazi dignitaries. The other was a portrait of Reinhard Heydrich in full SS uniform.

"Photographs of your husband, Frau von Osten," Frank said. He placed them on the table before her.

She looked at them. Her eyes grew wide. Her hand flew to her mouth and she cried, "But—oh, my God! I can tell you nothing! Nothing at all!"

XIV

Frank stared at the woman in dismay.

"But—why not, Frau von Osten? I don't understand. Why not?"

The woman pointed at the photograph on the table.

"That is *not my husband!*" she cried, an edge of hysteria tinging her voice. "I did not even know him!" Unconsciously she wrung her hands. "I had nothing to do with all that. Nothing." She looked up at Frank. "You want Lina Manninen. Not me. Not me."

"Lina Manninen?"

"Yes. *She* was married to—to that man." Again she pointed to the photograph of Reinhard Heydrich. "She has another name now. She married again. In 1965. A Finnish artist. He died four years later. It was in all the papers. *She* is the one you must talk to, if you want to know about *him*. Not me."

Frank felt the warm flush of embarrassment rise on the back of his neck. He was deeply chagrined. It was, of course, an incredible coincidence that there should be two women named Lina von Osten on the tiny island of Fehmarn. But there it was. He should have checked instead of simply wading in, taking it for granted that any woman on the island named Lina von Osten automatically would be the widow of Reinhard Heydrich. Awkwardly, he put the photographs back in his briefcase. He looked apologetically at Frau von Osten. She seemed to have regained her composure, although not her cordiality.

"I very much regret my mistake and any embarrassment it may have caused you, Frau von Osten," he said. "And I beg you to forgive me. But—when I saw the name in the telephone book I—I—" he shook his head.

"It was an honest mistake, Herr Brandenburg," she said, her voice noncommittal. "I do not fault you."

"Thank you." He looked at her. "Does—does Frau Manninen still live on the island?"

The woman nodded curtly. "In Todendorf. Only about four kilometers from here."

"Do you know if she has a telephone?" Frank pressed.

"I do not know. But we have a telephone and a telephone book. You may try." She turned to her daughter. "Anna. Show Mr. Brandenburg where the telephone is."

She turned away and began to busy herself with clearing the coffee cups from the table. It was all but a dismissal.

Frank followed her daughter to the little hallway, where a telephone stood on a small mahogany stand that had an attached bevelled–glass mirror above it and gleaming brass receptacles for umbrellas and canes on the sides. A keepsake from better days, Frank thought absentmindedly.

Anna pointed to a drawer in the stand.

"The telephone book is in there," she said. She turned on her heel and walked away.

Frank fished out the thin telephone book and thumbed through it.

Frau Lina Manninen was indeed listed, and she answered the phone on the first ring. Sheepishly, Frank told her about the mixup in names that had led him to the wrong Frau von Osten and asked her permission to visit her. Lina Manninen, formerly Lina Heydrich, wife of SS-Gruppenführer Reinhard Heydrich, assented at once.

The cold rain was coming down hard as Frank left the house and the two women and drove slowly along the deserted, unfamiliar country road.

As he stood in the gathering darkness before the Heydrich house, a cold rain pelting him and a gusty wind tearing angrily at the naked trees and rattling the peeling window shutters, banging them against the walls, he suddenly felt trapped, as if in a cheap mystery novel complete with mistaken identities and spooky old houses.

The Heydrich house itself was dark. It looked run–down and unkempt. A cracked sign hung askew on a wooden post:

PENSION IM GEHEGE

—a pitiful remembrance of better days, when Lina Heydrich had run a small guest house she had called "In the Copse."

Frank shivered. He huddled down in his overcoat, against the driving rain and the foreboding feeling of decay and gloom that began to creep over him.

A single feeble light barely illuminated the front door as he rang the bell. It was a dark and stormy night, he thought mirthlessly, the time–worn, oft–ridiculed arch–cliche for such circumstances.

But this wasn't a cliche.

The feeling of oppression was very real, so he was not surprised at the sight of the old woman who opened the door.

A witch, he thought automatically as he stared at her, a classic witch.

A deeply furrowed face, topped by a nearly bald pate with only a few strands of grey hair lying in disarray across the wrinkled, blotched skin, and with a large, hairy mole near the tip of the nose stared back at him with rheumy eyes. A single front tooth, yellowed to a mottled brown, was exposed behind thin, pasty lips when she said, "Come in!" her voice hoarse and gravelly. She wore no dentures, and her face had a sunken appearance that made Frank look away.

Was this Lina Heydrich? he thought, shaken despite himself, the once–beautiful widow of one of the Third Reich's most dashing, powerful, and ruthless leaders?

"Frau Heydrich—uh—Frau Manninen?" he enquired politely.

The woman nodded her ravaged head, dislodging a few of the grey strands of hair, which fell down over her eyes. She brushed them away with an impatient gesture that spoke of having been often repeated.

"*Bitte*," she said. "Please. I shall want to close the door against the rain." Frank had the feeling she meant against the rest of the world as well.

"I am Frank Brandenburg," he said as he stepped into the house. Lina Heydrich acknowledged his introduction with a mere nod. As she turned and shuffled into the dimly lit house on slippered feet, Frank watched her.

She wore what appeared to be a soiled, once–white nightgown with a high neck and frayed lace across the bosom and at the wrists. Her bare feet pushed the slippers, for which well–worn would be a charitable description, along the floor audibly, as she headed for a small sitting room lighted by a single weak bulb in a floor lamp. Another lamp on a small, cluttered desk remained dark. She indicated a threadbare easy chair.

"*Bitte*," she said. "Please. Sit down."

Frank did. He looked around. Prominently in one corner of the room stood a solid wooden chest with iron bands and fittings. On one wall, above a tall–backed wooden bench, a bust in dark bronze was mounted between a framed enlargement of a photograph of Lina and Reinhard, with their son and two daughters, and a large color print of a three–masted sailing ship. In the dim light Frank could not make out who the bust represented. He assumed it was Heydrich himself.

Lina sat down on a sagging sofa. She cocked her head and peered at Frank with her rheumy eyes.

"Why are you here, Herr Brandenburg?" she asked, her curiosity tinged with suspicion.

"I wanted to meet you, Frau Heydrich." He deliberately used her former married name. "I know so much about your husband, and I wanted to meet you."

In silence Lina Heydrich fixed him with her watery eyes.

"I wanted to talk a little with you," Frank continued. "About your husband, perhaps." He opened his briefcase and took out the photographs of Reinhard Heydrich. "And give you these," he held the photographs out to her, "as an inadequate little gift, which I beg you to accept."

Lina took the photographs. She held the portrait of Reinhard in front of her. Her eyes brimmed as she stared at it.

"It is a very good picture of my husband," she finally managed, her voice unsteady. "It was good of you to bring it." Unashamedly she let the tears run down her sunken cheeks. "Oh, if my Reinhard could only have been alive to see you come here. With his picture. To talk about him." She gave a little sob. "He would have been so pleased."

She wiped the tears from her eyes with her sleeve and clutched the photograph to her bosom. She looked up at Frank.

"What do you want to know?" she asked. "What can I tell you?"

"There are so many things, Frau Heydrich," Frank answered her.

"Your husband had so many responsibilities, he led such an interesting life." He paused. He looked straight at the old woman. "The Americans made a film about the Third Reich which they called 'The Holocaust,'" he continued disarmingly. "Perhaps you saw it?"

Lina shook her head.

"In that film they showed your husband involved in what they call 'the final solution to the Jewish problem.' What can you tell me about that?"

"You mean the extermination of the Jews," Lina said coldly. "I know what the Americans, and the British, say about Reinhard." Her hoarse voice grew angry. "But it is not true! Reinhard had nothing to do with all that. I would have known. He had much more important things to do."

"Then—what is sometimes said about him is not correct?"

"Correct!" She almost spat the word. "Most of what has been written and said about my husband is deceitful and distorted to conform to what is—required by the views of the present time." Angrily she wiped her eyes. "And such views change with the times. It is so easy to do. If something bothers your precious conscience, you just blame it on someone else. Someone who cannot defend himself. Someone—dead. That is what Germany is doing today.

"They have all been so—so unfair to Reinhard," she went on. "There was no reason for that—that Swiss diplomat, Burckhardt was his name, to call my husband 'The God of Death.'" Her brow knit angrily. "It was just for effect. Politics," she finished bitterly. She looked up at Frank.

"The Jews," she said. "They caused us so much grief. So much trouble. But Reinhard had nothing to do with your—your 'Holocaust.'"

She nodded toward the bronze bust on the wall. "That is his death mask," she said. "Reinhard's death mask. It is bronze. It was an SS ritual to make such a mask." She sighed. "You must look at it more closely. It is beautiful."

She got up from the sofa and walked to the desk. She turned the lamp on. It had a bright red light bulb in it that suddenly bathed the room in a crimson light. She turned to the death mask on the wall, now a dark red color.

"The man who was sent to Prague to catch Reinhard's assassins, a police officer whose name was Wehner, he said that Reinhard's death mask showed spirituality and beauty. Like a cardinal of the Renaissance, he said." She turned her runny eyes back to Frank. "Could such a man have done all the things they say he did?"

Frank stared at the mask. The only sounds in the room were the wind tearing at the trees outside, the rain drumming on the roof of the house, and the loose shutters slamming against the walls. He was acutely aware of the eeriness of the scene, of which the brooding death mask awash in red light was suddenly the center of attraction. Never mind the mystery novel, he thought, with a touch of gallows humor. I'm in the middle of a horror movie, witch and all. He tore his eyes away from the death mask and let them roam the room bathed in the red light from the desk lamp.

But he kept silent. It was best to let the woman talk.

"Yes," she went on, "the Jews. Today they are everywhere. Again." She smiled her toothless smile. It was more a grotesque grimace. "But I remember once, in Munich it was. Fifty years ago. Reinhard had been appointed commissioner of police, but it was the SA and the SS that had all the fun." Again she smiled in remembrance. "They were supposed to arrest political enemies and they caught up with the Jew, Lewy, who was the leader of the Jews in Munich. They chased him through the streets with dog whips, and they took his shoes and socks away from him and he had to run barefoot all the way home, so they could get his things." She peered at Frank. "But no one really harmed him."

She chuckled at the happy memories. She returned to the sofa and sat down. "They used to sing a little ditty in those days," she said. "It went like this:

> Hagenkreuz am Stahlhelm,
> Schwarz–weiss–rotes Band,
> Sturmabteilung Hitler,
> Werden wir genannt!
>
> Swastika on helmet,
> Black–white–red armband,
> Storm Division Hitler
> We're called throughout the land!"

Her rheumy eyes almost twinkled as she regarded Frank.

"Those were happier days, young man," she said. "Happier days. It was an old sailors' song they had rewritten."

"Yes," Frank said. "I know your husband was in the Navy."

Lina's eyes suddenly grew steely. "He was," she said tonelessly. "And they cashiered him. For some silly reason. Some ridiculous mixup. Only one year before his pension, they forced him to leave. It was so—so unfair."

Almost defiantly, she fixed Frank with her red–rimmed eyes. "He was a good man, my Reinhard," she said firmly.

For a moment they sat in silence, Lina seemingly lost in the memories Frank's visit had brought back to her.

"How did you meet him?" Frank asked.

Lina brightened. "Oh," she said. "It was at a dance. They said it had been arranged by a sailing club, or rowing club, so everyone thought there'd be a lot of young men there. I didn't really want to go, but the other girls at the pension talked me into it. I was going to the Technical High School in Kiel and I lived in a pension with a lot of other girls. There were mostly girls at the dance, and I was just about to leave when this tall, handsome Navy officer came up to me and asked me to dance." Her face fairly shone as she relived the past. "It was Reinhard. He took me home, and I was never the same again after meeting him. Something wonderful had happened to me. Reinhard had changed my life." She smiled her disconcerting smile. "And he obviously liked me too. Within a few days he proposed."

She turned to the little desk and picked up an ornate porcelain candlestick. "He gave me this," she said. "As a wedding gift. It is a *Julleuchter*. It was presented to Reinhard by the SS on some kind of special occasion." Impulsively she offered the candlestick to Frank. "Here," she said. "I want you to have it."

Frank stared at her. "Oh, no, Frau Heydrich. I couldn't. Your boy. Your daughters—"

Lina shook her head. Again a thin grey lock of hair fell down over her eyes, and again she brushed it away.

"No," she said firmly. "I want you to have it. I shall not be around much longer, and I know you will keep it safe and give it the place it deserves."

Frank did not know how to refuse without destroying the bond of candor that had developed between them. He took the candlestick.

"Thank you, Frau Heydrich, I am honored." He cast about in his mind for some way to change the subject. On the desk stood a framed photograph of Reinhard. A small plane could be seen in the background.

"Your husband was a pilot, was he not?" he asked, knowing the answer.

Lina nodded. "He loved to fly. He once said to me that he felt nearer to God when flying than when in church." She got up. "There is something else I want you to see."

She shuffled over to the big chest in the corner and opened it. From it she carefully brought out an SS officer's tunic. Cradling it in her arms as if it were a baby, she carried it over to Frank. He stared at it.

Its once–gleaming silver insignia were dull and tarnished with age. The black cloth had several jagged holes in it, and dark stains that looked a deep blood–red in the light from the crimson bulb dotted it.

"He wore it that day," Lina said quietly. It sounded like a prayer. She held it out to Frank. "You may touch it," she said.

Gingerly Frank touched the tips of his fingers to one of the stains. It felt stiff. All at once he was transported back into the past. He was touching history. Evil history. He was suddenly acutely aware of the forbidding death mask of Reinhard Heydrich glowering down at him from the wall with its dead eyes.

He removed his fingers.

"We had been to a concert that night," Lina said, her voice as soft as her hoarseness would permit. "In the Waldstein Palace in Prague. It was a chamber music quartet from Halle, Reinhard's home town. From the time when Reinhard's father had been director of the State Conservatory there. And they had even played a composition by his father. And Reinhard had been so proud and happy. And then, the next morning..." Again the tears began to flow from her sunken eyes.

Frank nodded. "The Czechs. The two Czech agents..."

Lina wiped her eyes. She glared at Frank.

"They threw the grenade," she said, her voice suddenly harsh. "Someone else killed him!"

Startled, Frank gaped at her. "Someone else, Frau Heydrich? Who?"

"The Führer."

"The Führer? Adolf Hitler?"

"Yes."

"But—how? Why?" Frank was incredulous. "You mean *Hitler* killed your husband?"

For a brief moment Lina looked at him, her eyes bleak. Then she slowly made her way back to the big chest—her personal reliquary— and tenderly, almost reverently, placed the lacerated SS tunic in it and closed the lid. In silence she returned to the sofa.

"The Führer was jealous of Reinhard," she said tonelessly. "He was envious because my husband's popularity, the acclaim bestowed on him, was beginning to exceed that of his own, and so he became distrustful of Reinhard." She rubbed her eyes. "Of course he did not kill my husband personally. He did not throw the damned grenade himself. He did not even arrange for Reinhard's assassination. The burden of that atrocity rests squarely on the Czech swine. The Führer wanted Reinhard out of the way, and he did not know how. But he was always quick to turn a situation, any situation, however impossible, to his own advantage. He wanted to rid himself of Reinhard—so he let him die. Helped him die."

"But—Frau Heydrich, several doctors worked to save your husband's life after the assassination attempt."

Lina nodded. "And he was surviving. Improving. Until Hitler sent his own medical team under one of his personal physicians, Dr. Gebhardt, to take charge of Reinhard's treatment." She looked Frank full in the face. "Four days later he was dead."

"And you think—you think they actually caused your husband's death?" Frank was intrigued.

Lina turned away. "I will say no more, young man," she said flatly.

"How? What did they do?" Frank persisted. "What else do you know? What other details can you give me?"

"I have said enough." She seemed to withdraw into herself.

Frank contemplated her. It was obvious that she was determined to say no more on the subject. Was she—afraid? Of someone? Something?

"One more question, *gnädige Frau*—gracious lady," he said. "After the war, several of your husband's associates were successful in escaping from Germany. Heinrich Müller, Josef Schwammberger, and Adolf Eichmann," he cited. "Franz Stangl, Alois Brunner, and Klaus Barbie; Walter Rauff, Anton Burger, and Josef Mengele. The list is a long one. What about Martin Bormann? Do you think he survived? Do you know anything about him?"

Lina shrugged her shoulders. "I am sure he did survive," she said disinterestedly. "If the others did, he would have too. But I have no direct knowledge of that." She gave Frank a sidelong glance. "Bormann was also jealous of Reinhard," she said. "He, too, wanted my husband out of his way. That I know." Her lips grew tight. "And he may still be alive. Safe in Argentina. While my Reinhard is dead."

"What makes you think Bormann is still alive, Frau Heydrich?"

Lina turned away from him. "I have said enough," she repeated.

"Nothing I can say now will bring my Reinhard back. Nor change the image the world has cast him in."

"The Führer exacted a terrible vengeance for his death."

She looked at him, a little crooked smile stretching her lips. "Lidice? It was an act of retribution well deserved," she said acidly.

She stood up. The meeting had come to an end. Frank also rose from his chair.

"Will you ever return to Prague?" he asked.

Lina stopped short on her way to the door. Slowly she turned back to face Frank.

Her eyes shone with a curiously feral glint in the light from the lamp with the red bulb. Her mouth grew tight around her sole remaining tooth.

"It is an accursed country," she said tonelessly. "Klaus, my firstborn son, was killed there. Run down by a car. And they robbed me of my husband."

Her eyes locked onto Frank's.

"I will not set foot in that country," she declared harshly, "until the streets of Prague are paved with the skulls of Czechs!"

The feeble light bulb outside above the front door had died. The night was dark.

Lina tried to light a candle, but it blew out.

"The weather on the island can be harsh," Lina Heydrich said. "But on his deathbed Reinhard said to me, 'Return to Fehmarn.' They were his last words to me, 'Return to Fehmarn.' And I am here."

In the darkness they said their goodbyes, and Frank, huddled against the wind and rain, headed for his car.

He was filled with depression. In coming face to face with the deterioration of Lina Heydrich, he felt he had confronted the depravity, the disintegration of the Third Reich itself.

And to the shame of his country, the Third Reich had been Germany. Once.

He suddenly remembered what day it was. It was November 18th, a religious holiday. It was *Buss–und–Bet–Tag*—the Day of Repentance and Prayer.

He felt a facetious fate had selected that particular day for his visit to the widow of Reinhard Heydrich.

Close by, a dog barked. It was a loud and angry bark. Frank started. He increased his pace as he hurried to his car.

He had always been afraid of big dogs.

✳   ✳   ✳

On August 14, 1985, less than two years after Frank's visit to Lina Heydrich, she died of the cancer that had been ravaging her.

Frank could not get Lina Heydrich's startling accusation that Hitler himself was to blame for her husband's death out of his mind. It seemed so—so far–fetched. It was a charge he had neither heard nor read about in his research before. Was is simply the delusion of a sick, lonely old woman? Or was it a secret so well guarded that no one knew?

Generaloberst Wolff might know.

At the first opportunity Frank went to see Wolff. Somehow, despite the great difference in their ages, or as Wolff had said, because of it, a strange bond of mutual rapport had sprung up between the old Nazi general and the young inquiring crusader whose quarry he was. Talking to Frank seemed to have a cathartic effect on Wolff, coupled with a desire to persuade young Frank to understand him and accept him. And his beliefs.

General Wolff now had a room in the home of a family named Ziegmann, a white, two–story house with brown shutters on Kirchenweg in Prien am Chiemsee, with a big garden and a fishpond with goldfish. The Ziegmanns lived downstairs, and Ziegmann's sister, Edeltraut, the friend of Wolff's he had met in Darmstadt, lived upstairs, where the general also had his room. He had brought with him his belongings from his apartment in Darmstadt, including the large oil painting of himself in full SS regalia and the game trophies he had shot while hunting with Göring on his Carinhall estate, as well as all his decorations and photographs from his time of service, so the room was quite cluttered.

Sitting in the downstairs living room, a typically Bavarian *Stube,* with old ornamented steins on the mantle of the tile oven and pewter plates on shelves on the walls, Frank told the general what Lina Heydrich had said.

Pensively Wolff watched him for a moment, an odd little smile tugging at his mouth. He seemed to be studying the intricate pattern of his heavy blue–and–white ski sweater.

"Schellenberg once told me," he said, "that Reinhard Heydrich was the puppetmaster of the Third Reich, the hidden pivot around which the regime revolved."

"Was he?"

"Hardly. But the fact that the chief of Secret Service police thought so is the point. The Führer may have thought so, too—in the sense that it was what Heydrich himself worked toward."

"Then Hitler *was* jealous of him."

Wolff slowly shook his head. "The Führer was above being jealous," he said. "But he might have felt that Heydrich was becoming a potential source of trouble. And his wont was to eradicate such potential trouble spots."

"Then you think Lina is right?"

Wolff pursed his lips as he briefly contemplated Frank.

"Let me tell you what I do know," he said. "Not my conjectures. Then you can make up your own mind."

XV

W hen Heydrich lay wounded in Prague," Wolff began, "Reichsführer SS Heinrich Himmler and Prof. Dr. Karl Gebhardt, the doctor Lina mentioned, went to the hospital where he had been admitted."

He looked at Frank.

"I was with them. I was there. It was the thirty-first of May. Heydrich had been wounded on the twenty-seventh."

"Did you see him? Talk to him?"

Wolff nodded. "He seemed to be doing well. He was in stable condition. He was in good spirits, already planning his return to his office, and the actions he'd take to revenge himself on his would–be assassins." He looked at Frank. "Himmler had a long private talk with him. I do not know what was said. Then Gebhardt was called in. He stayed in Prague, while Himmler and I returned to Berlin."

He paused.

"Heydrich was placed in the care of Dr. Gebhardt on the thirty-first of May. He was doing well."

Again he paused and looked soberly at Frank. "On June 4th, four days later, he was dead."

Frank was listening to what the general told him in fascination. Although the timetable of Heydrich's death was well known, he felt he was being made privy to some extraordinary inside knowledge.

"And do you think the Führer had something to do with it?" he asked. "Do you think he had given Himmler and Gebhardt orders to make certain Heydrich would die? to eliminate him as a source of potential trouble? in such a way that his death could be blamed on the Czechs? Do you think Lina Heydrich is right? What do *you* think?"

Wolff sighed. The curious little smile returned to his lips.

"What do *I* think, *mein lieber Junge*—my dear boy? I think that Lina Heydrich is a very astute lady!" he said slowly.

"And Himmler. He must have been in on it too," Frank said.

Wolff nodded. "I am sure he was. I am also sure that he left the— the particulars to Gebhardt. What particulars we will never know. Both men are dead. Himmler by his own hand, and Gebhardt, one of the so–called 'doctor killers,' who took part in the notorious medical 'experiments,' was sentenced to death at the trial known as the 'Doctors' Trial' in 1948, and hanged. I am certain that the Reichsführer SS delegated whatever measures were to be taken. For all his reputation as a man with ice water in his veins and nerves of steel, and despite being the head of the SS, the toughest organization the world has ever seen, the Reichsführer SS was curiously squeamish."

"Squeamish? What do you mean?"

Wolff steepled his fingers in front of him. "I remember once," he said, "when I was his adjutant, Himmler wanted to see how his men dealt with the task of executing certain—certain partisans. He went to Minsk to observe such a mass execution. I went with him."

He got a far–away look on his face. Frank could not tell if it was nostalgia or an effort to recall.

"The prisoners were kneeling at the edge of an open mass grave," Wolff went on. "There were men. And women. Of all ages. And the Reichsführer's SS men would walk up behind them and deliver the *Genickschuss*—the shot to the back of the head that made them topple into the grave.

"The Reichsführer was pretty pale as the executions he himself had ordered proceeded. And when one of the condemned men turned his head just as the shot was fired, and blood and brain matter splattered the Reichsführer's face, he nearly collapsed. I had to catch him and support him or he would have keeled over then and there. As it was,

I had to lead him away, holding him up all the way. His nerves of steel had suddenly become pretty rusty," he chuckled.

Slowly he shook his head. "He was a man of many doubts, many personal fears, our Reichsführer, despite his outward coldness."

"Just because he reacted to being splattered with—with gore?"

"No," Wolff shook his head. "That must have been pretty disagreeable. Although I do think he should have kept his composure in front of his men. No—I was thinking of other things. Less—dramatic, as it were."

"Are you going to tell me?"

Wolff shrugged. "I do not see why not," he said with his little smile. "If it interests you. By now it is spilled milk under the bridge anyway."

Again he gazed into space, remembering.

"It was something I ran into when I was chief of the Bureau of Ancestral Research." He looked at Frank. "Making certain that everyone of rank or influence had pure Aryan blood. That was important in those days. All–important. It still is." He gave a little snort. "Or should be."

"One day," he continued, "as I was going through some files, I found a document, a most curious document. Apparently our Reichsführer had been seriously concerned about his own ancestry. The document was marked SECRET and PERSONAL and had been sent directly to the Reichsführer SS."

"Himmler was concerned that he might not be pure Aryan?" Frank asked. "That there was a Jew in his family tree? Wasn't there—"

"No," Wolff shook his head. "Not a Jew."

"What then?"

"A witch!"

Frank gaped at him.

"Yes, a witch." Wolff barked a short laugh. "A witch named Margreth Himbler, who was burned at the stake in 1629! A direct ancestor."

"But—what could have happened to him if it had become known?"

Wolff shrugged. "I do not really know," he admitted. "It was so far back in time. But it would have been embarrassing for the Reichsführer, no doubt of that. He would have been ridiculed, especially by his enemies, his rivals—and he had plenty of those—and that was, of course, not to be tolerated. Perhaps he would have been required to prove she was an Aryan witch!" He laughed. "In any case, he was obviously extremely concerned."

"What happened?"

Again Wolff shrugged. "I do not know. Apparently they forwarded several documents pertaining to the case to him."

"What happened to them?"

"I do not know. It seems our Reichsführer was able to bury the whole story. Except for that one document that somehow found its way into our files."

"What happened to that one?"

"I pulled it," Wolff said. "As a matter of fact I still have it somewhere."

Frank's eyes lit up. "Really? May I see it?" he asked eagerly. "And—perhaps I could be allowed to make a photocopy of it?"

For a moment Wolff looked at him. "I will allow you to copy it," he said finally. "The world had been told that Heinrich Himmler was a human monster. That he may have had a witch as an ancestor will surprise no one."

"Thank you."

"I shall look for it and give it to you before you leave," Wolff nodded. "It is dated sometime in 1939."

"I shall be most interested."

Wolff studied him for a moment. "It occurred to me—" he stopped.

"Herr General?"

"You seem to be quite interested in the death of Heydrich," Wolff said. "And—uh, the involvement of the Führer and the Reichsführer, is that not so?"

Frank nodded. "It is. It is something I had not heard about before."

"It occurred to me that you might like to talk to someone, besides Lina Heydrich and me, someone who perhaps could give you some further—understanding of the matter."

"I should be most interested. Who?"

"His name is Höttl. Dr. Wilhelm Höttl."

"I do not know of Dr. Höttl."

"I did not expect you would, Frank. He is not a man whose name is bandied about. He is not a big fish. But his knowledge, his store of privileged information, is vastly greater than that of most of the names popular with the media."

"Who is he? What does he do?"

"It is what he used to do that is more to the point," Wolff smiled.

Frank gave a little laugh. "And what was that?"

"SS-Obersturmbannführer Höttl served under Schellenberg. In Amt VI—SD Ausland."

Frank was at once alert. He knew that Walter Schellenberg, who had died in 1952, had been the supreme head of all foreign espionage activities for the Third Reich, and had been a close associate of Reinhard Heydrich.

"He was Schellenberg's close confidant, Frank. And he was an intimate friend of Adolf Eichmann," Wolff finished.

"Does he live around here?" Frank asked eagerly.

"No," Wolff shook his head. "He lives in Austria. In Altaussee. Near Salzburg. But when you have a chance, you might call him on the telephone. Perhaps he might allow you to visit him. Perhaps he might talk to you."

Wolff stood up.

"I shall get his exact address for you," he said, "and his telephone number. I shall only be a minute." He left the room.

Frank was delighted. An intelligence officer of Höttl's standing was bound to have a lot of information. Wolff's comment about him being a little fish reminded him of what they said about the army, if you want to find out anything ask the sergeant, not his commanding officer. Perhaps Dr. Höttl would turn out to be a sergeant, a top sergeant. If he would talk. He knit his brow. If the general's name could be mentioned...

Wolff returned. He had two pieces of paper in his hand. He gave the smaller one to Frank.

"That is Höttl's address," he said, "and his telephone number. It is for your information. For your information only."

He handed Frank the other paper, a creased and discolored document.

"And that is the Himmler report I told you you could copy."

Frank took the paper. In awe he looked at the dog-eared document.

How ridiculous, Frank thought, to be worried about something that may or may not have happened three hundred years ago! That whole Third Reich obsession with ancestral research, with ancestral Aryan purity, was ridiculous. How far back did you have to go before it was safe to find a Jewish skeleton hanging on the family tree? A hundred years? A thousand? If you went back far enough you might find an apple on your family tree. Imagine a whole branch of a government devoted to such an inane endeavor as ancestral purity research? But then it was in line with some of the other Nazi excesses, he supposed.

He had read a lot about the preoccupation with racial purity in the

Der Reichsführer ⚡⚡
b-c Chef des Sicherheitshauptamtes

23. Mai 1939

II 21 / AZ. 6202/39.

Sp./Kä.

Geheim Persönlich!

An den
Reichsführer ⚡⚡

Geheim!

Persönlich!

B e r l i n SW 11

Prinz-Albrecht-Str. 8

Betr.: Möglichkeit einer Hexenerfassung in der
Ahnentafel des Reichsführer ⚡⚡.

Vorg.: Ohne.

Anl.: 1

Es besteht die Möglichkeit, dass nunmehr im Rahmen
der Erforschung des Hexenwesens im Sicherheits-
hauptamt eine Ahnfrau der Sippe H i m m l e r
als Hexe festgestellt wurde. Anliegend sind einig
Aktenangaben zur Verbrennung der Margreth H i m -
l e r aus Markelsheim bei Mergentheim (1629) bei
gefügt. Die Schreibweise mit b entspricht durchau
einem neuen hochdeutschen Doppel-m. Die Sippen-
linien der Familie Himmler erstrecken sich mit
in diese Gegend, so dass nunmehr durch eine genau
Vergleichung mit der Sippentafel festgestellt wer
den müsste, ob und welche Stellen in der Sippenta
fel die verbrannte Margreth H i m b l e r ein-
nimmt.

SS - Gruppenführer.

The Reichsführer SS
Chief of the Security Service Main Office
           II 21 / AZ. 6202/39   23. May 1939
                   Sp./Kä

                   SECRET PERSONAL!

To the   Secret!
Reichsführer SS   Personal!

Berlin SW 11
Prinz–Albrecht–Str. 8

Re: The possibility of a witch relationship in the
family tree of the Reichsführer SS.
Prev: Without.
Encl: 1

The possibility exists that, in the framework of
the research on witchcraft by the Security Service
Main Office at this time, a female ancestor of the
kinsman, Himmler, was arrested as a witch.
Enclosed are some documents of denunciation
pertaining to the burning of Margreth Himbler
from Markelsheim at Mergentheim (1629). The
writing style with 'b' corresponds throughout with
a new high-German double-m. The ancestral line
of the family Himmler reaches back into this area
so that henceforth it must be determined through
an accurate comparison with the ancestral table, if
and what place in the ancestral table the burned
Margreth Himbler occupies.

                          Heydrich

                          SS Major General

Third Reich. But not until now had the absurdity of it all really hit him. Concern, bordering on dread, over a witch dead three hundred years! *Unsinn!*—nonsense. In other countries people seemed to delight in being able to unearth such—such an aberrant branch on their family tree. In Australia it was an honor to be able to trace yourself back to one of the original convicts who settled the land, and in the United States of America finding an ancestor who had been hanged as a horse thief in the Old West appeared to be a distinction. But in Germany during Hitler's reign people dreaded finding someone like an accused witch hiding among their ancestors.

Or a Jew.

Himmler must have been greatly disturbed, Frank thought; the Reichsführer may have had both. He remembered reading somewhere that Himmler had been concerned about one of his forefathers, a man named Abraham Reinau, being a Jew. But Frank could not remember what the outcome of any investigation had been. If there had, indeed, been an outcome.

He said nothing. Carefully he put the document in his pocket.

"I shall return it to you as soon as I have copied it," he said.

Wolff nodded.

"There is one thing, Herr General."

"Yes?"

"When I call Dr. Höttl, may I be allowed to say that you suggested it?"

Wolff smiled at him. He nodded. "Of course you may. I suppose that does make a difference. In the cooperation you can expect to get."

For a brief moment he contemplated Frank.

"I believe," he finally said. "I believe you *are* seriously interested in—in the old days, Frank. I believe you do want to find out the truth of matters as they were. And as they are. I think it is about time I did something about it."

"What, Herr General?" Frank was puzzled.

Slowly Wolff reached into his pocket. He held his hand out to Frank.

"This!" he said.

Gruppenführer Albert Bormann with Adolf Hitler. (Ullstein)

Albert Bormann on trial. (Ullstein)

Luftwaffe Ace Oberst Hans-Ulrich Rudel, 1945. (Ullstein)

Hans-Ulrich Rudel with Frank Brandenburg.

Sculptor Arno Breker with Frank Brandenburg.

Generalmajor Otto Ernst Remer.

Otto Ernst Remer with Frank Brandenburg.

Hitler Youth Leader Baldur von Schirach with his wife. (Ullstein)

Reichsprotector SS-Obergruppenführer Reinhard Heydrich. (Ullstein)

Reichsprotector Reinhard Heydrich and his wife, Lina, attending the concert in the Wallenstein Palace in Prague on the evening before his assassination on May 27, 1942. (Bildarchiv Preussischer Kulterbesitz)

SS-Oberstgruppenführer Karl Wolff's ring, open to show the poison pill container.

Gudrun Himmler (married, Burwitz) with her mother, Margaret, in 1945. (Ullstein)

XVI

Frank stared. In the palm of the general's hand rested a ring.

"This ring," Wolff said. "It was mine. I give it to you."

Frank was overwhelmed. He did not know what to say. It was an act of acceptance he had not dreamt of achieving. A pang of shame flashed through his mind. He was not being completely honest with the old man. But it was only a flash.

He examined the ring. It was heavy, solid silver. It had a flat rectangular surface, its corners rounded, held by two tapering, intricately carved side prongs that joined to form the ring. On the flat surface the SS emblem had been etched, and underneath it LAH—Leibstandarte Adolf Hitler—Hitler's personal guard.

Frank was finally able to speak. "Thank you, Herr General," he managed. "I—I shall treasure it."

"And find good use for it, I trust. Of course, it does not guarantee cooperation. Those days are gone. But it may open wider a door or two that otherwise might be opened only a crack, or not at all." Wolff smiled at Frank. "A little 'Open Sesame,' if you like."

Frank turned the ring over and over in his hand. He noticed a small ridge on the underside at one end of the flat surface. He picked at it with his nail, and suddenly the top surface sprang up to reveal a small, hollow space. Startled, he turned to Wolff.

"A precaution, Frank," the general said. He sounded a little embarrassed. "Only a precaution. During the war. It was—it was best to be prepared for any contingency."

Frank peered at the little hollow receptacle. He could almost see the lethal pill. Would death have been instantaneous?

"Carry it with you, my boy," Wolff said solemnly. Then his face creased into a smile.

"But I suggest you do not wear it!"

Over the door a large white sign with ornately twisted black iron lettering spelled out:

Lichtersberg

194

Dr. Höttl

The new modern–Bavarian grey–white house in Altaussee stood only a few miles from Berchtesgaden and not far from Lake Toplitz, which supposedly held Nazi gold and treasure beyond imagination in its inaccessible depth, in the mountainous area known as the Alpine Fortress or National Redoubt, supposed to have been the last bastion of the Third Reich.

The man who opened the door was clad in black *Lederhosen* with plain suspenders, a light grey, open–necked shirt, and black socks drawn up to his bare knees. Greying hair, full over the ears, topped a craggy face. Looks a little like Curt Jürgens, Frank thought, in some Alpine adventure story.

"Dr. Höttl?" he asked politely.

"I am Dr. Höttl," the man said. He looked at Frank, his eyes noncommittal. "You must be Frank Brandenburg. Please come in." He stood aside to let Frank enter.

With reserved and formal courtesy the ex–SS–Obersturmbannführer showed Frank to his living room and offered him a chair.

The room was light and airy, with bright wallpaper, and was furnished with deep, leather–covered easy chairs. Several small tables held arrays of green plants and on a shelf on the wall above an ornate, bric–a–brac–covered cabinet stood a television set.

Höttl sat down in one of the leather–covered chairs. He folded his hands in front of him and languidly kneaded his fingers, as if he were washing them in slow motion. With his correct, noncommittal mien he studied Frank.

"I understand that Karl Wolff suggested that you see me, Herr Brandenburg," he said. "I must tell you, that although I do not know the general well, I have always found him to be most sympathetic." Pensively he watched his kneading fingers. "Years ago, when our paths crossed—uh, professionally, I found him to be in all respects a gentleman and an officer of the highest caliber." He gave Frank a searching look. "With what did the general suggest I could be of help to you?"

Frank shifted in the almost–too–comfortable chair. He met Höttl's steady gaze openly. In his pocket rested the ring that General Wolff had given him, and in his mind were the questions he wanted to ask the ex–intelligence officer. They were alone. Frank knew that Höttl was married, to the same woman since 1938, but if she was at home she did not join them.

Quietly, he began telling Höttl what both Lina Heydrich and Karl Wolff had told him about how Reinhard Heydrich died.

"The general felt," he finished, "that you, perhaps, might be able to tell me more about—about this most interesting question, which *he* feels is a distinct possibility."

For a moment Höttl again watched his slowly working fingers in silence, then he spoke.

"General Wolff is in error, Herr Brandenburg," he said deliberately. "That Hitler and Himmler had a hand in the death of SS-Obergruppenführer Reinhard Heydrich is not a possibility. It is a fact."

Frank was startled. "You have direct knowledge of this, Herr Doktor?"

Höttl gave a small, mirthless smile. "Only three people had *direct* knowledge, Herr Brandenburg. The Führer, the Reichsführer, and the physician they placed in charge of the Heydrich case. None of *them* are able to testify to the facts."

"Then—how—?"

"Logic, Herr Brandenburg. Logic and inside information." Again he smiled the thin little smile. "I was after all an intelligence officer."

Frank made no comment. He felt that Höttl was about to tell him what he knew. He was right.

"Let us look at the two men in whose power it was to do away with Reinhard Heydrich, and their relationships with the man: Hitler and Himmler. Himmler had a deep animosity toward Heydrich, and not without reason. As a case in point, let me tell you about one distasteful incident that I myself witnessed." He leaned back in his chair and unfolded his hands.

"It occurred at a party in SS-Obergruppenführer Heydrich's home in Berlin. It was in 1940 or '41. We were about twenty guests. Suddenly the telephone, which stood on the piano, rang, and Heydrich himself answered it. It at once became apparent that Reichsführer Himmler was at the other end. Heydrich said, '*Jawohl, Reichsführer!* Of course, *Reichsführer! Jawohl Reichsführer!*' Lina Heydrich walked up to stand behind her husband. And she began to mimic him. '*Jawohl, Reichsführer!* Of course, *Reichsführer!*' And she became embarrassingly vulgar, the woman. 'How deep are you up his rear now, Reinhard? *Jawohl, Reichsführer!* A little deeper, Reinhard! A little deeper!' We were, of course, appalled. I was only a lowly Hauptsturmführer at the time, but even I could see in what regard the Reichsführer was held in the Heydrich household."

He paused. "It is, of course, inconceivable that the Reichsführer was not informed of this—this display of vulgarity at his expense. His reaction to it I shall leave to your imagination. No, Herr Brandenburg, Himmler had no love for SS-Obergruppenführer Reinhard Heydrich."

It made sense, Frank thought. He could not help wondering how much Lina Heydrich's performance might have contributed to her husband's death. And there was another reason. Heydrich knew of Himmler's disturbing "witch" ancestor. Perhaps the only one who knew. It was he who had signed the strictly confidential personal report to Himmler. Dead, he could not reveal his knowledge.

"As for the Führer," Höttl continued. "Schellenberg told me—" he stopped and looked inquiringly at Frank. "You do know who Walter Schellenberg was, do you not?"

"I do, Herr Doktor. SS-Gruppenführer Schellenberg was the Chief of Amt VI of the Reichssicherheitshauptamt—espionage in foreign countries. He was Reichsführer Himmler's right–hand man toward the end of the war." Frank was glad he'd done his homework. "And as I remember, it was he who went to Lisbon to kidnap the Duke and Duchess of Windsor, a mission that failed. And he—"

"Yes, yes, yes," Höttl interrupted him. "*Schon gut*—enough. Then you also know that Schellenberg died in 1952. In Italy. But before that, he had told me that Reinhard Heydrich, sometime in 1942, shortly before he was assassinated, had taken Schellenberg aside and confided in him that it was his strong belief that the Führer was insane and had to be replaced." He looked gravely at Frank. "I have told no one this before, but it is my firm belief that Schellenberg told Himmler, who in turn informed the Führer. It was, after all, a report with which he could grievously harm the object of his animosity, Reinhard Heydrich. The Führer's reaction to this intelligence need not be questioned, you agree, Herr Brandenburg?"

Frank nodded. "I do, Herr Doktor."

"You may also believe me when I tell you that it took considerably lesser transgressions than those committed by Heydrich to lose one's life in the Third Reich."

Frank believed him.

"From what you have told me, Herr Doktor, there seems to be little doubt that both the Führer and Reichsführer Himmler had good reason to want to see Heydrich dead. And yet, from the recorded actions of terrible reprisals, the world believes that the Führer lost a trusted friend."

Höttl laughed. An explosive sound more like a bark.

"The world believes a lot of falsehoods, a lot of lies," he said. "Someday, perhaps, the truth will out, and the world will have a different, a true picture of the Third Reich and the ideals it stood for. But not yet. Today few care about the truth."

"I do," Frank said.

Höttl fixed him with his steady, somehow disturbing eyes. "Perhaps," he said. "You may well be an exception to the generally abysmal quality of our youth today. Without morals. Without ideals. Without backbone. Without character. Not like the youth of *our* time. The Hitler Youth. The girls in the BDM. *They* had character. *They* had ideals. *They* were the future of the world. But the world destroyed them— egged on by those least worthy of inheriting it." He spoke with an eerie, cold dispassion, but with deep conviction. He leaned toward Frank. "If you are like those valiant youths of *our* day, then *that* is the message I want to see you carry with you when you leave here."

Frank listened to him. He felt increasingly uncomfortable. Somehow he felt there was an "if you are not" threat lurking in the ex–SS Obersturmbannführer's speech. Höttl made him feel uneasy. The man was too controlled. Too much in charge. He felt the ex–intelligence officer could see right through him. He had a flash vision of the man walking into another room—and returning with a gun.

"You—you said that—that the world believed in other falsehoods, Herr Doktor," he managed.

Höttl nodded. "When you called me on the telephone, you talked to me about a television show, which claimed that a total of some ten million people or more were killed by us. Systematically. It is, of course, a lie, a gross exaggeration." He folded his fingers before him and began his slow–motion massage. "You undoubtedly know that Adolf Eichmann was one of my closest friends. We spent many a wonderful time together in the old days. In fact, I provided a hiding place for him, in 1945, right here, before he went to Argentina. And I warned him when he was over there in South America that Israeli agents were on to him, that they were getting close. Too close. He did not listen to me. But no one knew better than SS-Obersturm-bannführer Adolf Eichmann the correct figure of such executions. True undesirables, criminals, and other misfits were—removed. But Eich-mann told me only six million Jews were exterminated."

Frank kept quiet. There was nothing to say.

"Of course, I personally knew nothing about what was going on in the so–called concentration camps. They were work camps, as far as I knew. Not until Eichmann told me did I know."

Frank looked at him. Once again he wondered how it had been possible for so many millions of people to have been systematically killed, with so few in the Nazi hierarchy knowing anything about it.

"Actually, his original report to Himmler had stated that four million Jews had been eliminated in the camps, but the Reichsführer had said to him, so few? it must have been more, so Eichmann made a reevalu-ation of six million. So you see, the accusations of today are vastly exaggerated.

"And Bormann," Höttl continued. "Reichsleiter Martin Bormann. The world has been told by experts that his bones were miraculously unearthed from the rubble of a shattered Berlin. It is, of course, not true. Those—remains are not those of Martin Bormann."

"Then, if Bormann is not dead, where is he?"

Höttl gave Frank a sharp look. His fingers stopped moving. "I have no contact with Reichsleiter Bormann," he said curtly. "I am merely convinced that the announcement of the discovery of his skeleton in Berlin is a falsehood. I am told he escaped to South America."

"I understand you still have friends in South America, Herr Doktor, as well as here. Friends from the old days. Have any of them ever mentioned having had contact with Martin Bormann?"

For a brief moment Höttl studied Frank, his eyes unfathomable. "Please be careful, Herr Brandenburg," he said, his voice a flat monotone. "You are encroaching upon a critical subject. I am willing to help you with your research. Primarily because of the recommendation by Karl Wolff. But I must caution you to—be very careful. And not only here, with me, Herr Brandenburg. Not only here."

Frank felt a sudden gusty chill. Perhaps it was only his imagination. "Of course, Herr Doktor," he said contritely. "I—I was only wondering if Martin Bormann had escaped from Germany via one of the known escape routes. ODESSA. Or *Die Spinne*."

Again Höttl gave his bark–like laugh. *"Die Spinne,"* he said. "The Spider. Another fabrication of sensation–hungry chroniclers."

"You mean, there was no rescue, no escape organization called Die Spinne?" Frank was startled.

"I mean it has been glorified and glamorized, Herr Brandenburg." He leaned back in his chair. "Would you like to know how Die Spinne was born?"

"Very much, Herr Doktor."

"Shortly after the war," Höttl told him, "I began to work with the *Amis*. The CIC. The counterintelligence corps of their army."

"The Americans? You worked with the Americans?"

"Many of us did. It is commonly known. The *Amis* said to us, if we help you, if we leave you alone, what can you do for us? It was simple. We could do a great deal for them. We knew more than anyone about the really important 'mandatory arrestees,' as they called the individuals who were their prime targets. We were—unimportant, in the scheme of things. And we were, of course, all strongly anti–Bolshevik, anti–Communist, that was the catchword, and already had several anti–Soviet operations in place. Yes, indeed, Herr Brandenburg, we could be of considerable value to the *Amis*, who were just beginning to find out how perfidious their Russian 'allies' were. I still have copies of several documents regarding such intelligence matters that passed between the *Ami* CIC and me. I shall show them to you before you leave."

He gave a raspy chortle in remembrance. "Of course," he went on,

"I had already been in contact with certain *Amis* in Switzerland. And with the Swiss. Months before the war came to an end."

"You were in Switzerland?"

"During the month of February 1945. And again in March and April."

"For what purpose?"

"There are always—negotiations between warring powers going on in neutral countries, Herr Brandenburg. Especially when the end of hostilities draws near, and there are—arrangements to be made. It was within my province, within the province of Amt VI, to be involved. At that time the *Amis* were terrified at what we might be able to do with a fortified Alpine Fortress, impregnable to their conventional forces, and the Swiss were afraid that the Allies would force them to supply Alpine troops to defeat us there. It was fertile ground for negotiations. And it was personally beneficial for me and my family."

"How?"

"We lived in Vienna, Herr Brandenburg. The Russians were knocking at our door. And no one wanted to become a Russian prisoner of war. But, where to go, Herr Brandenburg? Where to go? Where would we be safe from the Russian onslaught? The *Amis* helped us. Those of us who had expressed a willingness, and had the ability to cooperate with them. They let us know which sectors of Austria would not be occupied by the Bolsheviks. And that is where we resettled." He nodded. "It is not by accident that I and many of my friends are settled here in the Ausseeland."

He smiled a curiously meaningless smile at Frank. "And it was right here, right here in Altaussee, that Die Spinne was born. I had brought an old friend and colleague of mine, Erich Kernmayr, an avid anti–Bolshevik, to work with me as we cooperated with the CIC. Erich was determined to be of as much help as he could to those who had to escape from Germany to avoid being arrested by the occupation forces, and one day he pointed out to me that I could contribute greatly toward this goal, sitting as I did here in Altaussee, in safety, able to pull a whole network of strings. I was like a spider in its web, he said. So you see, Herr Brandenburg, I—Wilhelm Höttl—am Die Spinne!"

He laughed.

"We were, in fact, able to be helpful to many of our friends. Right here in sleepy little Altaussee."

"But—I understood that Die Spinne was active all over Germany. Internationally, in fact."

Höttl smiled.

"Our *Spinne* was much localized right here." He shrugged, another slow–motion gesture. "Of course, as others became involved, the—uh, reputation of the organization grew. And as more and more escapees succeeded in reaching safety, more and more such cases were attributed to Die Spinne, some justifiably so, others not. But Die Spinne achieved international fame."

"Others, Herr Doktor? What others became involved in Die Spinne?"

"The Catholic Church, Herr Brandenburg," Höttl said blandly.

"Oh. Bishop Hudal."

Höttl nodded. "You are familiar with the help the Bishop gave us," he acknowledged. "It was a most valuable association. But there were others. Bishop von Brixen, for example, and the Franciscan Father, Franz Pobitzer. He ran the *Anlaufstelle*—the escape route stop—in Bolzano in Italy."

Frank nodded. "I understand that the escape route ran through Bolzano. And Merano. To Rome. And Genoa."

"*Stimmt*—correct. And with their help, and that of the American CIC, we were able to get certain of our people out of Allied detention."

"The CIC?"

"As long as they told the CIC interrogators everything they knew about the Russians, the CIC cared nothing about who the people were whom we brought to them, or what happened to them afterward. We were able to get many of them to safety."

For a moment he contemplated his folded hands and his slowly moving fingers.

"In retrospect," he said, "it was a curious triumvirate. Former SS members, the *Ami* CIC, and the Catholic Church. Curious indeed."

It was, Frank mentally agreed. He wondered how much of it was true, and how much was due to a biased memory. He realized by now that the Catholic Church had been involved in helping Nazi war criminals escape arrest by the Allies. But was it only a handful of individuals, or was it done on a wider, more official scale? And he realized that it would have been extremely valuable at the time for the American CIC to acquire the not inconsiderable knowledge possessed by its Nazi counterpart, and that some concessions would have to be made to obtain it. But was it done in as cavalier a manner as Höttl suggested? Would he ever know? Would anyone ever know?

"It was all many years ago, Herr Brandenburg, long before your time," Höttl said, almost patronizingly. "And for all those years, I and my family have lived here in Altaussee, quietly and unobtrusively." He looked at Frank. "For many of those years, since 1952, my wife Elfriede and I ran a boy's school here. The Ramgut by name. We tried to instill in our youths some of the values of old. I hope we succeeded. Today—we are retired, the school is no more."

He stood up. The interview had come to an end.

"I never had to face a court, Herr Brandenburg," he said, an air of self–righteousness about him. "Either German or Allied. I was, of course, arrested, because of my rank and position. For investigative purposes. But the examiners soon realized that I was an *anständiger Mensch*—a respectable person, and I was released. Furthermore, the Allied authorities de–Nazified me, as they called it." He gave his short bark of a laugh. "Be that as it may."

He gave Frank his hand.

"*Servus*, Herr Brandenburg," he said, using the popular Austrian parting, "it was my pleasure to talk with you and to meet someone who is genuinely interested in our Third Reich and our beliefs."

As Frank walked from the house with the beautiful view of the Dachstein Mountains, his mind was flooded with what he had read about this respected, de–Nazified recent schoolmaster, who had run an organization of former SS officers with the dual purpose of assisting the American CIC with intelligence about the Russians and helping as many fugitive Nazis and war criminals as possible escape justice.

Although Austrian, Wilhelm Höttl had joined the Hitler Youth already in 1931, and he held the Golden Emblem of Honor. Three years later he became a member of the SS. He had been a close friend of mass murderers Adolf Eichmann and Ernst Kaltenbrunner. According to documentation, the fate of Vienna's Jews had rested in his hands when, as Inspecteur der Sicherheitspolizei und des SD, he had held a high police and security post in that city. A close collaborator of the notorious Gestapo chief of Rome, SS-Obersturmführer Herbert Kappler, and in 1944 in charge of the mass arrests and deportations of citizens of Hungary; in fact, in 1961 the Hungarian authorities had demanded his extradition. Austria had refused. Wilhelm Höttl, a man still with close ties to former Nazis and war criminals, both in South America and in Europe.

An *anständiger Mensch.*

Frank decided to stop off in Munich on his way back to Travemünde, and pay a visit to General Baur in Herrsching am Ammersee. There was that matter of Operation Seraglio, which Christa Schroeder had told him about. And the missing documents. If anyone would know what had happened to them and to the plane, it would be General Baur.

Baur received him cordially, obviously pleased to see him. And he listened attentively to Frank's account of what Christa Schroeder had told him.

For a moment he sat in silent thought, his face cloudy.

"*Geheimoperation Serail*," he said finally. "Of course I remember it."

He looked at Frank, his eyes dark.

"I wish you had not asked me about—Operation Seraglio."

Frank was genuinely disturbed. "Herr General," he said. "I—I'm sorry. I did not—"

Baur held up a hand to silence him. "You could not have known, my boy," he said soberly. "But *Serail* is a—a very painful memory for me. I have been asked about it before. I have always refused any comment." He fell silent for a moment, then he looked up.

"Frank," he said. "I shall tell you about Secret Operation Seraglio."

XVII

By the end of April 1945," Baur began, "it was becoming obvious to even the most fanatic optimist in the Bunker that Germany and Berlin would go down to defeat. It was no longer a question of if but of when, and the when seemed only a few days away.

"There were a good many people in the Führerbunker, Frank, people of importance, many of them whose presence was no longer necessary nor even desirable, who could be evacuated by air and flown to safety in the south, with the possibility of continued service to the Reich and the ideals of *unser Vati*. That evacuation operation became *Geheimoperation Serail*, and it would include bringing to safety a large number of sensitive and secret documents, which the Führer wanted preserved for the future. I was placed in charge of that operation."

"Do you know what those documents were, Herr General?"

Baur shook his head. "I was told some were transcripts of *unser Vati*'s comments, made at various times. But I believe those were not the really important ones nor the secret ones. There were other documents, but I was not informed what they were. They were all securely sealed in several heavy crates, ten or more of them.

"The first plane took off from Gatow Airport, which was still in

159

our hands, on April 20th, shortly after 2100 hours, and eight more departed during the following hours until midnight. Christa Schroeder, the secretary you talked to, was on one of those planes. So was another of *unser Vati*'s secretaries, Johanna Wolf, and Martin Bormann's brother, Albert. Those nine planes all arrived safely and on schedule at their destinations in Munich and Salzburg."

He stopped. His lips tightened into a straight, hard line. It was obviously difficult for him to express what he remembered.

"The last plane, a JU–352, had engine trouble. It was aboard that plane that the crates of documents had been loaded. Its departure was delayed until the early hours of the morning of the twenty-first, about 0500, when it finally was able to take off."

Again he stopped. He swallowed, and looked at Frank, his eyes bleak.

"That plane, my boy, never did arrive."

"What happened to it?"

"I do not know," Baur said, his voice hoarse, "I—do not know. I— I had to tell *unser Vati* that the plane was lost, that my Operation Seraglio was a failure. He was shaken, Frank. He took it hard. He had tears in his eyes. 'It had to be the plane with the crates,' he said bitterly, 'with the documents that would have been so important for the world of the future.' And when I had to tell him that his personal servant, a young sergeant named Wilhelm Arndt, of whom *unser Vati* had grown quite fond, had also been on board the plane, he cried, my boy. He cried."

"Was the plane, or the wreck, ever found?"

Baur shook his head. "There was talk of people, some Bavarian farmers, who had heard a crash. The Luftwaffe Graves Registration investigated. Some time after the war. But they found no eyewitnesses. No wreck. No documents."

He sighed. His bleak eyes met Frank's.

"What I have told you has been told before. By others. But I have kept my silence about it. Perhaps you can understand. It was *my* operation. And it failed."

Frank started to protest, but Baur silenced him.

"I know," he said. "Nine of the ten planes did arrive safely at their destination. But the tenth did not. *My* plane, Frank, as truly as if I had piloted it myself. Shot down. Crashed. Destroyed—with all aboard."

He looked almost pleadingly at Frank. "And I had been assuring *unser Vati* that I could fly him to safety. Pleading with him to leave Berlin—

with me. In one of my planes. Like the one that was lost. I gave *unser Vati* my guarantee that I could fly him to safety. My solemn word. It has taken me many years to be able to live with my—betrayal. And betrayal it was. My word had been hollow. Make no mistake about it, my boy, if the pilot of that ill–fated JU–352 that disappeared in the wartime skies of our Fatherland could not have avoided disaster— neither could I. Gundelfinger was a *prima* pilot."

"Was that the name of the pilot?"

Baur nodded. "Major Friedrich Gundelfinger."

A few weeks later, Frank was home in Hildesheim for a few days. He and Herta had plans to attend a party to be given by one of their friends.

The story of the lost plane and the vanished documents had really excited his imagination.

He realized that the direction of his search for information had changed completely. He could see that he had been naive in setting out to learn the facts about the Holocaust. It had been only because he himself had not known. The world had known the truth for decades, and that knowledge had been available to him as well, had he only known where to look for it. He did not for a moment regret the time or effort he had spent in learning for himself what he could have learned at second hand. He had been, and still was, fascinated by the different versions of the "facts" that had been told him. The final verdict was, of course, that the accounts of the Holocaust which had so disturbed him were true. But in the course of his quest, other much more exciting, much more enigmatic questions had arisen. What was the fate of Reichsleiter Martin Bormann? How strong was the influence and power of the Nazis today? And what had happened to the vanished JU–352 and its cargo of secret documents?

He had gone through all his research books trying to find references to *Geheimoperation Serail*. Several had mentioned it only in passing, but one source gave a more complete account, which largely corresponded to what Baur had told him. It was *The Bunker*, by James P. O'Donnell, a former United States intelligence officer in the war, former American State Department official, and noted journalist.

In his book, O'Donnell concluded that the JU–352 had crashed in Bavaria, although while Baur had told him the flight was during the night of April 21st, O'Donnell placed the event a full day later. Frank was inclined to believe the general.

All aboard the plane had been killed instantly, according to the book, and their bodies, as well as the plane itself and its entire cargo, had been consumed by fire.

But O'Donnell also broached the possibility that some of the crates might have survived the flames—and might today lie forgotten in some Bavarian hayloft or chicken coop. Or even pigsty.

Frank's curiosity had been aroused. What if...?

On the off chance that something further might have been learned in the intervening years, he had written to WASt, Die Deutsche Dienststelle für die Benachrichtigung der nächsten Angehörigen von Gefallenen der ehemaligen Deutschen Wehrmacht—The German Agency for Notification of the Nearest Relatives of Fallen Former Members of the German Armed Forces—in Berlin. He had asked two questions: Firstly, What happened to the JU–352 that left Berlin during the night of April 21, 1945? And secondly, What is known about the death of Luftwaffe Maj. Friedrich Gundelfinger? The name was unusual enough that he hoped to get results without knowing the officer's service serial number.

A week later he had received his answer.

"We regret to have to inform you that we unfortunately cannot give you the information you requested regarding the airplane crash of 21. 4.1945, because such information does not exist in our records."

So much for that. But there was more.

"We learned of the crash of 21.4.1945 only from a register in the Criminal Police Department in Glashütte, dated 18.11.1948. This entry concerned only the pilot, Maj. Friedrich Gundelfinger, born 19.5.1900 in Munich. Fallen 21.4.1945 at 6:00 A.M. near Börnersdorf, county Dippoldswalde. Buried: Börnersdorf Cemetery."

Börnersdorf.

The name had a familiar ring. Börnersdorf. Börnersdorf. Where had he seen that name before?

And he remembered.

The English historian High Trevor–Roper had told of a JU–352 carrying secret documents that went down near Börnersdorf, documents supposedly including the famous phony Hitler diaries. That was where he had read about Börnersdorf. According to Trevor–Roper the plane, which was en route to Salzburg, was shot down by an American fighter plane in the early morning hours of April 21st. The British historian had stated that a Wehrmacht officer had retrieved and concealed the documents in a hayloft for thirty–five years! They were then smuggled out of East Germany and stored in a Swiss bank, and in 1980, three years earlier, while living in Switzerland, this officer had given the documents, including the Hitler diaries, to the journalist Gerd Heidemann. Heidemann, in turn, had claimed to have traced this Wehrmacht officer from Börnersdorf through Western Europe to South America. But Heidemann had, of course, been proven a forger. It was a confused story at best.

Was this the same plane that, according to the historian James P. O'Donnell, had crashed and burned in Bavaria? Was this the *Serail* JU–352? Or was it another plane?

The picture was hopelessly confused. Baur had told him that the last *Serail* plane left well past midnight of April 20th–21st and crashed hours later. O'Donnell stated that the plane took off at 1:00 A.M. on April 23rd and crashed in Bavaria. Trevor–Roper wrote that the plane departed on the morning of April 21st and crashed shortly thereafter, and the WASt records quoted the pilot of a plane shot down at 6:00 A.M. on the twenty-first. Two different dates and times. Were they all talking about the same plane?

Which one was the *Serail* plane? What *had* happened to the documents?

The officer described by WASt *had* to be the pilot of the Operation Seraglio plane, mentioned by Baur. There could not possibly have been two Major Friedrich Gundelfingers who died in plane crashes during that same time.

The answers would lie in Börnersdorf. He was sure of it. That was where he would have to go if he wanted to find out about the vanished Seraglio documents. But Börnersdorf was in the Erz Mountains southeast of Dresden on the northern border of Czechoslovakia in the Deutsche Demokratische Republik—East Germany—hundreds of miles from where O'Donnell said the plane went down, and a *Bundesbürger*— a West German—couldn't just cross over the *Sperrzone*—the Iron Curtain—on a whim. It took permits, travel papers, identification documents—and a legitimate reason. But there had to be a way.

There was.

In his capacity of researcher he decided to visit Auschwitz, one of the most infamous of the Nazi extermination camps. It was a perfectly reasonable purpose, and since Auschwitz was located in Poland about sixty kilometers west of the city of Krakow, it would be necessary for him to cross East Germany by car. This was quite possible with the proper papers. He would travel to Auschwitz via Dresden in East Germany and Breslau or Wroclaw, in Poland, and he at once set out to get all the various documents and affidavits that were needed for the trip through the DDR. They all had to be in perfect order and up to date. His passport and his driver's license, his car registration and his green–card proof of insurance. At the border he would get the special transit visa. By the time all was arranged, he had made his plans.

He had requested and received permission to enter the DDR via the transit highway over Magdeburg, skirt Berlin, and head south toward Dresden and from there east toward Breslau and Auschwitz. He had requested and received permission to leave the DDR after his visit to the camp via the E–40, the highway transit that runs past Dresden through Karl Marx Stadt and Plauen, exiting the DDR just before Hof in West Germany. The reason he had given for wanting to take this route was that he had business in Munich in Bavaria after his visit to Auschwitz. The E–40 ran within thirty or forty kilometers of Börnersdorf; he'd play it by ear when he got there. From the little pamphlet *Reisen in der DDR*—Travels in the DDR, which listed the dos and don'ts—mostly don'ts—of driving in the DDR, and which had been given him with his papers in preparation for his trip, he knew that it was strictly forbidden for drivers travelling on special transit visas to leave the transit highways, but he had decided to take the chance, if at all possible.

His trip through the DDR had been uneventful. He had driven carefully, obeying all rules and regulations and dutifully presenting his permits and identification documents at all checkpoints. Auschwitz, or Oswiecim, which was the Polish name for the town and the camp, lay a few kilometers down the road.

Auschwitz. A name that had become synonymous with hell, and the mention of which for five long years had sent a surge of dread through millions of innocent people.

The twin camps of Auschwitz–Birkenau were the largest extermination camp compound of the Third Reich. Auschwitz was designated a *Konzentrationslager*, KL-Auschwitz I, and Birkenau, or Brzezinka in Polish, three kilometers to the east, was called KL-Auschwitz II. Here some four million victims, men, women, and children had been exterminated by the Nazi regime.

Silently Frank stood gazing at the cynical message in large letters over the main gate:

ARBEIT MACHT FREI

—Work Makes You Free.

It was true.

Free from the horrors and terrors of the camp. Free from an inhuman life of unimaginable suffering. Free—when death finally released you.

He had seen the sign in hundreds of photographs. But none of them had had the same chilling effect on him as seeing it in stark reality.

The black iron gates, hanging from their massive gateposts, stood wide open between two sets of double wooden marker posts, tall and painted black–and–white, barber–pole fashion; but a barrier boom had been lowered across the roadway. A sign atop the boom read: *HALT. Ausweise Vorzeigen*—STOP. Show Permits. At the road's edge stood a wooden post with another sign: *VORSICHT. Hochspannung. Lebensgefahr*—CAUTION. High Voltage. Mortal Danger. A thick red lightning bolt had been painted across it. To Frank it looked like a slash of blood.

He ducked under the boom and began to walk down the deserted road flanked by solid, grim, two–story red–brick buildings.

The original camp had been constructed around a group of abandoned Polish military barracks at Oswiecim, which the Nazis had renamed Auschwitz after the conquest of Poland in 1939. The barracks stood outside the city limits and therefore afforded the possibility of expansion, while still taking advantage of the fact that the town was an important rail center.

In 1940 construction of the concentration camp was completed, and SS-Hauptsturmführer Rudolf Hoess, an officer who had served at both Dachau and Sachsenhausen concentration camps to the satisfaction of his immediate superiors and Reichsführer SS Himmler, was appointed commandant. In June of that year the first inmates arrived, 728 Poles from the city of Tarnow, to be interned for political reasons. Over the next four years this number would swell to several millions, and in January of 1942 the extermination program began in the by now vastly expanded complex.

Victims arrived from all over Europe, some after spending as much as ten days and ten nights without food or water, travelling as much as two thousand miles, standing crammed into railroad cattle–cars without relief of any kind.

Most of those who arrived alive were killed at once in the gas chambers and cremated in the ovens of the crematoria: about eighty percent. The remaining twenty percent were used as slave labor as long as they could last.

The camp complex was evacuated in January 1945, when Russian troops were approaching, and the remaining inmates were sent on death marches to other concentration camps inside the Third Reich.

When the camp was overrun much of it had been destroyed by the fleeing Nazis in order to hide the enormity of their misdeeds: gas chambers, crematoria, torture chambers. But enough remained to establish a monstrous indictment.

These thoughts ran through Frank's mind as he walked through the nearly deserted camp streets, a feeling of uneasy depression heavy on his shoulders.

He rounded a corner of a barracks and stopped.

At the far end of the street between the two buildings, a tall brick wall had been erected across the roadway. Unlike the windows in the other buildings in the camp, the windows in the two buildings flanking the street were covered with heavy wooden shutters.

Half way down the street, on a short flight of stairs, sat a figure, head bowed, one hand resting on a step for support.

It was a woman. Her face was hidden from him, but she had a crown of short, reddish hair. In what appeared to be a light blue pants suit dotted with tiny white flowers, she looked startlingly out of place in the drab, somber surroundings.

She sat absolutely motionless.

For a while Frank watched her. She never moved. He began to be concerned. Was she all right? Did she need help? He walked up to her.

"Excuse me," he said. "Are you all right?"

The woman looked up at him: the round, pleasant face of a woman in her sixties.

"Yes. I am," she said. "I was only seeking a moment of peace, where none was to be found so long ago."

She stood up. She nodded toward the wall at the far end of the street.

"That is the *Todeswand*—the Wall of Death," she said quietly. "Tens of thousands were shot against that wall by the SS guards. Men and women. One of them was my friend. Rachel."

She stopped. For a time she stood gazing at the wall. Frank remained silent. He did not want to intrude. In awe he looked at the woman. He knew he was looking at a survivor of the hellish place. On the inside of her left forearm he had glimpsed a tattoo. The letter A, followed by a number.

"She was a gold retriever," the woman said softly.

"A—gold retriever?" Frank asked, puzzled.

The woman nodded. "She retrieved the gold in the teeth of the *Häftlinge*—the inmates. After they had been gassed and hosed down to clean them of the feces and blood that covered them in their death throes, and before they were drained of their blood and burned. She had to pull all the teeth with gold in them, and fill her quota of buckets."

Unnerved, Frank stared at the woman. She had delivered her account of abysmal atrocities in a flat, matter–of–fact tone of voice, devoid of emotion.

"Why—why was she shot?"

"She had committed an unpardonable crime," the woman told him. She spoke in a curious, toneless voice, as if trying to be coldly uninvolved. Frank guessed that she could not afford to let herself relive her memories too intimately. "She kept a gold crown," the woman went on. "It could be bartered for a slice of bread. Some of the guards could be bribed. A kapo saw her and turned her in."

"Kapo?"

"An inmate trustee. There were such. They had traded their souls for a little better treatment."

"I—I am sorry for your friend," Frank said. It sounded inane, but he did not know what else to say.

"I am not," the woman exclaimed. "There were worse ways to die than being shot. Much worse." She pointed off to her right. "Over there. In Block Eighteen," she continued. "You were put in a cell and left there unattended until you starved to death lying in your own waste. Or you were placed in a cell in total darkness and with no air, slowly to die of suffocation. And in Block Twenty–two they had their four little punitive bunkers."

"What were they?"

"They were boxes, only ninety by ninety by ninety centimeters. You could only fit in there by curling yourself into a small ball. For days they kept you there. Even if you died, you stayed in there until your sentence was up."

Frank stared at the woman, appalled. "What—what could an inmate have done to deserve such inhuman cruelty? What could he possibly have done?"

"He may have picked up an apple core discarded by a guard," the woman said, her voice flat. "Or needed to relieve himself during work hours, or been found to have done so, unable to hold back and fearful of punishment. Or he may simply not have worked fast enough to satisfy a guard. For those lesser offenses there were lesser forms of punishment. Beating. Starvation. Round–the–clock work shifts. Or they would hang an offender by his arms, turned back. For hours. Until they were forced from their sockets. Those were the kinds of punishments for the ordinary violations of camp rules. A few committed far more serious crimes, such as prying out one of their own teeth that had a gold filling, to trade it for food. That was always punishable by death." She looked toward the wall, her eyes hooded. "If they were lucky they would die like Rachel. She was nineteen." The woman fell silent.

"And you," Frank said. "You must have been her age."

"Eighteen. When I first got here."

"Did you—did you also retrieve gold?"

The woman shook her head. "No," she said. "I was a harvester. I harvested hair. Mostly from women. Before the corpses were burned, their heads were shorn," she explained unemotionally. "I was one of those who did that."

"Why?"

"The really fine strands were used in instruments," the woman said. "The rest was processed for mattresses and such." She looked bleakly at Frank. "I was told that when the camp was liberated they found fourteen thousand pounds of human hair stored in sacks. That was what they had not been able to ship to the manufacturers in Germany before they had to leave. I was also told that analysis of the hair revealed the strong presence of Zyklon B."

"That was the poison gas used to—to kill the inmates, was it not?"

The woman nodded, her face grim. "It was. It took about twenty minutes to kill everyone in the largest gas chamber. It could hold two thousand inmates at a time. Men, women, and children. All of them had been ordered to remove their clothing. They were told they were to be given a shower before being shown to their quarters. That way there was no resistance. No panic. It was very efficient."

She rubbed her forehead with the back of her hand.

"There was only one small problem. The ovens in the crematoria could burn only 350 corpses every twenty–four hours. That meant that there were always heaps of bodies stacked outside. They could burn two bodies per oven of the newcomers, and four per oven of the inmates who had worked and died in the camp. The inmates, especially the women, weighed only between forty–five and sixty pounds. They took up less room and burned quickly. Especially after being drained of blood. And even robbed of their gold teeth and their hair, they were still of some value. Their ashes were used as fertilizer on the farms in Germany."

Frank had been listening to the woman in horror. He had read about much of what she was saying, but hearing it told, dispassionately and matter–of–factly by someone who had lived through the horrors, chilled him. He wondered why the woman talked so much, and then he understood. It was all inside of her. Locked away in her mind. It had to come out. And once the floodgates had been breached it would be hard to dam them up again.

"Have you been here before?" he said. "I mean—after–"

The woman shook her head. "No. I had not the courage. Not until now." Slowly she looked around her. "Look," she said. "Those wooden shutters. They were to keep the inmates in the barracks from seeing what went on at the *Todeswand*." Despite herself her eyes grew moist. "But they could hear," she whispered. "They could hear."

She turned to Frank. "No," she said, "I have not been back here before. But—I felt I owed it to all of us who can never return. I owed it to them to come here. And remember them."

Impulsively she held out her hand to Frank. "I am Sarah," she said.* "Walk with me. Be my link to today."

Frank took her hand.

Together they walked down the street, away from the Wall of Death.

Together they walked past the guard towers that now loomed dead and empty. Past the electrified barbed–wire fence strung on curiously graceful swan–neck cement poles, all inclined toward the camp area and the horrors that went on inside, as if they were hanging their heads in shame.

"There," Sarah pointed to a spot near the fence. "That is where the

* The name has been changed to protect the privacy of the former Auschwitz inmate.

school teacher Geller died. So desperate, he was, that he tried to climb the fence. He was electrocuted. They let him lie there, right there, in the sun. For four days, they let him lie there in his threadbare zebra suit, until the stench became too great."

And as they walked past a long, wooden, shack–like building, she said: "That is like my block. Where I stayed. We slept four to a bunk of wooden slats that were meant to hold two. Lying on rotten, befouled straw, we could not move. There were three tiers of bunks. It was not pleasant when someone above you had dysentery."

She took Frank's arm, as if seeking comfort and safety.

"Miriam died there," she said softly. "She was twenty–two. They had taken her baby when she arrived, and killed it. One evening, early it was, just after we had bedded down, she died. She was lying right next to me. All night, she lay right next to me. Close to me. And grew cold. So very cold."

"Roll call was held right here," Sarah said, as they were walking along the broad main street between the barracks. "Every day, you stood here. Sometimes you shivered in the bitter cold, at other times you sweltered in the hot sun."

She stopped. For a moment she stood in silence, looking straight ahead—into the past.

"There were punitive roll calls as well," she said. "You were forced to stand here. For hours. The longest punitive roll call lasted nineteen hours. Sometimes they brought a portable gallows, and you had to watch someone being hanged. Sometimes a friend. Sometimes you were forced to kneel, or to stand with your arms in the air, or to squat with your knees bent. That was the worst. Those who collapsed or changed position were beaten. Sometimes killed."

Slowly she began to walk down the street, Frank at her side.

"That was the *Krankenbau*—the hospital." She nodded toward a drab building. "We called it the antechamber to the crematorium. There was little room for the sick, so they were eliminated. Usually with an injection of Phenolin right into the heart. Those who were actually hospitalized were worse off. There were more rats than medical supplies, and vermin everywhere. And there was always the risk of becoming part of a medical experiment, usually fatal after a time of agony." Her face clouded over. It was the first time Frank had seen her affected by what she told him.

"I knew a woman," Sarah went on. "They had used her to try to find a quick and effective way of sterilizing the undesirable. They had injected a strong acid into her uterus. Burned it out. When they let her go—she killed herself."

She looked away from the building. "It was there Mengele did his experiments on twins," she said. "Every set of twins, adults and children, that arrived here, was at once sent to him. To that building."

There was a sudden, sharp noise, as someone in the distance dropped a pail or a bucket.

Sarah started violently. For a split moment Frank saw raw terror blaze in her eyes. For an instant he looked down into the fear, the never–forgotten horror that still festered in the woman's mind.

Abruptly Sarah turned away. "Come," she said. "I will show you where it was that I arrived here."

The railroad siding was overgrown with weeds; the once–shining rails were dull and rusty. Sarah pointed to the tracks.

"There," she said. "That is where the train stopped. And right here, where we now stand, is where Mengele stood. Right!—Left!—Right!—Left!—he selected those who were to die at once, and those who looked young and strong enough to be useful before they died." Again she pointed. "And over there a little group of musicians played waltzes and marches and bright popular songs, to welcome the new arrivals."

For a moment she stood lost in thought, as if she could still hear that macabre music.

She sighed. A deep, unconscious sigh. Her voice was less steady, less detached than before.

"All the children, except the twins, were put to death at once. They were of no use," she went on. "They were gassed, or they were killed by injections into the heart. In many cases the parents died with them. In others, the children were simply taken from them. But all of them died. All of them. Eventually even the twins."

Frank stood gazing at the empty, unkempt railroad platform. His mind was playing tricks on him. He seemed to see the empty platform before him crammed with people. Men, women, and children. Old and young. Short and tall. People. And suddenly all the photographs he had seen were no longer shades of ink on paper, the people in them no longer shadows—they were flesh and blood.

Like Sarah.

"I was sent to be tattooed," Sarah said. Absentmindedly she rubbed her left arm. "And photographed. Many of us were. But most were put in those stalls over there." Again she pointed. "Stables. They were originally built to house fifty–two horses of the Polish cavalry, when the camp was a Polish military camp. Fifty–two horses. The SS crammed a thousand people in there. To wait for transportation to the gas chamber." She looked up at Frank. "Did you know that Auschwitz was the only extermination camp where the inmates were tattooed?"

Abruptly she turned and walked away, following the rusty, weedy railroad tracks toward the big brick tower and gaping archway through which the rails led into the camp area.

Frank followed her. And with him, he felt, marched the unseen presences of millions of long–dead camp victims, making him one of them. He felt the true horror, the true monstrousness of the camp, as if he had actually experienced it. In a way he had.

He had visited the nightmarish past and seen its abominations through the eyes of a woman named Sarah, with a number tattooed on her arm.

Sarah stood outside the tower gate in the middle of the railroad tracks. Quietly Frank went up to her. Tears were welling up in her eyes and rolling down her cheeks, as she wept silently. She looked up at him, attempting a wan little smile. She took his hand. She said nothing.

There was nothing to say....

Frank was tooling down the prescribed transit highway on his way back from Auschwitz. He had just passed the Dresden interchange. It was a few minutes past two o'clock. He would be in Börnersdorf— if all went well—later in the afternoon.

The memory of his visit to the extermination camp and his meeting with Sarah was still raw in his mind. He tried to put it behind him. For now. He was about to take a risk, the potentially serious risk of venturing into forbidden territory in the DDR, in his search for information. Börnersdorf. And the *Serail* documents. He wanted to have a totally clear head.

He was just about to pass a huge truck loaded with gravel when he felt a jar, and his car suddenly acted as if it were driving across a giant washboard.

Dammit! A flat. Right front.

He slowed down and pulled over to the side.

And as traffic whizzed by on the highway he began to change his flat tire for the spare in his trunk. It took him half an hour. No big deal.

As he resumed his journey, he had a sudden, chilling thought. What if it happened again? This time he would not have a spare, and he would be stuck. What if it happened while he was illegally off the transit highway?

There was only one thing to do. He had to get the flat repaired. He began to look for an off–ramp.

He left the transit highway at the next exit and quickly found a gas station with a mechanic on duty.

While the mechanic fixed the flat—forty–five minutes, he said— Frank went to a small cafe across the road for a cup of coffee.

When he returned to the gas station, he found his car on the rack, the right front wheel off, and an array of tools and parts strewn on the ground below.

Shocked, he confronted the mechanic. The man shrugged. When Frank had hit whatever it was he hit to cause the flat, the man informed him, he had also damaged the steering arm. Couldn't possibly drive the car the way it was. Wasn't around, so he decided to go ahead and fix it. Wasn't anything major. But ran into problems with parts. Car was a Toyota. Only had parts for a Warburg or a Trabi. Could adapt parts carried by outfit in Dresden. They were on the way. Shouldn't be more than a couple of hours. Cafe across the road serves a nice dinner. Sauerbraten is good.

Frank was furious. He had no doubt that the man was making the whole thing up. There had been nothing wrong with his steering arm. Absolutely nothing. It was a scam so that the man could fleece him of some westmarks by inflating his bill, since all repair bills by Western tourists had to be paid in hard–to–get West German currency. But there was not a thing he could do about it.

It was dusk and the station was closing down when Frank finally drove off. It was already dark when, after a couple of hours, he at last saw the sign; Börnersdorf Kreis Pirna, Bezirk Dresden.

He parked his car at the side of the road just outside the village and turned off the lights. For a moment he sat and watched the black shapes of the houses and barns before him, black on black as they melted together in the dark. The night was partly cloudy and the waning moon provided little more light than did the patches of stars in the night sky. The village itself showed no lights. Like farmers the world over, the Börnersdorfers retired early.

He put his little camera in his pocket and cursed himself for not having thought of bringing a flashlight. He got out of the car and walked into the village along the road, which became its main street. The night air was cool, and the sleeping hamlet was quiet and hushed. In the distance a dog barked. Frank started. He walked on. It was far away. But somehow the sound brought his position clearly to his mind. His position of very real danger. What would happen to him if he were caught? Prison? For how long? His little booklet said two years. Two years! He suddenly remembered the horror stories he had read in the papers about people who had been in the DDR illegally and had been caught. Spies. No matter who they were or why they were there, they were called spies. And the East Germans dealt harshly with spies. He shivered. Suddenly the cold darkness round him had become sinister and foreboding.

He looked at his watch. He could barely make out the time, 2137 hours. It wasn't that late. He had not anticipated finding no one awake to talk to. It had been a mistake.

He walked between the dark and shuttered houses. From a partly open barn door up ahead he could see a yellow light spilling out into the dark, being absorbed by the black night. Someone was awake. He quickened his steps.

He reached the barn. Cautiously he stepped through the door.

"*Holla!*" he called. "Is anyone here?"

There was no response, but a couple of horses half–hidden in their stalls stirred uneasily.

"*Holla!*" Frank called again. "Anyone?"

The light came from a kerosene lamp that hung from a large, rusty nail on a post. He walked over to it.

"*Holla!*"

He walked up to one of the stalls and leaned over, peering into it.

"*Was suchen Sie hier?*—what are you doing here?"

Startled, Frank whirled toward the voice.

Behind him stood a burly man, his face grim, a pitchfork held firmly before him, the sharp, wear–polished points of its teeth glinting in the glow from the lamp like a multitusked bayonet fixed on a gun.

XVIII

Frank stood staring at the pitchfork. He made no move.

"What do you want here?" the man asked once again. The pitchfork stayed pointed at Frank. "Who are you?"

Frank told him. He told the farmer that he was a historian doing research, looking for information about a plane crash that had taken place near Börnersdorf, back in the war, in 1945. He told him he was looking for anyone in the village who might be able to give him any such information.

The farmer listened. He lowered the pitchfork. "You are from the West." It was not a question. "Do the authorities know you are here?"

"They do," Frank assured him. It was only a little lie. "I have the proper permits and travel papers."

The farmer nodded. "I have heard about that plane crash you talk about," he said slowly. "But I, myself, was born the year after the war was over. I know nothing."

He put the pitchfork aside. He scratched his head.

"Rost," he said. "Anton Rost.* He can help."

"Rost?"

---

* The name is an alias to protect the real farmer.

"He's an old–timer. Over seventy–five, they say."

"And he knows about—about the crash?"

The farmer shrugged. "If anyone knows, Rost knows," he said firmly. "And Rost stays awake late. Sometimes he is still awake at midnight, they say." He shook his head. "I want to take a look at Lotte. My mare. She is about to drop her foal. Tonight. Or tomorrow."

He took the lamp from the nail, walked to a far stall and peered into it. He returned to Frank.

"Tomorrow," he said. "Come. I will take you to Rost."

The *Bauernstube* in the modest little house that belonged to the farmer, Rost, was typical of any such room in any small farmer's house, East or West, Frank thought. Rough wooden furniture, a bare worn floor, a black wood–burning stove, and open shelves with sturdy but cracked or dented cookware.

Rost, too, was typical, a small wiry man with the kind of furrowed face that results from working out of doors and which made him look anywhere between sixty and a hundred and sixty.

"It was a long time ago," Rost said. "I was still a young man." He cackled, showing yellowed, uneven teeth. "And that *is* a long time ago!" He nodded sagely. "But I do remember. I do remember the plane that crashed here, only a few miles from the village; I, myself, was the first one out there."

"Tell me about it."

Rost eyed Frank speculatively. "There is little to tell," he shrugged. "The plane had crashed. It was burning."

"But—you do remember when? You do remember the date?"

Rost nodded emphatically. "It was the day before my wife—God rest her soul—it was the day before she used the last three eggs from the water–glass barrel. For our supper. It was early in the morning of the twenty-first of April in the year of 1945."

"Did anyone of the crew survive?" Frank asked. "What about the pilot, Major Gundelfinger?" He knew the answer, of course.

Rost looked at him closely. "You—you know about the Major, young man?"

Frank nodded. "It is because of him that I am here," he said. It was true.

Rost nodded. "They all died," he said, "except two, and one of them died two days later. He was an SS-Rottenführer—an SS Corporal. As I recall, his name was Becker. Or something like that."

"And the other one?"

"He was badly hurt, he was. I myself took him home from the wreck. He was brought to the *Militärlazarett* in Bad Gottleuba."

"What happened to him?"

Rost shrugged. "It was a time of much happening," he said. "I do not know."

"Do you remember his name?"

Rost drew himself up. "A man is apt to remember the name of someone whose life he saved," he said solemnly. "His name was Westermaier. Franz Westermaier. He had been the tail gunner on the plane."

"And the plane itself, it was totally burned up?"

Rost nodded. "Everything that could burn, burned. There was a lot of scrap metal lying about, of course. That was all that remained." He paused. "Except for the crates."

Frank tensed. "The crates?"

"*Gewiss*—sure," Rost nodded again. "The plane had broken in two at the impact, and the least damaged part, the tail section it was, it did not burn as fiercely as the other section, and a lot of wooden crates had spilled out."

"What happened to those crates?"

"We—salvaged them. All but one of them that had broken open in the crash. It was burning. And so were all the papers in it."

"But the others—how many were there?"

Rost shrugged elaborately. "Ten I think. Perhaps a dozen. I do not remember."

"What did you do with them?"

"They had markings on them," Rost said. "Important markings. And they were sealed. They were Government property, we all agreed. And they should not fall into the hands of the enemy, the Russians. If they got here."

"I understand," Frank said, curbing his impatience only with difficulty. "But what did you *do* with them?"

"We took them to the parson's house," Rost said. "We hid them."

Frank stared at the farmer, a simple old man who did not know that he was proving some of the world's leading reporters and historians wrong! The missing *Geheimoperation Serail* JU–352 did not crash in Bavaria, but far earlier in its flight. Not everyone on the plane was killed. There was one survivor. And the fabled crates filled with the Führer's documents were not consumed by flames, but hidden in safety in a village parson's house!

Frank hardly dared ask his next, obvious question.

"Are they—are they still there?"

Rost looked at him.

"It was many, many years ago, young man."

"I know—but are they?"

Rost shook his head. "For a day they were," he said. "Then a group of men came. And they asked about the crates. And we gave them to them."

"A group of men?" Frank asked. "Who were they?"

Rost shrugged. "I do not know who they were. It is long ago. They were soldiers. Wehrmacht, I believe. We did not ask. One does not question authority. They knew about the crates. They described them, so we knew they were theirs. And we gave them to them."

"What did they do with them?"

"They loaded them on a truck. They drove off with them. To Dresden, I think."

Frank's disappointment tasted bitter in his mouth. "Thank you, Herr Rost," he said. "Your information is most interesting."

The old man grinned at him. "I will bet that you would rather have found a parson's house full of crates than a cemetery full of bodies, *ja?*" He cackled.

"Cemetery?" Frank asked. "What—bodies?"

"The bodies of the ones who died in the crash, young man. Most of them we could identify by their discs, with their service serial numbers. We have a memorial plot in our cemetery. We buried what was left of them there." Again he cackled. "And *they* are all still there."

Frank was at once alert. Here might be tangible proof of what Rost had told him.

"Herr Rost," he said. "I must return tonight, before my permit expires. But I should very much like to visit the memorial in your cemetery, if it is possible. However, it is still very dark outside, and I have no flashlight. Is there perhaps a possibility that you could lend me one? I shall return it at once."

Rost shook his head. "I have no flashlight, young man. But I will lend you a kerosene lamp. And you need not return it tonight. I shall be asleep. Just hang it on the tree at the memorial plot, and I will pick it up tomorrow."

Frank stood up. He extended his hand to the old farmer. Rost took it. His hand was rough and hard. "Take the road through town and turn right at the second side road. The cemetery is right there. You cannot miss it."

The Börnersdorf cemetery was a small, wooded tract of land off the road. In an untended plot under a forked tree Frank found the memorial stone, a slab of black granite with carved white lettering, headed:

ZUM GEDENKEN—IN MEMORIAM

There were sixteen names on the marker. The name in the middle read:

Friedrich Gundelfinger, 19.5.1900—21.4.1945

The pilot of the Geheimoperation Serail JU–352.

Seven of the names on the stone were followed by dates other than April 21—probably men from Börnersdorf, fallen in the war. The other names were those of the plane crew—and Wilhelm Arndt, the Führer's favorite servant.

By the light of his borrowed kerosene lamp Frank recorded the names of the other seven listed on the marker: Eugen Bassler. Unknown woman. Wilhelm Budack. Unknown woman. Hermann Schleef. Unknown soldier. And Max Fiebes. With SS-Rottenführer Becker and the sole survivor, Westermaier, there had been eleven people on board the JU–352.

He suddenly remembered his camera. He could take a picture. He had a flash, and he could use the self–timer, so he could be in the shot himself. He carefully placed the camera on a flat stone facing the memorial marker. He looked around. On a grave nearby fresh flowers had been placed. He borrowed a few. Yellow, and red. He set the timer and knelt by the stone.

It was the last exposure on the film in his camera, but luckily he had a spare roll in his pocket. He changed film and checked the focus. He'd better bracket it a lot. Circumstances were impossible at best. Six exposures later he replaced the flowers on the grave from which he had borrowed them, hung the kerosene lamp on the tree, and extinguished it. The cemetery was suddenly shrouded in Stygian darkness.

It took him a few minutes to regain his ability to see, then slowly he made his way among the tombstones to his car, and drove off toward the transit highway—and legitimacy.

He was driving along a country road, approaching a main road which, according to his map, would take him to a transit highway on–ramp. He was elated. All had gone swimmingly, and he had obtained some invaluable information. He could hardly wait to return to Hildesheim and follow up his leads.

There was the name of that tail gunner, the survivor Franz Westermaier. If he could be tracked down. And who were the men who had carted away the crates?

It was dawn and growing light as he neared the main road, and he had turned off his headlights.

The side road joined the main road on a slight incline, and as he was about to crest it, he took a look in both directions.

A chill surged through him. Not a hundred feet away a car was driving slowly, almost searchingly, along the road, bearing down on him.

A Lada, it bore the distinctive beige–and–green markings of the VOPO—the *Volkspolizei*. The East German People's Police.

Even as he watched, the blue light blinked on.

XIX

His thoughts jangled through Frank's mind in helter–skelter panic. Had they seen him? It would be impossible that they hadn't. Could he back down out of sight? It would do no good; they'd come after him. Should he drive up onto the road and onward, as if nothing was wrong? He'd be stopped. He was certain of that. His car had West German plates. Should he make a run for it? His chances would be nil. Should he just remain where he was? They'd investigate. No. Whatever he did would be suspicious.

Except one thing.

He jumped from his car, ran up on the road, and waved his arms frantically, flagging down the approaching police car. It came to a halt. Frank ran up to it.

"Bitte!" he said breathlessly. "I need help. I am lost."

The two policemen in the car climbed out. In their unfamiliar green uniforms, their VOPO number shields gleaming on their visored caps, they looked ominous to Frank. Glowering, they confronted him.

"Papiere, bitte—papers, please!" one of them growled. Frank handed him his papers. "I am sorry," he said apologetically, "but—"

The VOPO held up his hand, silencing him. "Moment," he said sharply. He studied Frank's papers, each document in turn. He looked up. "Hildesheim," he said. It sounded like a major accusation. He handed the papers to his partner, who began examining them.

"Yes," Frank nodded. "I have been in Poland," he explained. "I am on *Durchreise*—I am passing through the DDR on my way back. It is in my papers, there. I have permis—"

"We have seen the papers, Herr Brandenburg," the second officer said curtly. He glared at Frank. "You are a long way from the transit highway." His voice was cold. "And you are in a zone where it is illegal for you to be. Do you not know that it is forbidden to you to leave the transit highway?"

Frank nodded earnestly. "Yes, officer. I do know that. But—please. Let me explain. That is why I stopped you. To get help. May I explain?"

In silence the two VOPOs scowled at him. He took it as permission to go on.

"I had a flat," he said. "On the transit highway below Dresden, headed for Karl Marx Stadt. And something went wrong with my car. I had to get it fixed. I—" He fished the receipt for the repair on his steering arm from his pocket and gave it to one of the police officers. "Here is the bill for it. You can see the date. It was a gas station just off the transit highway. It took—"

Again the VOPO held up his hand to silence him. Frank stopped in mid–sentence. The police officer showed the receipt to his partner, who took it and returned to his car. He picked up the mike and began to talk.

"What else have you to say?" the remaining VOPO said to Frank.

"It—it took hours to fix the car," Frank said. In his mind he thanked God for having placed him in the hands of a crook. "By the time I could go on it was already growing dark. And I—I lost my way. For a while I drove around looking for—"

"What were you doing on the side road?" The VOPO nodded toward Frank's car.

"Oh, I—I drove about looking for a way to get back on the transit highway, and it got awfully late. I was very tired, and I did not think it was safe for me to drive, so I drove off the road to take a nap. I— I just woke up when I saw you coming, and realized that I could ask you for help."

The other officer returned. He nodded to his partner. The officer took the receipt. "They remember you," he said to Frank.

As well they should, Frank thought.

The VOPO held out his hand. "Your keys," he said.

"They are in the car."

"Wait here," the VOPO ordered him.

As Frank waited by the police vehicle, the two VOPOs went over to his car. He watched as they looked through it, opened the trunk, and rummaged through his luggage. Quickly he searched his mind. Was there anything incriminating in his belongings? He could think of nothing.

Presently the two officers returned. One of them had his camera. He held it out to Frank. "You have been taking pictures?"

Frank nodded. "Yes. About half a dozen."

"There are things that it is forbidden to photograph."

"Nothing like that," Frank said quickly. "Nothing like that at all. Only—country scenes. Things like that."

The VOPO studied the camera. "Six exposures," he said. "We will have to make certain they are not illegal."

"They are not important," Frank said. He hoped he had the proper noncommittal tone of voice. "Please take the film out. It is of little consequence."

The VOPOs looked at one another. Then one of them opened the camera and removed the film. He gave the camera back to Frank.

"You are about seven kilometers from a transit highway on–ramp," he said gruffly. "Follow us. We will take you there."

"Thank you," Frank said. "Thank you very much."

Ten minutes later he was once again tooling down the transit highway.

If the East Germans ever bothered to check his film and wondered what he'd been doing in Börnersdorf, way off the transit highway, he'd be long gone. But in his pocket rested the roll of exposed film he had taken out of his camera in the cemetery. The one with the snapshots he had taken in Auschwitz.

And one flash exposure of the Börnersdorf cemetery memorial marker.

Out of focus, dammit! It was all there, the tree, the flowers, the memorial marker with the names, and he, himself, kneeling next to it in the dark Börnersdorf cemetery. You could read the names all right, but they were out of focus. He cursed having had to sacrifice the bracketed shots, but he still considered himself lucky to have escaped an at best awkward situation with no greater penalty than the loss of a few snapshots. At least he had one left.

As soon as he had returned to Hildesheim he had once again made contact with WASt in Berlin, the agency which already had been helpful to him. Through them he was able to learn that Tail Gunner Franz Westermaier had died in 1980, and how to locate his widow. She lived in the little town of Simbach/Inn near Braunau in Bavaria.

He had called her at once to arrange a meeting. He had told her that he was doing a study on the men aboard the JU–352 that had crashed at Börnersdorf, and asked if he could be permitted to come visit her.

There had been a long pause on the phone. He had thought she would hang up. Then she said, "I do not think so. The—memories of those days are too painful for me. I think it is best—"

"Frau Westermaier," he interrupted her gently. "I do realize that. And I know your husband passed away only three years ago. But there are relatives of the others aboard that plane, Frau Westermaier. Relatives of your husband's comrades, who would be grateful to know that the mission for which their loved ones gave their lives had been a worthwhile one. Won't you please help?"

Again there was a pause—then an audible sigh.

"I—I cannot see you," the woman said. "But—perhaps I can answer a few of your questions on the phone. What do you want to know?"

"Thank you, Frau Westermaier. It is much appreciated. Your husband was a member of the crew of the JU–352, was he not?"

"Yes. He was the *Bordschütze*—the tail gunner."

"And the plane was shot down."

"No. It was not shot down."

"Then what—"

"Franz said they had been delayed in taking off, because of some engine trouble. They did not leave Berlin until around five o'clock in the morning, and it was already beginning to get light." She paused. It was obviously difficult for her to retell the story. "He told me that because they—they had lost the cover of darkness," she went on. "They flew very low to avoid detection, and when they flew over the

Erzgebirge—the Erz Mountains—I do not know why, but it could have been because of the engine trouble they had had earlier, or low clouds, but a wing tip of the plane clipped the top of a tall fir tree—and they crashed."

"But your husband survived."

"Yes. He was the only survivor of the crew. One other man, they had several passengers, one other man also survived, but he died a couple of days later."

"Your husband was wounded in the crash, was he not?"

"Yes. He was very badly hurt."

"What happened to him?"

"A farmer saved him. He was taken to a hospital. In Bad Gottleuba."

"Did your husband tell you the man's name?"

"Yes. It was a Herr Rost."

"Frau Westermaier, did your husband ever mention anything to you about the crates that were carried on the plane?"

Again a pause. "He told me they had been there. He told me they were of importance." And again the sigh. "He told me that as soon as he could, he called the *Führerhauptquartier* in Berlin, and told them about the—"

"Do you know with whom he talked?"

"I do not know for a fact, but I think it may have been someone in Reichsleiter Martin Bormann's office."

"Did he tell you what was said?"

"No. Only—" She stopped.

"Yes, Frau Westermaier?"

"Well—Franz told me later that he had found out that a team of intelligence officers had gone to Börnersdorf to get the crates. The villagers had kept them safe."

There it was. Full corroboration of farmer Rost's story.

"Did he tell you what was done with them?" he asked.

"No, no. I do not even know when those people went there. Or who they were."

"Did he tell you how he found out? From whom?"

"No. He did not."

"Do you know if—"

"Please," the woman pleaded. "No more questions. I have told you all I know."

"I want to thank you, Frau—"

"*Schon gut*," the woman said. She sounded tired. "*Schon gut*—that's all right." She hung up.

For a moment Frank sat in silence staring at the telephone. He had not learned anything new, but the Westermaier woman had corroborated Rost's account.

As for the documents, he would probably never find out what happened to them.

But he'd sure try. He'd sure as hell try.

The stone hit the leaden surface of the little lake with a soft plop. Quickly the concentric rings on the satiny water spread on ever–widening circles from the point of impact.

Frank watched in silence. He leaned against a tree and looked up at the darkening sky. It was dusk, that hour of the day when time itself seemed to slow its pace, making ready to rest. It was his favorite time of day, but as he stood on the bank of the lake in the near–deserted park, he felt none of the wonted peacefulness and relaxation.

He turned from the rippling water to look at Herta, who stood quietly beside him. They had met in Hildesheim to come to grips, the two of them, with the fact that they were steadily growing apart; he coming from his studies in Lübeck, she from Bremen, where she was learning hotel and restaurant management, one day, perhaps, to take over a restaurant owned by her parents. They had both sensed that the meeting would be a crucial one.

"Please, Herta," Frank said. "Please try to understand. I—I *have* to go on."

"Why?"

He looked at her, his eyes as bleak as the cold, waning day. "I—I just do," he said miserably.

"We hardly see each other anymore," Herta said. "We used to have such fun together. We used to go dancing. Or to a show. Or—just be with each other. We don't anymore. While everyone else is having a good time, you are hanging around railroad stations or visiting with—with all kinds of disreputable people. It's practically all you do." Earnestly she looked at him, obviously concerned. "You are letting it eat you, Frank." There was a sadness in her voice he had not heard before. "You are letting it eat—us."

"I do not want that to happen."

"Then give it up, Frank. Let it be all. You have already learned so much."

He sighed. "But—not enough, Herta. Don't you see, not enough. Not yet. There are still so many things, more now than when I began. So much I want to know. Need to know."

"What?" There was a quiet defiance in Herta's voice. "What?"

For a moment Frank stood in silence.

"You are right," he said. "I have learned a lot. The reason I originally got involved in the search for the truth, the question of the Holocaust, is really no longer the reason I have to go on."

"Then what is?"

"Other more compelling, more disturbing questions have taken its place."

"What questions, Frank? What reasons are so important, so strong that they can take over your life? What is it you must know? And why?"

He frowned. "I do not really know why," he said slowly. "All I know is that I must do all I can to find out. There is something in me that drives me on. There is the question of what really happened to Martin Bormann. *Someone* knows. *I* want to know. And what really did happen to the *Serail* documents? And there are other questions like that. And more important, perhaps, why *are* they questions? Why the mystery? For what reasons the secrecy? I—I feel it is important to try to find out. Important to me. To my relationship to the past, to the past of my place of birth, Herta." Beseechingly he looked at her. "I cannot explain it any better. And I cannot help it. But—but please understand."

Herta looked at him in silence, and he went on.

"You know how I am. I just cannot leave anything I start half done. Whatever it is. Whatever I do, I have to finish. If I do not it drives me out of my mind. You know that. And—and right now, I feel I— I have not finished my search. And it is tearing me. I have to go on— until I know I have gone as far as I can. And time is running out for me, Herta. Many of the people I want to talk to are old people. They will not be around much longer. It is—it is a last chance."

Earnestly he watched her. "And it's more than that. More than Bormann. More than the missing documents. More than all the people I've talked to. Wolff. Baur. All of them. It is what they represent.

A chapter in my country's past. My heritage. My roots. *Our* roots, Herta. I *must* come to terms with that. Understand it. And what I am doing is the only way I know how to do that. Please, Herta," he implored. "Please understand."

Herta watched him, her eyes unnaturally bright. She walked up close to him.

"I do understand, Frank," she whispered softly, a trace of resignation in her voice. "I do understand."

For a brief moment her words hung mistily in the cold air between them.

Gently she hugged him. She turned and slowly began to walk away from the ever–blacker lake. Frank followed.

In both their minds remained a host of thoughts. Of regrets. Of desires. But they remained unspoken. Frank knew that they would always be friends.

He quickened his step and caught up with her. He took her arm. Together, in silence, they walked toward home.

But even now, with his arm linked with hers, Frank found his thoughts straying ahead. Ahead two days, to the town of Erkrath near Düsseldorf and his meeting with SS-Obergruppenführer Dr. Werner Best, former chief of Section I of the RSHA—the Main Security Office of the Reich—and notorious Reich Commissioner for Occupied Denmark, a man whose address Karl Wolff had given him and suggested he see.

Frank knew quite a lot about Dr. Werner Best, enough to know that the man was at the same time one of the most illustrious figures of the Third Reich and one of the most ambiguous and enigmatic.

Frank had written him, with no result. He had finally made a telephone call and been granted a meeting.

He had no concept of what to expect when that meeting took place.

XX

I t had not been easy to find Dr. Best in the town of Erkrath. Best and his wife had moved, and Frank had to go to the *Einwohner-meldeamt*—the Resident Report Office—in Mülheim an der Ruhr, where the Bests had lived before, to get their new address. It turned out to be a retirement hotel called Rosenhof. He was startled, until he remembered that Dr. Best was eighty years of age and had been in ill health for several years, a fact that had helped keep him out of prison.

The Rosenhof was a pleasant terraced building surrounded by woods and reached across an extensive, well kept lawn. Each apartment had its own little balcony. Frank parked his car, a Toyota PKW, in the parking area. He had brought a potted plant from the nursery in Hildesheim for Mrs. Best. It had a novel, self–regulating watering device stuck into the soil. As he walked along the path across the lawn he glanced up to the apartments on the third floor. In one of them lived the Bests. He wondered which one.

Former Reich Plenipotentiary Commissioner for Occupied Denmark, former SS-Obergruppenführer Dr. Werner Best met Frank in the lobby. A relatively short man, clad in an open–neck shirt and slacks, practically bald, with a sharp nose, curiously penetrating blue eyes, and a strained straight smile on his lips, Dr. Best did not cut an imposing figure.

Holding his potted plant awkwardly with one arm, Frank shook the man's offered hand, suddenly acutely aware of the fact that forty years before, that hand, with a stroke of a pen, had held the power of life and death over millions of people in Europe. He hoped Best did not notice the abruptness with which he withdrew his hand.

As they rode up in the elevator together, Frank suddenly knew how he would spend his time with the man. Forget about the usual discussion regarding Best's time as Reich Commissioner in Denmark; it was a subject already well covered, and he—Frank—would learn nothing new.

However, Best had had close personal contact with the top Third Reich personalities, the "Big H's": Himmler, whom he had known and worked with for twelve years; Heydrich, who had been his immediate superior on the Gestapo for five years; and Hitler himself. Talking informally with Best would give him an excellent opportunity to get a more personal impression of these three men, who had affected the world so greatly. He glanced at Best. It would not be easy, he thought uncomfortably. The man was aloofly reserved, with no visible hint of communicative openness.

His wife, Frank thought, was a female carbon copy of her husband, correct and cool. Politely she had accepted his gift, and perfunctorily she had served fruit juice, as they sat down in the living room. The bald little man who perched stiffly and tight–lipped across from Frank had once been the equal of Heydrich, Kaltenbrunner, and Himmler. Their malevolent spirits seemed to Frank to hover over the little group.

"You wanted to see me," Best said, a hint of resentment in his voice. "I can tell you that I consented only because of the recommendation by Karl Wolff. The Oberstgruppenführer was always a dear friend of mine. Otherwise—I see no one. I have had threats against my life—" he fixed Frank with his sharp eyes, as if he were to blame "—and have even had to have police protection. I still get requests from journalists and historians. I refuse them all. What do *you* want with me? What do *you* want to discuss? My reprehensible Gestapo days? My unsavory actions in occupied Denmark? What, Herr Brandenburg?"

Best glared at Frank with suspicious, barely concealed bitterness. Frank could feel the latent hostility lashing at him like a chill gust of arctic wind. He had his work cut out for him, he realized, before he might get the man to relax and open up. The legal term "hostile witness" flashed through his mind. He wondered exactly what kind of witness the former SS-Obergruppenführer had been at his several trials and examinations.

"Nothing like that, Herr Doktor," he said with a disarming smile. "Enough has been said and written about that." He dismissed it with a deprecating wave of his hand. "I simply wanted to meet you. After all, you *are* an important part of our history. And I wanted to talk to you, informally, about some of the other important people in the Third Reich whom you knew. Get your impression, your opinion of them. Your relationship with them. That is what I hope to do."

For a moment Best contemplated him. "That, at least, is refreshing," he said drily. "Not out to scoop the world, even at this late date, with some new heinous revelations. Refreshing." He again fixed Frank with his piercing eyes. "And you know how to use flattery as well," he said with amused sarcasm. "I suppose that should be rewarded. Very well. Which of the—uh, other important individuals would you like to discuss first?"

Frank felt himself beginning to blush. Had he been that obvious? Apparently he had. "Perhaps—perhaps the Führer himself, Herr Doktor?" Dammit! That sounded like flattery, too.

Best coughed a little laugh. "The Führer himself," he said. "Of course." He leaned back in his chair.

"Contrary to what you may think, young man, I was never captivated by Adolf Hitler—or by one of his—uh, missionaries. I had my own ideas, my own ideals, if you wish. And I spoke my mind. Even when it did not agree with that of the Führer. I had my share of uh, run–ins with him."

"May I know one of them, Herr Doktor?"

"One of my disagreements with the Führer?" Best shrugged. "I see no reason why not." He pursed his thin lips in recollection.

"I remember one time," he said. "There had been some trouble with terrorists in Denmark. The Führer had ordered me to make reprisals— counterterrorism, as it were. In the ratio of five to one. And if that was not sufficient to stop the terror attacks, ten to one. Ten Danish hostages shot for each German killed." He ran his hand over his bald pate, a remembered gesture from earlier days, when a full head of hair might have needed grooming.

"I did not follow his orders," he continued. "I knew that executing hostages only created martyrs. And we did not need martyrs in Denmark. Instead I had the apprehended terrorists tried before a military court. Because of that, and the fact that the Communists in the country had called a general strike, a strike quite shortlived, I might add, I was denounced to the Führer and ordered to report to him at the Berghof on Obertsalzberg in Berchtesgaden."

He stopped and took a deep breath. "Von Ribbentrop was there, too. The Führer, in his gruff voice, thundered his anger at me for a full quarter of an hour. He accused me of willfully disobeying his direct orders. He threatened to imprison me. He fixed both me and von Ribbentrop with those cold eyes of his, which were sometimes filled with scorn and sometimes had the disturbing, mesmerizing stare of a serpent." Again he fixed Frank with his own disconcerting stare. "A habit of his," he said, "which incidentally never affected me."

Frank sat silent, listening.

"The Führer snapped at us: '*Die Herren wollen immer klüger sein als ich!*—You gentlemen always want to be wiser than I am!' When I finally was able to get a word in and asked him if I could be permitted to say something, the Führer screamed at me: '*Ich will nichts hören. Raus!*—I will listen to nothing! Out!'"

For a moment Best sat in silence, slowly shaking his head. "When I left the Berghof," he said at last, "I had in mind something the Reichsführer SS Heinrich Himmler once said to me. 'Do not ever contradict the Führer or point out to him any mistakes he might have made, or he will become despondent, and the brilliant concepts created by his genius may be disturbed.' I took 'genius' to mean 'prophet,' for the Führer was the hallowed prophet to many, such as the Reichsführer SS." He sighed. "But infinitely more disquieting than that was the conviction that overtook me then, the conviction that the Führer was no longer his normal self. That he was now mentally deranged. His unchecked rage, his stereotyped repetition of meaningless arguments, his refusal to listen to anyone or anything he did not wish to hear at the moment, convinced me. The Führer had become what I thought of as the *rasende*—the raving—*Prophet*."

He fell silent, and absentmindedly stroked his pate.

"Were you often at odds with the Führer regarding the administration of Denmark?" Frank asked.

"At times we disagreed on policy," Best said. "I tried to—uh, correct any misjudgments whenever possible. Others I had to carry out, as they were matters of protocol."

"Protocol?"

"Yes. Such as the Führer's order to me totally to ignore the King of Denmark and the entire royal family. All because the Führer had taken violent offence at what he, undoubtedly correctly, perceived as a deliberate insult to him by the king."

"King Christian insulted the Führer?"

"So it would seem," Best nodded. "With his telegram."

"What telegram?"

"You do not know the story?"

Frank shook his head.

"The Führer had sent a long, flowery telegram to the King congratulating him on his birthday. At long last the King's acknowledgement arrived. A telegram with the single word, *Tak*—which means 'thanks'!"

Frank laughed.

"You think that is amusing, Herr Brandenburg?" Best asked sharply, fixing Frank with his penetrating eyes.

Frank stopped. Had he offended the general? What if he had?

"Yes," he said.

"So do I," Best chuckled. "So do I. But not nearly as amusing as another story about the Führer and the Danish king."

"Another true story?"

"Perhaps. There were many stories and anecdotes told about King Christian X, it is the measure of a popular man. Some of them were true, some were not. But true or not, the significant fact is that they were told at all. They showed the high regard in which the people of Denmark held their wartime king."

"What is the story?" Frank was curious.

"It was said that the Führer sent King Christian a long dispatch in which he suggested that the two Germanic sister countries of Germany and Denmark become one nation. Receiving no reply, he repeated his suggestion, and once again awaited the King's answer. When no reply was forthcoming, he fired off a telegram demanding an answer. He got it. King Christian is supposed to have wired back: 'I have given your suggestion much thought. But at my age, I think I am too old to rule over two countries.'"

They laughed together. Even Frau Best joined in. Gradually the atmosphere of wariness in the room was changing. Best seemed to be warming to his subject. It was obvious that he enjoyed telling a good story.

"At other times," he went on, "the Führer did agree with me. Once, when Generalfeldmarschall Keitel, the chief of staff of the High Command of the Armed Forces, suggested that the food rations for the Danes be cut to the bare bone, and I strongly disagreed with him, the Führer sided with me." He gave Frank a sidelong look. "Curiously enough, by quoting from the Hebrew Bible: *Thou shalt not muzzle the ox when he treadeth out the grain.*"

"You were Reich Commissioner for Denmark for more than two years, Herr Doktor. What impressed you the most?"

"Two years Reich Commissioner, Herr Brandenburg, from February 1943 to May 1945—and six years thereafter in a prison cell. *That* is what impressed me the most." The bitterness crept back into his voice.

"That cell in the Citadel was a far cry from our lovely villa we called Rydhaven, north of Charlottenlund just outside Copenhagen. It was so peaceful there. So comfortable." He sighed. "Sitting in that cell, young man, I asked myself what had gone wrong in the years between our glorious emergence in 1939 and our ignominious defeat in 1945."

"What do you think went wrong?"

"Primarily one single flaw, Herr Brandenburg. One serious, fundamental flaw in the Führer's psyche. Of course, there were many flaws and errors that contributed to the catastrophe, but without that basic flaw of the Führer's, all of them together would have meant nothing." He stroked his pate. "Six years gave me ample time to arrive at my conclusion, you may be assured."

"One flaw? You refer to the Führer's anti–Semitism?"

Best shook his head irritably. "No, no," he said. "Not at all." He paused, as if organizing his thoughts. Frank was about to prod him when he continued.

"The flaw to which I refer," Best went on, "is one of concept, and the resulting relationship between the Reich and any given territory annexed by the Reich. The Führer was not able to think in terms of the population of such a territory, or country, as a whole, but only as individuals or special groups of individuals. He had no realization of the importance, the power of the spirit of the national common-alty. Except in Germany. He did not realize that it was equally strong among the 'inferior' people of the nations he conquered. That power is not centered in short–lived individuals, but in the timeless common people. I call it the 'populace principle' of command. The Führer did not realize that individuals, or small groups of individuals, do not act or react in the same manner as the populace as a whole."

He leaned forward in his chair, intent on explaining his theory.

"So. While eliminating individual opponents or threats to his authority the Führer at the same time—uh, helotized the country, he made serfs or slaves of the *populace*, Herr Brandenburg, the populace as a whole.

"Let me give you some concrete examples. The Führer's flaw, his inability to recognize the populace principle, was first manifested in 1939, with the subjugation of Czechoslovakia. By creating a menial, a lackey nation, helotizing and degrading the populace—he insured affront, discontent, and resistance, instead of laying a foundation on which to build a growing positive relationship. Disregard of the populace principle, not so?

"After the blitz victory in Poland it was the same. And in France—where up to one hundred and fifty of the populace were executed in retaliation for each German killed by the resistance. A violation of the populace principle, which led to greater resistance and a vastly diminished opportunity for positive interaction with the people.

"And in the Ukraine, Herr Brandenburg, I had been in contact with anti–Communist leaders since 1939. If the Führer had assured them a national state of their own they would have mustered in excess of two million soldiers to fight on the side of the Reich, soldiers who knew how to fight in the vastness of Russia. It would have meant victory for Germany. But instead, the Führer chose to subjugate, to helotize the Ukrainian people, thereby creating an army of populace partisans that fought to the death against him, ensuring defeat."

He spread his hands and fixed his eyes on Frank.

"So you see, Herr Brandenburg, the Führer's disregard for the populace principle cost him the war—and the Reich."

He leaned back in his chair. "You wanted a thumbnail sketch of Adolf Hitler, young man. You have it."

He stroked his pate. "Now," he said brightly. "Who is next?"

It was obvious that the former SS-Obergruppenführer was enjoying having his say.

"You mentioned Reichsführer SS Heinrich Himmler, Herr Doktor,"

Frank said. "When he cautioned you against contradicting the Führer. What was your impression of the Reichsführer?"

"Ah! Himmler. I would have bet he would be your next subject." He thought for a moment.

"My first impression of him was very favorable. He seemed to be a reasonable man. He made political sense, and his thoughts and plans appeared to be on a grand scale. But even from the first I recognized his predilection to—uh, lecture you. If Adolf Hitler was the prophet Heinrich Himmler was the schoolmaster. That is how I came to think of him. He did possess the characteristics of the schoolmaster, so typical in Germany, and probably elsewhere as well, characteristics that manifested themselves in many ways during his political career."

"You mean the Reichsführer SS was scholarly? knowledgeable?"

"I mean he was a disciplinarian, Herr Brandenburg. I mean that he lectured rather than conversed. A case in point, during the early years, 1934 in fact, was his explanation, expounded to a group of leaders in the SS, of the reasons for the action taken against the SA that year."

"I read about that," Frank exclaimed. "That was when the Führer had several men from the Sturmabteilung shot. Including Röhm, the SA chief of staff. Because they were homosexual, *nicht wahr?*"

"Precisely. The so colorfully named Night of the Long Knives. Close to two hundred dead. Including Ernst Röhm. The Reichsführer not only rationalized the—uh, rather overplayed scenario of that night, but delivered a stirring lecture on the evils of homosexuality. He recited a long biological–political sermon, pointing out to us all that the SA had been on the way to becoming a society of sodomites, a threat to the German people, and he explained to us in detail how and why homosexuality was the source of corruption and the way to destruction. Homosexuals were easy prey for foreign agents, he stressed. Homosexuality was filthy, an abomination in the eyes of nature, patently abnormal, promiscuous behavior. And I remember a rather curious thing he said. 'What may be harmless as far as little secretaries are concerned, when officers are involved, it means catastrophe for the State.' At the time it seemed a rather muddled dictum. Still does. But it shows the way the Reichsführer SS thought, especially since it was all delivered as a lecture in the precise manner of a schoolmaster lecturing a class of students on the evils of smoking. Himmler valued an orderly mind highly."

"Then the good relationship that existed between you and the Reichsführer may have been strengthened because of the fact that you had a doctorate in law."

Best laughed. "Because of it!" he snorted. "Rather in spite of it. Himmler had a deep distrust of lawyers. All jurists. He felt that they totally lacked a healthy understanding of people, and thus lacked the ability to think and act in a politically correct manner. It was a prejudice that often colored his decisions when lawyers were involved. If you wanted to prevail with the Reichsführer, your arguments would have to be cloaked in political rather than legal terms. He thoroughly disliked lawyers. There was only one other class of people he disliked as much. Pessimists. In order to function well, the Reichsführer had to work in an up–beat atmosphere of optimism. He would suffer if you poured water in the wine of his enthusiasm."

He leaned back in his chair with a nostalgic look on his face.

"I remember once, in the spring of 1935, I brought to him the text of a newly enacted law pertaining to the Gestapo, a text with which he was very satisfied. However, I felt it was my duty to point out to him certain—uh, short–comings, and to advise caution, which I did. Himmler at once grew angry with me and dismissed me with the words: 'You can rob one of all pleasure!' He was really a simple man, Herr Brandenburg. To him, one was either very good or very bad."

"That is rather simplistic, is it not?"

Best nodded. "Simplistic—in the mold of the stereotyped schoolmaster. The Reichsführer *was* a simplistic man. As in the matter of racial purity."

"I know he believed in the supremacy of the Aryan race."

"To the hilt, Herr Brandenburg. To the hilt. Quite surprisingly so."

"Why surprising?"

"Let me tell you a little anecdote about the Reichsführer and his racial idol. It happened to my wife, as a matter of fact." He nodded toward his wife, who gave him a quick smile back. "The Reichsführer's ideal German was tall and athletic, blond and blue–eyed, with an oval–shaped cranium to house a superior intellect, as opposed to the stocky, round–headed, dark–eyed and dark–haired races. We were at a party, as a matter of fact it was in the home of the Japanese ambassador, Oshima, and my wife sat next to the Reichsführer SS, who lectured her on the importance of keeping the German race pure, in the image of his Nordic ideal, and that the youth of the Reich should

be made aware of this importance. My wife suggested that such indoctrination might be dangerous. 'How?' the Reichsführer asked,
startled. 'Because,' my incautious wife replied, 'if those requirements
did become reality, the Reich would lose most of its top leaders: Dr.
Goebbels, the Führer, and you, yourself, Herr Reichsführer!'"

"What happened?"

"The Reichsführer peered through his steel–rimmed glasses at my
wife for a long moment," Best said, his eyes twinkling with remembered amusement. "And then he delivered himself of one of his
characteristic prevarications: 'Even a round cranium may hold an
elongated brain,' he said. Presto! A dark–haired, dark–eyed, stocky
Aryan by sleight of mind!"

Frank laughed.

"Himmler did have some—uh, unorthodox beliefs as well," Best
continued. "He apparently believed in a God; at least he issued an
edict that everyone belonging to the SS must be *Gottglaübig*—believe
in God, although which God was never defined. It could have been
an ancient Nordic God such as Odin or Thor. What he himself actually
believed was always unclear. Only one thing was certain, he was
something of a romantic mystic complete with superstitions and the
use of their jargons. He believed in such things as astrology and
graphology, in Mesmerism and black magic. There were certain times
of the year when he would retire and would make no plans, no
decisions, because for him it was a 'time of adversity.' Quite a curious
role model, Reichsführer SS Heinrich Himmler, to be emulated by
the finest of Germany's young men, the rank and file of the SS. A
man who let his life and his activities be influenced by soothsayers
and charlatans."

He stroked his bald head pensively. "Of course," he mused, "he
was not unlike the Führer in that respect. The Führer also believed
in astrology. In fact, there were several other similarities between the
two of them. Hitler despised lawyers and pessimists as well. He was
disgusted by homosexuals, and he hardly looked like the Aryan paragon."

He licked the inside of his mouth in the manner of old people
bothered by dry mouth. "You know, Herr Brandenburg," he said. "I
often thought Himmler was much like Robespierre, the French
revolutionary, Maximilien Robespierre, from Arras. Like Himmler,
Robespierre, although a jurist, was the dogmatic schoolmaster type.

He, too, was a romantic who wanted to renew the virtues of the Roman Republic. He too believed in a pedagogical ideal and tolerated no disobedience of it. He too considered it his duty to annihilate all opponents of these doctrines and principles. He too was neither an egoist who sought power for his own personal gain nor a sadist who tortured and killed out of cruelty. He was simply the unrelenting, pitiless, dogmatic schoolmaster of the French Revolution. Exactly like the Reichsführer SS, whose firm belief was that there had to be a leader—a Führer, and that that Führer was always right. Consequently Himmler and his SS would follow and obey that Führer's every order, every wish. *Meine Ehre Heisst Treue* was the motto of the SS, 'My Honor Means Faithfulness."

"Yet toward the end the Reichsführer did go against the Führer's wishes," Frank pointed out. "When he entered into surrender negotiations behind Hitler's back. With the Swedish count Folke Bernadotte. The Führer himself called him a traitor."

Best nodded solemnly. "So he did," he acknowledged. "But by that time the Reichsführer had convinced himself that Hitler was ill, and no longer could function as—uh, the Führer. The Reichsführer simply carried out what he saw as the doctrine to be followed." He sighed, a wistful sigh.

"I remember him saying to me, 'If I could only sit down with Eisenhower for just two hours, I could convince him that we *have* to fight the Russians together!' That is what he wanted to do. That was in 1945."

He gave Frank a long look. "You know, Herr Brandenburg, already in 1944, in September, I received via Sweden a message from the British government, requesting that I arrange contact between them and Reichsführer SS Himmler, whom they—according to their message—considered '*besser als sein Ruf*—better than his reputation,' with the sole condition that Hitler remain completely uninformed. The Reichsführer's reply was, '*Nein. Zur Zeit nicht*—No. Not at this time.'"

"When did you see the Reichsführer SS for the last time?"

"It was the night of the second and third of May in 1945. I had been ordered to report to the headquarters of Admiral Doenitz, the new head of state after the Führer's death. It was in Plön, a few kilometers southeast of Kiel. When I arrived the headquarters was already in the process of moving to Flensburg on the Danish border.

I ran into the Reichsführer SS, who suggested that I drive up with him so we could discuss a few things on the way."

"And did you?"

"I did. The Reichsführer himself drove the car. We had to skirt Kiel because of the air raids, and we did not reach our destination near Flensburg until the next morning.

"I asked him how our Fatherland could have come to such a disastrous end, and he gave me the stock answer that the Führer had not been—uh, himself for some time. Out of curiosity I asked him why he had turned down the British feeler of six months earlier, and he told me that at that time he had still felt that he had a duty to inform the Führer of the situation. He had done so. However, it had only resulted in a explosion of rage on the Führer's part—and a strengthening of his suspicions about the Reichsführer SS."

He gave Frank one of his piercing looks. "So you see, Herr Brandenburg, it was not the Reichsführer SS who turned down the British request—it was the Führer himself.

"Toward the end Himmler was a confused, a broken man, Herr Brandenburg, a man to be pitied. His world of dogma was crumbling around him. His enemies in the Reich hierarchy, the generals of the OKW—the Army High Command—and Reichsleiter Bormann, used their influence with Hitler to denounce him.

"Himmler has been judged a bloodhound and a mass murderer by history, young man, as has Robespierre. It is an unjust verdict. But even as the *Doktrinär*—the dogmatist from Arras, the bloodstained schoolmaster of the French Revolution, can be understood and judged only when viewed as an intolerant teacher–type—because that is exactly what a dogmatist is—a teacher–type who by accident found in his hands, instead of the disciplinary cane of the classroom, the unlimited power of a great state and the means of executing that power, and who used this omnipotence consistently and pedantically to follow his infallible doctrines—if *he* can be judged in this manner, so can the bloodstained schoolmaster in the black uniform of the SS!"

"But—what about the concentration camps, the extermination camps? Himmler was—"

"Fact is, Herr Brandenburg," Best interrupted sharply. "There were about twenty thousand inmates in those camps when the war broke out, no more—and of those more than half were criminals, not—uh, political prisoners. The war, Herr Brandenburg, the war swelled their ranks with such dire consequences. But the Reichsführer SS did not conduct the war. He merely carried out the orders and the wishes of his Führer, who was always right."

Abruptly he fell silent. His tone of voice had clearly said: subject closed.

Frank felt it wisest to change the subject completely.

"There is another high–ranking officer I should like you to talk about, Herr Doktor. SS-Gruppenführer, Reichsprotector Reinhard Heydrich."

"Ah, yes. Reinhard Heydrich." A small frown crept over Best's forehead. "Nietzsche's *blond Bestie*—blond beast. I shall tell you about Reinhard Heydrich. The *real* Reinhard Heydrich." He gave Frank one of his piercing looks. "If you are ready to listen to the story of a—uh, rather repugnant individual from your Fatherland's past."

XXI

Best clasped his hands in front of him, as if for support. It was obvious to Frank that the SS-Obergruppenführer's memories were becoming painful for him.

"Heydrich was my immediate superior for five years, as you undoubtedly know. Because of that, or in spite of it, I find it difficult to—um, characterize the man. Heydrich cannot be typified as easily as Hitler, the prophet, or Himmler, the schoolmaster. His—uh, makeup was considerably more complex. Heydrich possessed a—a demoniacal personality, he was, perhaps, the most demoniacal of the entire Reich leadership. Perhaps 'the demon' would describe him best."

"In what way demoniacal, Herr Doktor?"

Best pursed his lips. "It is not easy to define," he said slowly, "in a few words. There was a coldness about him, a total lack of compassion. It was not that he denied the compassion in him, it simply was not there. For example, he was deeply involved in the notorious so–called 'final solution to the Jewish problem,' but he had no—uh, hate for the Jewish people. I do not think he even thought of them as human beings. Only as pawns to be used in schemes and plans to insure the greatness of the Third Reich. Heydrich's inhumanity and cruelty did not stem from a conscious doctrine, as in the case of Hitler and Himmler, but rather from an unconscious, instinctive, and natural force—demoniacal, if you wish—that propelled him onward, and had no provision for responsibilities concerning those who were plowed under in the process."

He paused and slowly stroked his pate.

"Heydrich was intelligent," he continued. "Highly intelligent. But it was the intelligence of the hunter, the fencing–master, the conqueror. He approached problems with a Gordian Knot mentality, often discerning and delivering the decisive strike quickly and effectively, and with utter disregard for those who might be cut down because of his actions. He had no personal friends. Other people were either obstacles in his way or means to further his own goals, and they were treated accordingly. He used them as he saw fit."

Frank listened, spellbound. Best had been in practically daily contact with the infamous Heydrich for five years. His evaluation of the man was priceless. Exactly the kind of first–hand information he sought.

"I first met Reinhard Heydrich toward the end of 1933," Best went on. "When I was called to Berlin to take over the leadership of Abteilung I des Geheimen Staatspolizeiamtes—Section I of the Gestapo, under Heydrich. Section I was where administrative and legal matters were handled. To my astonishment I found that every one of Heydrich's subordinates feared him. Every single one, Herr Brandenburg. And his equals as well. A fear that was tinged with awe and a certain grudging admiration. Even high–ranking officials would inquire about Heydrich's mood apprehensively before approaching him.

"With his tall, slender build, blue eyes, blond hair, and haughtily aquiline features he was the personification of the Aryan look, in contrast to Hitler and Himmler. It mattered not that he was somewhat broad in the—uh, hips, that the long, sharp nose dominated his narrow face, that his blue eyes were too closely set and usually glinted with cold, calculating suspicion and were irritating because of their constant shifting about; Heydrich was still a pure Aryan figure.

"He was completely, inexorably ruthless, Herr Brandenburg. He would project his own characteristics onto those he perceived as his enemies, or enemies of the State, and he would fight them accordingly. He would look upon them as being as devious and dangerous as he himself would have been in their place. He measured all people by his own measure, and he sought adversaries behind every bush, where he himself would have been lying in wait."

"What—what motivates a man like that? What drives him?"

"Power, Herr Brandenburg. The desire for pure power. Not materialistic prosperity. Not the furthering of theoretical doctrines. Only power. Justification of his own personality. Heydrich had a burning need to be the best. Number one. In everything he came to grips with. Both on the intellectual–political level and on the strictly physical level. He flung himself into competitive sports and had to excel in everything. Skeet–shooting, flying, horseback riding—although he was less successful in that sport, since he was just as unable to relate to the horses as he was to people—gymnastics, and especially fencing, a sport which mirrored his entire life style with its thrusts and parries, feints and hits, lunges and ripostes. Because that is exactly how he dealt with those around him. Including me."

"You, Herr Doktor?"

"Very much so, Herr Brandenburg, very much so. Heydrich saw in me his archrival. He firmly believed that I was scheming to oust him from his position and take his place."

"Would you have wanted to replace him?"

"Under no condition," Best said firmly. "Had I been asked, I would have declined. But Heydrich had no doubt that that was exactly what I conspired to do. Especially when he learned that several of his subordinates would confide their problems to me rather than to him, simply because they feared direct contact with him so much that they attempted to avoid it as much as possible. He was utterly convinced that with deceitful cunning and the aid of the ministerial bureaucracy, Dr. Frick, Göring, Canaris, and others whom he considered his enemies, I was plotting to capitalize on the situation and take over his position and his power. It is precisely what he would have done had our roles been reversed. Consequently, his animosity—his hostility toward me grew in intensity daily. I tried to assuage his suspicions, to no avail, of course."

"Did the situation ever come to a head?"

"It did. Toward the end of our—um, association. I had infuriated Heydrich, and incidentally Himmler as well, by serving my military enlistment in the Wehrmacht rather than in the Waffen SS. I served during June and July of 1940 in the 115th Infantry Regiment, Herr Brandenburg. When I was discharged I was appointed to the position of Chief of the Civil Administration in France. My five nerve–racking years with Heydrich had come to an end.

"We had one final confrontation however, Heydrich and I. He accused me of acting as—uh, as a brake on him and his endeavors, and from having prevented him from functioning at his best. He almost whined when he said to me, 'Whenever I had a good idea, I always risked that you would turn up and prove to me with your legal arguments why it could not work, or why it had to be done in a different way.'"

Best gave a little disdainful snort. "I told him that I had been fully aware of acting as a brake on him and his excesses. That it had been quite deliberate on my part. That a personality such as his needed a brake to keep him from getting himself and others into trouble!"

"Was that the last contact you had with SS-Obergruppenführer Heydrich?"

"No. The last time I saw him was in the spring of 1942. In Paris. There was a conference we both had to attend. By that time Heydrich's animosity toward me had turned to hate."

"What happened?"

"We treated each other with icy politeness. I knew at that time that Heydrich was doing everything in his power to undermine me and my work in France. I tried to see him privately to—uh, clear the decks, as it were. He refused. As he had refused all my other attempts to meet with him." Absentmindedly, he made the chewing motion with his mouth characteristic of old age. "Later it was reported to me," he said, "that Heydrich, among other vilifications of me, had stated that he would do everything he could to have me sent to the Russian front, and had said that that would be the surest way of solving *Problem Best!*"

He leaned back in his chair. "You know, Herr Brandenburg, I have a theory about Reinhard Heydrich."

He spoke in a confidential, almost conspiratorial tone of voice. Frank could not help marvelling at how the man's attitude had changed. From overt hostility toward him to treating him like a long–lost friend or a member of the family. It was not the first time it had happened. Frank realized that despite the protestations of his subjects that they did not want to talk about the past, once they did so the need to talk about it was irresistible.

"A theory?" he said.

Best nodded. "A possible explanation of why Reinhard Heydrich had such an overwhelming need to succeed, to—uh, be the best. Why he was so hypersensitive to any criticism; his compulsion to influence, really to control others. In other words, the prima donna syndrome. I believe that these traits, common to actors and other performers, may all have been manifestations in him of qualities inherited from his parents, and perhaps to some extent reinforced by them."

"What do you mean?"

"Reinhard's father, Bruno Heydrich, was a musician, Herr Brandenburg. At one time an opera singer, who had studied with Cosima Wagner in Bayreuth and performed successfully in such cities as Stettin, Aachen and Köln, where for four years he sang such Wagnerian roles as Tristan, Siegmund, and Siegfried to increasing acclaim. Reinhard's mother, Elizabeth, was an actress. As so often is the case, I believe that the—uh, performer's characteristics of the parents were fully manifested in the offspring, in this case Reinhard, who inherited all those performer traits, but without the talent to go with them, although he did play the violin.

"But Reinhard Heydrich cannot be categorized as the customary actor–type, only as possessing the traits and needs. The resulting exaltation and domination was enough for him, without bothering with the performance. I also believe he was influenced by his father's operatic roles, the forceful, righteous, God–like heroes of Richard Wagner, portrayed by his father on the stage, and to be emulated by his son in life. Consciously or unconsciously he saw himself as a noble Wagnerian hero, a man of strength and grandness, a man cast in the mold of an invincible Norman or Viking—the pure Aryan. For make no mistake about it, Herr Brandenburg, race and racial purity were of extreme importance to Reinhard Heydrich. His ideal was a pure Aryan family devoted to the Third Reich."

"I saw Frau Lina Heydrich just a few months ago," Frank said. "You must have known her, Herr Doktor, met her many times. What did you think of her?"

"I knew her only marginally. I formed no opinion of Frau Heydrich."

"She apparently loved her husband very much."

For a moment Best fixed Frank with his penetrating eyes.

"Even a rotten apple can be loved, Herr Brandenburg," he said. "By a worm."

He started to get up from his chair.

"One more question, Herr Doktor," Frank said. "I am interested in the fate of Reichsleiter Martin Bormann. What can you tell me about him? Did he survive?"

Best gazed at Frank for a moment. Then he looked away.

"On that subject, Herr Brandenburg," he said flatly, "I have nothing to say."

He stood up. The interview had come to an end.

As Frank walked across the vast lawn in front of the Rosenhof retirement hotel his eyes swept the orderly green expanse. Like Germany today, he thought. A manicured spring domain, clean and fresh. But if you dug down to the roots beneath the green surface you could still find the decaying remains of the winter past.

The talk with Best still buzzed in his mind. He knew he had been privy to a frank and unconstrained appraisal of some of the top personalities of the Third Reich. It had been, of course, the judgement of one person, and therefore bound to be colored by bias, but it had been rendered by one of their peers.

SS-Obergruppenführer Dr. Werner Best had had a remarkable career in the hierarchy of the Reich, a career cloaked in contradiction and ambiguity.

During his five years as a collaborator of Heydrich's he had helped ensure the smooth operation of a system of unequalled terror and worked to increase the power of the infamous Gestapo and the Sicherheitsdienst—the Security Service, and as chief of Section I he had been charged with complicity in the murder of many thousands of Jews and Polish intellectuals. During his two years as chief of civil administration in France, he had been closely involved with combating the French Resistance, with hostage reprisals, and with the deportation of Jews to labor and concentration camps. But during his three years as Reich Plenipotentiary Commissioner in Denmark, he had apparently sought to sabotage orders by Hitler and Himmler directed against the Jews in that country, in one instance issuing his own orders that forbade German troops to break into Jewish homes.

He had been sentenced to death by a Danish court in 1948, but his sentence had been commuted to five years, and he had been granted a clemency release in 1951. On several occasions between 1958 and 1972 he had been charged with war crimes, including mass murder, by West German authorities, but he had always been released on medical grounds, although the charges were never dropped. But one thing was clear to Frank; Best's past activities as a top SS officer made his opinions and evaluations worthy of serious consideration.

One thing stuck in his mind. It was Best's conviction that Hitler had lost the war because of his underestimation, his disregard for the importance of what Best had called the "populace principle." It had seemed logical, and it had brought to Frank's mind another report about the Führer's disdain for vital concerns that did not fit in his own scheme of things.

In his research Frank had read about the Third Reich's attempt to develop an atomic bomb.

Already in 1939 a physical chemist, Professor Paul Harteck, had written a report to the Ministry of War concerning the newest development in atomic physics, which could produce a bomb vastly more effective than the most powerful conventional bomb. An atomic bomb. The country that first made use of such a bomb, he had pointed out, would win the war.

Hitler had, of course, been excited. He had at once inquired about the research. Who was responsible for it, he had wanted to know.

But as names were ticked off to him—Prof. Albert Einstein, Prof. Lise Meitner, Dr. Eugen Wigner, Dr. Leo Szilard, Prof. Victor Weiskopf, and the Hungarian–born Dr. Edward Teller, all of them Jews, as well as more Jewish scientists who had fled Germany or were forbidden to conduct research in the Reich, Hitler had become increasingly outraged. "Jews!" he had screamed. "A science developed by decadent Jews!" And he had angrily declared that Germany, the German people, need not rely on Jews. He would have nothing to do with *Judenphysik*— Jew Physics. And for three years atomic bomb research had had a very low priority in the Reich, until finally the necessity to develop such an atomic bomb had become apparent.

But it had been too late. Although the Nazi scientists went all–out to perfect the bomb, it had been too late.

The Führer's own anti–Semitism had caused a delay in a crucial race between Allied—including Jewish—scientists, and the Third Reich. A race that had been lost.

Two major but seemingly inconsequential decisions by the Führer had brought disaster to the Nazi cause.

In the *Rise and Fall of the Third Reich* the author holds one man responsible for both the Rise. And the Fall.
Adolf Hitler.

The sun was a cool yellow in the sky and the ground was covered with a thin blanket of crisp new snow. The doors to the greenhouses were kept tightly shut against the cold, one's breath was visible in the frigid air, and the Christmas lights were still up.

Frank was home on his vacation from his studies at Gartenbaubetrieb Wulf in Lübeck. It felt good to be home, even if it were only for a couple of weeks. He had seen Herta once and it had been like old times, but she had to stay in Bremen and help out in her parents' hotel during the holidays.

He had spent a warm and cheerful Christmas eve with his family, and General Wolff had called to wish him a merry Christmas.

And he had had a chance to rearrange the display items in his bunker. He had acquired several more objects of interest to him, besides the *Julleuchter* given him by Lina Heydrich Manninen, and a watercolor by Arno Breker called "The Sitter," which he had acquired after his visit to the artist. He also now had a Hitler self–portrait in pencil with a note of authentication signed by Gruppenführer Albert Bormann on the back. It had been given to him by Karl Wolff. And he had acquired a silver gravy ladle once owned by Hermann Göring as well as bricks and tiles he had picked up from the Berghof and the Wolfsschanze, and many more autographed photographs hung on the walls.

He had had a chance to bring his card file up to date. He had started it after he had read Simon Wiesenthal's book *The Murderers Among Us*. Who better to ask about what really went on during the time of the Third Reich, than the murderers among us? he had thought. So he had made a list of people he would try to find. Already several names on the list had been crossed out.

And he had been able to squeeze in a visit to Generalleutnant der Luftwaffe Adolf Galland, whose name had been given him by Hans Ulrich Rudel. He had visited the general in the office he, although retired, maintained on Gotenstrasse in Bonn. As a gift he had brought the general a small potted palm tree. He had thought it appropriate for the season.

General Galland was a famous Luftwaffe ace, like Rudel, and had been commander–in–chief of the Luftwaffe Fighter Arm from 1941 to the end of the war. He had been a highly visible figure in the postwar period, and Frank had simply wanted to meet him. Frank had expected that he would learn nothing new from him.

He had been right.

Frank knew that Galland had served in the famous Condor Legion in the Spanish Civil War during 1937 and 1938, flying more than three hundred missions and developing new techniques of close aerial support. He knew that the general had had an illustrious career in the Luftwaffe during World War II, earning many honors and high decorations, and he knew that the fighter ace had left Germany in 1945 immediately after the war and had spent six years in Argentina as technical advisor to Peron's air force.

Galland had begun the interview with obvious small–talk, as if sizing Frank up.

One little incident had puzzled Frank. They had been talking about one of Galland's meetings with Hitler at the Wolfsschanze. The Führer had had his dogs along, and Galland had pointed out how fond the Führer had been of dogs.

"He had, of course, those three great German shepherds," Galland had said. "What were their names again?"

"Blondie," Frank had said.

"Right! And Wolf. And the big black one, what was that third dog's name?"

"I don't know," Frank had told him. "I don't think I ever knew."

"No matter." Galland had dismissed it. And the rather inane conversation had continued.

But Frank had had a feeling of a certain reserve in the man's attitude, which was one of polite noninvolvement. It had puzzled him.

And while Galland acknowledged that he still had many German friends in Argentina, he refused to discuss them. And he did not even comment when Frank asked him if he had met Martin Bormann.

In fact, Frank had found this jowly, unimposing man in his seventies, sporting a small Führer-like moustache and wearing a conservative light grey suit with a bright red tie, sitting across from him behind a large desk, exceedingly reserved and difficult to communicate with. And Galland had flatly refused to talk about the days of the Third Reich.

Frank had been reduced to admiring the models of World War II planes that adorned the office and the large portrait of the general that dominated it. And to receiving the intelligence that Galland felt that Reichsmarschall Göring's mishandling of the Luftwaffe contributed to a great extent to the defeat of Germany, and that he had not known anything about the concentration camps until after the war.

The interview had been an exercise in total futility.

But he *had* met the man.

Back in Hildesheim, he had looked up some of his old classmates from the Freiherr–vom–Stein Realschule.

It had been a mistake.

XXII

ull of enthusiasm, Frank had told his friends about some of the experiences he had had, about his meetings and talks with people who had helped shape his and their country's past. He had expected them to share his interest, his excitement at the confidences shared with him by these people, whose names at one time had been on the lips of every German.

This, too, had been a mistake.

At first his schoolmates had seemed fascinated. They had asked him a thousand questions and urged him to talk. And then they had scoffed at him. They had not believed him. They had more than suggested that he was exaggerating his exploits greatly—if not in fact making everything up to make himself important. They had laughed at him.

Frank had been devastated—and suddenly he was eleven years old. That was the year he had had his first male teacher in school. Up until that time all his teachers had been women.

Frank and his new teacher did not get along well. Frank was an intent child, and his teacher would belittle him. He rode him mercilessly and ridiculed him in front of his comrades. And as children will, many of them followed the teacher's lead. Frank was made to sit in the last chair at the last desk in back of the classroom, where—according to his teacher—he belonged. He would repeatedly be kept after class, sitting in his chair in the back, as his classmates left. And when he had been forced to repeat the fifth class, they had derisively called him the *Sitzenbleiber*—he who is left sitting behind. Frank had been devastated. He had felt himself to be a complete outsider.

But as he sat by himself on that last chair in the back of the room, he quietly resolved that if he were indeed an outsider he would be a very special outsider. And with a tenacity born of that decision he rose above his schoolmates' taunts. Later, as he pursued his interest in his country's past, triggered by "The Holocaust," he would draw upon that same tenacity when confronted with difficulties.

He realized that he had missed some of his childhood years: he had become an adult too soon. But he had no regrets. What he had set out to do, what he was doing, was worth doing. He was certain of it.

Almost.

As he watched his schoolmates once again having fun at his expense that little doubt took an extra gnaw at the edge of his mind.

He dismissed it.

He had one visit to pay on his way back to Travemünde and his studies in Lübeck, a man whose name had been given him by the sculptor Arno Breker, who had been of the opinion that Frank would find him interesting to talk to. The man was a prominent architect, Professor Hermann Giesler, Hitler's former Generalbaurat for Munich, *Baurat* meaning Construction Counselor, a government title bestowed on outstanding architects.

Generalbaurat Hermann Giesler lived in a modern two–story villa on Im Dämmergrund in Düsseldorf. His son let Frank in and took him to the living room where his father was waiting for him. After introducing Frank, he left.

Frank stared at the man who laboriously rose to greet him. A short, wizened old man, bald, with a pair of glasses riding high on his pate, a sallow, sunken face with small, rheumy eyes and a slit mouth; a scrawny neck too skinny for the collar of the white shirt and black tie that hung loosely on his slight frame under a black–checked jacket that seemed at least two sizes too large. Hermann Giesler looked much older than his eighty–six years. There was a cadaverous look about him. Frank had the instant chilly feeling that he was looking at a man whom Death had already staked out. It was difficult for him to see in that gaunt, wasted figure the once vital, robust, brilliant, and authoritative Generalbaurat from the days of the Third Reich.

Hermann Giesler came from a family of architects. His father, his grandfather on his mother's side, and his brother were all architects. Hermann had actively joined the Nazi Party already in 1930 and designed and constructed several buildings for the Party. In 1937 he won a Grand Prix and a Gold Medal at the Paris World's Fair for his architectural work, and the year after, Hitler appointed him Generalbaurat and entrusted him with designing and constructing the buildings on Obersalzberg.

When Hitler invaded Poland, Giesler's work took on a more military aspect. He became active in Luftwaffe construction projects, led Baugruppe Giesler in the Balkans, and was leader of the OT– Einsatzgruppe Russland–Nord, the Todt Organization Operations Group, Russia—North. The Todt Organization, named after Dr. Fritz Todt, Reichsminister of Armament and Munitions until his death in a plane crash in 1942 and founder of the organization, was a semi-military construction organization. Todt, as Inspector–General of Roads, and his organization had been responsible for creating and building the autobahns, and also constructed the Siegfried Line and the Channel coast fortifications. The Todt Organization had been responsible for building military roads in the occupied territories from the northern tip of Norway to the southern coast of France, as well as a network of military roads for the invasion of Russia, all accomplished by the use of expendable slave labor.

After his mission as leader of the OT–Einsatzgruppe Russland–Nord Giesler had become leader of the OT–Einsatzgruppe Deutschland VI— Bayern und Donaugau, in charge of construction projects in Germany, in Bavaria, and along the Danube, in which work he distinguished himself, earning the gratitude of the Führer.

After the war, Giesler had been a U.S. prisoner of war and was interned for two years. He was set free only to be sentenced to life with hard labor by the Dachau Military Court as a war criminal. He was released in 1952.

It had all been a long time ago. Judging by the look of the man, Frank thought, at least a century.

He glanced around the room. Although sparsely furnished with heavy antique furniture and obviously valuable oil paintings on the walls, the room still had a solid look of respectability.

Giesler extended his bony hand to Frank, who took it. The firmness of the old man's handshake surprised him.

Giesler had noticed Frank's look. "You must excuse the meagerness of my furnishings," he said apologetically. "Most of my furniture is still impounded by the federal authorities after my—trouble with them. They took it over from the American occupation forces. I am still waiting to get it back." He pointed to one of the heavy old chairs. "Meanwhile, please make use of what I do have. Sit down."

Frank did so, as Giesler returned to his own chair.

"In your letter to me," Giesler continued, "you wrote that you were doing research on conditions during the Third Reich. What an interesting pursuit. And that you were talking with as many of the important personalities from that time as are still around. I am wondering, young man, I am wondering why you chose me. I am quite unimportant, you know."

"Not so, Herr Professor," Frank objected. "I am well aware of your accomplishments in the architectural world. Both the projects that were built and the ones you designed for the Führer, which unfortunately were not built." He reached for his briefcase and removed a drawing mounted on cardboard. "As a matter of fact," he said, "I took the liberty of mounting a reproduction of a sketch for one of those projects, designed by you, Herr Professor, and I should be most pleased if you would sign it for me."

Giesler looked flattered. "Of course, young man," he said. "Of course. I shall be honored to do so."

Frank brought the mounted sketch to him. It was a rendering of the new main railroad station to have been built in Munich, surrounded by sketches of several other famous structures, such as the Eiffel Tower, St. Peter's, the Pyramid of Cheops, and the Washington Monument, for comparison.

Giesler took one look at the sketch, and his face at once clouded over.

"No," he said curtly. "I very much regret it, but I will not sign that sketch."

Totally taken aback, Frank exclaimed. "Why not?"

"Because, young man, I do not recognize it as mine. I do not accept it as my work!"

"But—"

Giesler held up his hand. "I know it appears in a book that includes my work. Purportedly includes my work, I should say. *Eine Stadt für 1000 Jahre—A City for 1000 Years,* not so? I reject it. That sketch was made by the Bonatz Bureau without my knowledge and without my instigation. And later it was distorted, falsified, Herr Brandenburg, *falsified*, by adding a 285–meter dome!" Angrily he stabbed a knobby finger at the sketch. "Not mine," he said. "Not mine!"

Frank quickly put the sketch away. A good start, he thought. Off to a terrific start.

"Please excuse me," he said. "I did not know. I do know, however, that you are one of the two most illustrious architects that the Third Reich produced. You and Reichsminister Albert Speer. I—"

"Please, young man," Giesler interrupted him again. He waved a delicate hand. "I shall thank you not to compare me with Albert Speer. I did not like that man. He was two–faced. Two–faced. I did not like him."

Frank gaped at the old man. How deep could he dig himself in? He was about once more to say he was sorry, but he caught himself. He was falling into a rut.

"For better or for worse, Herr Professor, Speer was an intimate of the Führer's. As were you, yourself."

The old man nodded, suddenly mollified. "I was," he said. "I was." He smiled at Frank. "I was the one the Führer called to the Wolfsschanze after the attempt to assassinate him. I was the one."

He looked pleadingly at Frank. "You must forgive me, my dear young man," he said, "if I sounded harsh. But the disagreeable matter of this published falsification of my work has caused me deep annoyance. I beg you to understand that I cannot sign such a forgery."

"Of course I understand, Herr Professor," Frank quickly assured him. "And I regret the error."

Giesler waved his bony hands. "Not at all. Not at all."

"At the Wolfsschanze," Frank asked, "what did the Führer say to you?"

"He was, of course, shaken," Giesler answered him. "But he told me he was not surprised. There were traitors and subversives all around him." He leaned forward with the intent eagerness of a small child. "He said to me that if I wanted to hear a really shocking story of treason in the highest places, Rattenhuber could tell it to me. SS Brigadeführer Hans Rattenhuber, of the Reichssicherheitsdienst," he explained. "All I had to do was ask him."

"And did you?"

"I did. Rattenhuber told me that when they had searched the entire fortification at the Wolfsschanze, they had found a secret, direct telephone line to somewhere in Switzerland concealed in the quarters of a high–ranking officer, who apparently had used it to transmit messages to Russian agents in that country, so that the Bolshevik forces knew everything the Führer was planning. The man had already been questioned and had admitted everything." He peered at Frank with the glee of a small boy telling another a naughty secret. "The officer's name was General Erich Fellgiebel, the chief Army signal officer in charge of all military communications! Imagine—the shame of it!"

Frank had anticipated Giesler's revelation. He remembered the story that Generalmajor Otto Ernst Remer had told him of Fellgiebel's sabotage of the secret weapon he had called *Die Tonne*, and also that he had mentioned the officer's secret line to Russian agents in Switzerland. He was about to tell Giesler that he had already known about Fellgiebel and his treachery, but he decided to keep silent. The old man was taking such a delight in telling him.

"Of course he paid for his treason with his life," Giesler said solemnly. "As was proper."

"Probably an easier death than if he had been sent to a concentration camp," Frank commented.

Giesler looked up, a sudden steely glint in his rheumy eyes, which he quickly controlled.

"Ah. Yes. The camps." He shook his head in gentle admonition. "You must not let yourself be duped, my dear young man," he said. "The death camps, the crematoriums were never built during the Third Reich. I would have known. Dachau is only a few kilometers from Munich, after all. There were labor camps. The ovens were built later." The old man's voice became excited and incensed. "No one was cremated. No one. Those human ashes and splinters of bone that were found in the ovens, they were all fake. Fake! my dear young man. Analysis has shown that they were not human at all. All those human cremation stories you have heard are propaganda lies. Lies against the Third Reich and our vision of the future."

He stopped, composing himself after his impassioned speech.

Frank stared at him. Did the man really believe that? Did the others who had told him similar stories really believe it? Or was it a way to relieve their feelings of guilt?

"It must have been interesting to be with the Führer so soon after his escape from assassination," Frank said.

"It was, young man, it was. History that would live in posterity was being written at that place in those few days. Of course the Führer had much to do, and my time with him was limited. I spent a great deal of my time at the Wolfsschanze in the office of Reichsleiter Bormann. When the Führer was busy with his generals on military matters. The war had to go on, after all, not so?"

Giesler nodded solemnly. "An astounding man, the Reichsleiter," he said. "I never saw anyone else work so tirelessly for the Führer and for the Reich." He nodded as for emphasis. "I liked the man, Herr Brandenburg. I admired him."

"Did he die in Berlin, Herr Professor? Or did he survive?"

For a moment Giesler sat in silence, his mouth working slowly.

"Let us say, my dear young man, that I have no direct knowledge in this matter." His lips split in a thin smile. "Let us also say that as far as I am concerned Martin Bormann was the ultimate survivor. And let us say no more about it."

"You were with the Führer at other times, on other occasions than at the Wolfsschanze, were you not?"

Giesler nodded emphatically. "Many times. Many times, when we discussed the rebuilding of our country. And the Führer did me the honor of asking me to design and build his mausoleum. And take charge of a magnificent rebuilding project at Linz." His rheumy eyes twinkled. "And once, in a moment of special confidentiality, he confided in me the name of the man he wanted to succeed him, when the time came."

"Who was that, Herr Professor?"

"Only a man who beyond a doubt had proven his courage, his devotion to the German cause and country, would have that right, the Führer said. Only a man with the undisputed qualities of leadership and the power of communication. Only someone who could think wisely and logically under stress, and who was of unquestioned character.

Only someone who had fought bravely for his Fatherland. Only such a man would have the right to succeed the Führer."

"Who was that man, Herr Professor? Bormann?"

With a little smile Giesler shook his head.

"No, my dear young man, not Bormann."

"Then who?"

"I think," Giesler said, "I think the answer will surprise you."

XXIII

F rank's curiosity was piqued. If not Bormann, who? Himmler? Göring? Hitler had denounced them both toward the end. Hess was imprisoned in England. Surely not Goebbels? One of his top generals? Unlikely.

"Who, Herr Professor?"

Triumphantly Giesler gave him the answer: "Oberst Hans-Ulrich Rudel!"

"Rudel? You mean—the Luftwaffe ace?" Frank was genuinely startled. Openly he gaped at the old man, who was thoroughly enjoying himself.

Giesler emitted a dry cackle. "I thought you would be surprised, my dear young man," he said, pleased with Frank's reaction.

"I have met Colonel Rudel," Frank said. "I was impressed with him. But—" he let the sentence hang.

"A remarkable man," Giesler said. "I am glad you had a chance to meet him. Of course," he went on, "the Führer knew it was quite impossible. Rudel would never have been accepted. But that was the man he really would have wanted to take his place. Rudel fitted the Führer's criteria perfectly."

"Did Rudel ever know this?"

"I do not know. I doubt it. The Führer often liked and trusted the younger officers more than he did the older, established officer corps. He never did like the *Junker*."

He seemed to have a sudden idea.

"As a matter of fact, Herr Brandenburg," he said brightly. "I happen to know one of these young officers. Young in the nineteen–forties, that is, of course. We have all grown a little older, not so?" He gave his dry cackle. "I think you ought to talk to him."

"I should be most interested, Herr Professor."

"Good. His name is Schulze–Kossens. SS-Obersturmbannführer Richard Schulze–Kossens."

"I know of the officer," Frank said. "I have, in fact, corresponded with him. I wanted to meet him, but I have not been successful."

Giesler lifted a skeletal hand and shook a skin–and–bone finger at Frank.

"You tell Schulze–Kossens that I suggested that he see you, Herr Brandenburg. You tell him that."

Generalbaurat Hermann Giesler had reawakened Frank's desire to meet the last surviving German officer present at the signing of the notorious Soviet–German Nonaggression Pact in Moscow in 1939; the Führer's personal Waffen SS-Adjutant, SS-Obersturmbannführer Richard Schulze–Kossens, who lived in Düsseldorf. Frank's letter to him in 1981 and subsequent correspondence had resulted only in a series of postcards from Schulze–Kossens with excuses and explanations of why a meeting could not be arranged, because of a series of trips both in and out of Germany that prevented the former adjutant to the Führer from seeing Frank.

Once more Frank wrote, requesting a meeting, mentioning that Generalbaurat Giesler had suggested it, and this time he was successful. A meeting in Schulze–Kossens' home on Karl Müller Strasse was set up.

The house was a duplex, nicely furnished, with a fireplace, deep–pile rugs, and paintings on the walls. Schulze–Kossens had an office upstairs and that is where he and Frank talked, leaving Frau Schulze–Kossens downstairs taking care of the flowers Frank had brought her and preparing coffee and cake for later.

Frank had at once been impressed by this tall, slender man in his seventies, who carried himself with an erect military bearing. His office mirrored the man. Prominently displayed in a cabinet were all his medals and decorations and a large signed photograph of the Führer. Bookcases held a copy of *Mein Kampf* and many books from the Third Reich era, and there were framed documents and photographs of Schulze–Kossens with Hitler and von Ribbentrop, with Mussolini, and, from the signing of the Moscow Pact, with Molotov and Stalin; and there were signed photographs of other once–prominent personalities, among them Arno Breker and Otto Günsche.

"Sit, Herr Brandenburg," Schulze–Kossens said, pointing to a chair. "And make yourself comfortable."

After having been put off by him for so many months, Frank was surprised at the man's polite, disarming charm.

As if reading Frank's mind, Schulze–Kossens said, "You must forgive me for having had to postpone this little meeting of ours so many times, but as you may know, I am very active in HIAG, and do much travelling on behalf of that organization." He looked up at Frank. "You are familiar with HIAG?"

Frank nodded. "I am, Sir," he said. "The Hilfsorganisation auf Gegenseitigkeit der ehemaligen Angehörigen der Waffen SS."

"An organization to help old Waffen SS comrades who may have suffered because of their patriotism," Schulze–Kossens nodded. "There is still need for such help," he said, "and it does take up a good deal of my time. But it is, of course, of importance." He looked at Frank with curiosity. "Why?" he asked. "Tell me why you have been so— so anxious, so persistent in your wish to meet with me? What can I do for you?"

"There are two or three things I should like to ask you about," Frank began. He nodded toward a framed photograph of Bormann. "First, I was wondering what you might be able to tell me about the fate of Reichsleiter Martin Bormann?"

Schulze–Kossens remained silent. He just gazed at Frank, an enigmatic look on his face.

"When I asked Professor Giesler," Frank went on, "he told me that as far as he was concerned, Bormann was the 'ultimate survivor.' But he had no factual knowledge. He suggested that you might. Do you?" he pressed. "Do you know what happened to the Reichsleiter?"

Unblinkingly, Schulze–Kossens looked him straight in the eye. "No comment," he said flatly. Then he broke into a broad smile. "We are off to a good start, are we not?" he said. "What is your next question?"

"I—I was wondering if you would tell me something about the signing of the Soviet–German Nonaggression Pact. I—"

Schulze–Kossens laughed. "Yes, of course," he nodded. "I *am* the only 'leftover,' am I not?" He sounded slightly sarcastic. "It was a dull affair. Protocol. Boring protocol. They were all dull. Stalin, Molotov. Schaposchnikow, the chief of the general staff of the Red Army. Dull. The lot. It was all dull, at least as far as my role in the proceedings was concerned."

"But the pact itself was of importance, was it not? It—"

"It did exactly what the Führer wanted it to do. No more. No less."

"And that was?"

"Simply to buy time. Time to invade and crush any resistance in Poland, without Russian interference. Time to extend the power of the Reich in both territory and armament strength, making the inevitable attack on the Soviets possible long before they had had the time to do the same." He smiled at Frank. "And confusion. Confusion in the naive minds of the Allies, who had thought it self–evident that Russia would be a partner against the Reich, because of the presumably unreconcilable ideological differences between the Soviets and the Germans. And confusion among the Russians themselves. Propagandized after the pact to believe Germany an ally, they needed precious time to adapt psychologically to resist the attack on them by the Reich, when it came."

"Germany had to make concessions, too, did she not?"

"Unimportant ones. Agreement to recognize Russian influence over or annexation of certain territories. Finland. The Baltic States. Bessarabia. An agreement that would be nullified automatically when the Reich ultimately attacked Russia. As planned."

"Was it not—unconscionable of the Führer," Frank ventured, "to feign a treaty, when actually planning an attack?"

Schulze–Kossens shrugged.

"Is there not a saying that all is fair in love and war? In any case the pact turned out to be an embarrassment for the Russians."

"How so?"

"At the Nürnberg Trials," Schulze–Kossens told him. "I was a witness. As such, I was able unequivocally to authenticate a document introduced by Dr. Seidl, the lawyer for Rudolf Hess, which spelled out in detail how Germany and Russia would divide Poland between them after the war. It was a great embarrassment to the Communists," he said, a half–smile of pleasant memories tugging at his lips. "Inasmuch as they had postured as friends and protectors of the Polish people."

"You were the Führer's Waffen SS-Adjutant, were you not?"

"I was. I had been adjutant to the minister of foreign affairs, Joachim von Ribbentrop. It was in that capacity I went to Moscow. In 1942 the Führer made me his personal adjutant. From then on I was in constant attendance. Sat in on practically every military meeting."

"What was the Führer like? to work for?"

"Challenging. Unpredictable. Dangerous."

"Dangerous?"

"Case in point would be Fritz Darges."

"I am not familiar with Fritz Darges. Who is he?"

"SS-Obersturmbannführer Darges was one of the Führer's—entourage, if you will. Once, at an outdoor conference in the field, sometime in early July of 1944, the mosquitos were bothering the Führer. Ineffectually he kept slapping at them and fanning his ears. Darges made the mistake of laughing at the sight. Irascibly, the Führer ordered him to get rid of the mosquitos. When the poor man failed, the Führer screamed at him: 'A miserable, low submariner can sink a cruiser with a one–man torpedo, but you, a Sturmbannführer, cannot even dispatch a mosquito! Get out! Report to your regiment at the Russian front at once! I never want to see you again!'"

"*Was* he sent to the Russian front?"

"He was. Miraculously, he survived.

Schulze–Kossens once again gave Frank one of his infectious smiles. "You should have a talk with Fritz Darges," he said. "The man keeps to himself. Shuns anyone who even smells like a reporter. But I will get you an introduction."

"Thank you," Frank said. He decided to make a point of calling on SS-Obersturmbannführer Fritz Darges.

"It has been pleasant talking to you, Brandenburg," Schulze–Kossens said. "But I must get back to work." He began to get up.

"Just a couple of quick questions, please."

"Quick ones. Fire away."

"The concentration camps, the extermination camps, do you believe they existed?"

"I do. It is not a pretty tale. I, personally, knew nothing about them until after the war. Next?"

Frank believed him. "Do you miss the old days?" he asked.

"Should I not miss the best years of my life?" Schulze–Kossens stood up.

"One final request. I see you have a photograph of SS-Sturmbannführer Otto Günsche. The Führer's SS-Adjutant. Do you know him?"

"I do."

"Would you give me an introduction to him as well?"

Schulze–Kossens contemplated Frank for a moment.

"Done," he said.

Back in his room in Travemünde, Frank was entering the record of his interview with SS-Obersturmbannführer Richard Schulze –Kossens in his master card file, and making a new card for SS-Obersturmbannführer Fritz Darges for future action, when he came across a card bearing the legend "Gauleiter Jordan, Rudolf." It was blank, except for the notation "Baur."

Flugkapitän Hans Baur had told him about Jordan, the former Gauleiter of Halle and Magdeburg, Reichsstatthalter of Anhalt and Braunschweig, who had been his prison mate for most of the ten years Baur had spent in Russian detention as a prisoner of war.

Rudolf Jordan, Baur had told him, was a man Frank would find interesting to talk to. He lived in Munich, and Frank had had no chance to go there to see him as yet, but he decided to set up a meeting on a weekend in the near future. So far, Baur's recommendations had been well worth following up. Frank was certain Rudolf Jordan would be no exception.

The Jordan home was a second–floor apartment in a dismal old apartment house that had survived the war. It was located at There-sienwiese, the square in front of the hundred–foot–tall bronze statue, *Bavaria,* where the famed Munich Oktoberfest takes place.

But the run–down building Frank entered looked far from festive.

He climbed the stone steps, made smooth by decades of footsteps, and rang the bell.

After a short wait the door was opened a few inches. Through the gap Frank could see a heavy chain.

"Yes? Who is it?" It was a woman's voice.

"My name is Frank Brandenburg," Frank said. "I am here to see Herr Jordan."

The door closed. Frank could hear the chain being removed. The door opened again, this time wide enough to let him enter. The elderly woman who stood just inside glanced quickly out onto the empty landing behind Frank.

"Come in," she said. "Come in." There was urgency in her voice rather than hospitality.

Frank entered. The woman closed the door behind him and replaced the chain. "I am Frau Jordan," she said noncommittally. "I shall take you to my husband."

The room to which Frau Jordan took Frank had the high ceiling customary to old houses, and was sparsely and simply furnished, with a few pictures scattered in what appeared to be a haphazard arrangement on the walls. The balding man who rose laboriously from a straight wooden chair at a round table covered with a plain white cloth looked frail. Clad in a black suit with an overly wide yellow tie with black polka dots, he stood unsteadily, holding onto the table. His face looked harried and apprehensive.

He greeted Frank without offering him his hand, which Frank noted trembled uncontrollably. The man's speech was slightly slurred and it was obviously difficult for him to speak.

And Frank remembered what Baur had told him. Rudolf Jordan had suffered a stroke.

"What do you want with me?" the former Gauleiter said plaintively. "I never give interviews. To anyone. What do you want?"

"Please sit down, Herr Brandenburg," Jordan's wife said. There was resentment in her voice. She pointed to a chair.

Frank sat down, and as the woman left the room Jordan also seated himself. "What do you want here?" he repeated his question.

Frank felt terribly uncomfortable. "Herr Jordan," he said. "General Baur suggested that I visit you. Just to meet you. And have a little talk."

"Ah. Yes. Hans Baur. It is only because he is a good and old friend that I agreed to talk to you." He peered at Frank. "I never give interviews."

"So I understand," Frank said. "And I very much appreciate your seeing me." He reached into his briefcase and took out a blowup of a photograph taken at a celebration in a town called Quedlinburg in Jordan's former *Gau*. It showed Himmler, Heydrich, Wolff, and Jordan himself. "I brought you a little gift, Herr Jordan, that I thought you might like to have." He handed the photograph to Jordan.

Jordan glanced at it. Quickly he looked up at Frank, a suddenly frightened expression on his face.

"Why?" he exclaimed. "Why are you giving me this?"

Taken aback, Frank explained. "You are in it, Herr Jordan. It was taken at the festival in connection with the reinterment of the tenth–century king Heinrich I at Quedlinburg in your *Gau*. See?" He pointed to Jordan in the picture.

"That is not me!" Jordan said, shaking his head emphatically. "That is not me!" His trembling was getting more pronounced. "Why would you give that to me? What do you want?"

Frank took the photograph and put it back in his briefcase.

"I am very sorry, Herr Jordan," he said. "I must have made a mistake."

He stole a glance at the agitated old man. It was difficult to recognize the once powerful Gauleiter and Reichsstatthalter, who had joined the Nazi Party in 1925 and reached the high rank of SA Obergruppenführer a mere twelve years later, in the trembling eighty–two–year–old perched anxiously on the plain wooden chair before him. He was, of course, the person in the photograph he had been shown. Why would he deny it? What fears kept him from recognizing or acknowledging his past?

"What do I want?" Frank said pleasantly. "Only to reminisce with you about the past. You *were* one of the loyal, early followers of the Führer."

Jordan's eyes shifted uneasily. "It had to come," he said defensively.

"What had to come?"

"The revolution. There was no choice for me other than to join it. The time was ripe for revolution. I was not wrong in joining it."

"You mean, when Adolf Hitler came to power?"

Jordan nodded. "The revolution." He peered at Frank. "Do you know how to tell when the time is ripe for revolution?"

"How?"

"When the top dogs no longer give a damn—and the underdogs can't. That is when. And that is when Adolf Hitler took over."

"Let me ask you a couple of specific questions, Herr Jordan." The old man eyed him apprehensively. "About the concentration camps," Frank went on. "The extermination camps. What can you tell me about them? I understand one or two of them were located in your *Gau*. Nordhausen was one of them, was it not? Where they had the underground factories that made V–2 rockets?"

Jordan looked alarmed. His frightened eyes darted around the room. He put a trembling finger to his mouth and hissed: "Ssshhh!…SSShhh!"

Frank watched him in amazement. He decided to try another tack. "What about Reichsleiter Bormann?" he asked. "What can you tell me about him?"

Jordan sat motionless on his chair, staring at Frank, fear in his eyes. He did not answer.

Frank studied the man. He acted as if every answer he might give, every statement he might make, would result in some kind of dire misfortune for him. Was it the result of ten years in a Russian prison? Ten years of Russian interrogation? Perhaps he saw in his present interviewer one of his Russian inquisitors. He had to be careful not to sound too insistent.

"Herr Jordan," he said quietly, "please answer my question."

"He called me," Jordan said. "In the middle of the night. I was fast asleep, and he woke me up. He told me he was dead. And that everything now would be right."

"Who was dead? The Führer?"

Jordan flinched as if he had been struck. "No!" he cried. "No, no! Roosevelt! The American warmonger. He told me that the Führer, that all of them, were certain the war would be turned around, and we would win." Sadly he shook his head. "They were wrong." He looked up at Frank, almost pleadingly. "I know what it is to be dead," he said. "But I was *not* dead."

Puzzled, Frank frowned at him. "What do you mean?"

"They *said* I was dead. But it was not true!"

"Who said you were dead?"

"The County Court. Right here—in Munich. In 1951 they declared me dead, and they said that people had seen me being executed in Magdeburg after the war. And they declared me dead. But it was not true." He peered earnestly at Frank as if to persuade him that he was telling the truth. "It was not true," he repeated. "But not until three years later did they admit that I was alive."

"That happened during the time you were in the Lubjanka Prison in Moscow, did it not? The authorities here did not know that?" Frank was incredulous.

"No. They said I was dead." Fearfully Jordan looked around him. "There are still prisoners in Russia," he whispered hoarsely. "Behind bars." He put his trembling hand up in front of him as if grabbing two prison cell bars. Violently he shook them, terror in his eyes. "Bars," he rasped. "Behind iron bars. Koch. Erich Koch. Gauleiter Erich Koch. *He* is still behind bars. In Poland. And there are others. Others—behind bars…"

"Do you know who?"

Jordan suddenly stopped. With alarm he snapped his head back and looked intently at Frank.

"Who?" he repeated. "I know no one. I see no one from the old days. No one. I know nothing. About anyone. Nothing." Plaintively he looked at Frank. "Why do you want to know all this?" he asked. "Why are you asking me all these questions?"

"I told you, Herr Jordan," Frank replied. "I am doing research, I want to learn."

Jordan leaned toward him. He lowered his voice. "Do not learn too much," he cautioned. "Do not learn too much—and be careful. Things may not always be what they seem to be. The Führer was afraid of that, too."

"Afraid of things not being what they seem to be? How so?"

"Hess," Jordan whispered.

"Rudolf Hess? You mean, whether he flew to England with the Führer's knowledge or without it?"

"No, no," Jordan said irritably. "Hess betrayed the Führer. The Führer said so, himself."

"Then—what?"

"The broadcasts."

"What broadcasts?"

"Over the enemy radio transmitters. The Führer feared that there would be radio broadcasts to Germany with Hess denouncing him and the Reich." He shook his head. "But he was certain that Hess would not do that, whatever his reasons for flying to the enemy were."

"Then why—"

"It would *seem* to be the voice of Rudolf Hess," Jordan said. "But it would in fact be the voice of a clever impersonator. And with everyone knowing that Hess was in fact in England, they would believe it was his voice. That is what the Führer feared. And that is why he had Hess declared insane. So that if his voice were heard, it would be the voice of a madman."

Frau Jordan appeared in the door to the room. It was evident that Frank's talk with her husband had ended.

As Frank rose to take his leave, Jordan raised a trembling hand toward him.

"Be careful," he said. "Tell no one that you saw me. No one..." (Jordan died in Munich in October 1988.)

Frank was genuinely disturbed. Jordan's behavior did not make any sense to him. The old man had seemed in constant fear. Of what? Of whom? Was he afraid of being indicted once again? Was his erratic behavior the result of his ten years in Russian imprisonment? Or was it caused by his stroke? Or merely his age? Probably a little of each, he thought.

Frank knew that Jordan had written and published a book about his life, both as a Gauleiter and as a Russian POW. It had been available by subscription only, but it had been written, and it had been published. Then why now the obvious fear of discussing the past? It did not make sense.

Was there something to be afraid of? Now, more than a couple of decades ago, when Jordan wrote his memoirs?

If so, where was his own involvement, his increasingly probing quest leading him? and to what?

He knew something about the man who Jordan had said was still imprisoned in Poland, Gauleiter Erich Koch.

Koch, Gauleiter of East Prussia, Reich Commissioner of the Ukraine from 1941 to 1944, and honorary SS-Gruppenführer, was an avid believer in the German master race with a vast contempt for the Slav "subhumans," and had been one of Hitler's most cruel and inhuman satraps in the conquered eastern territories. He had directly caused the deaths of hundred of thousands of innocent men, women, and children who had been sent to extermination camps, their villages burned to the ground, and he had been responsible for the killing of at least four hundred thousand Poles. In 1958 he had been turned over to the Polish authorities, and eight years later he was sentenced to death. He was in ill health, and because of a special article in the Polish Penal Code that forbids the execution of bedridden prisoners, his sentence was commuted to life imprisonment.

That same day Frank called the Polish Embassy in Cologne and asked for information about the war criminal Erich Koch, imprisoned in Poland. He was informed that Koch had been held for several years

in a prison in Barczewo/Wartenburg. The embassy had little information about Koch, he was told. Outside what was available in the
Federal Archives, they could refer him to a man named Georg Stein,
a historian who was supposed to have considerable knowledge about
the Gauleiter. And he was further informed that Erich Koch had
recently died.

End of trail.

All the way back to Travemünde on the train he dozed fitfully.

His mind turned to Gauleiter Koch. What kind of man could in cold
blood ship hundreds of thousands of innocent people to slaughter in
extermination camps? crammed into railroad cars?

He had a sudden unpleasant thought. How many such shipments
had traveled along the very same tracks over which he at this moment
was travelling? He remembered reading somewhere that payments to
the Reichsbahn—the National Railroad—for those shipments of concentration camp victims had been handled by the Reich Travel Bureau
in the same way as vacation travel for other Germans. Then and today.
The money had come from the valuables confiscated from the Jewish
victims, who in this manner paid for their transportation to their own
torment and extermination. The very railroad system that today carried
thousands of vacationers and travellers such as himself reliably and
comfortably all over Europe was the same system that equally efficiently transported millions to their deaths in the gas chambers of the
extermination camps.

Rest was suddenly impossible. When he arrived home he was
exhausted.

That evening he was asleep before his troubled head hit the pillow.

Slowly he opened his eyes. Something had awakened him. He sat
up in bed, wholly alert.

The room was dark; only the faintest night light seeped in through
the curtained windows. The air was heavy and thick, and he found
it difficult to breathe.

What had awakened him?

A noise. An unfamiliar noise. The kind of sound that however faint
will wake you simply because it *is* unfamiliar, and therefore a threat.

What had it been? He listened. Nothing.

And then, suddenly, this time wide awake, he heard it again. Crying.

It was the soft, pitiful sound of someone crying, weeping bitterly. A heart–rending sound punctuated by wracking sobs.

And it came from outside his door.

Mystified, the beginning of fear stirring in him and making his heart beat faster, he got out of bed. Slowly he walked to the door. The crying outside was getting more insistent.

He opened the door.

Frank Brandenburg with Dr. Wilhelm Höttl.

Frank with the plane crash memorial in the Börnersdorf cemetery.

SS-Obergruppenführer Werner Best during Nürnberg war crimes trial of 1946. (Ullstein)

Dr. Werner Best with Frank Brandenburg.

Luftwaffe Ace General Adolf
Galland.

Generalbaurat Hermann Giesler.

Professor Hermann Giesler with Frank Brandenburg.

SS-Obersturmbannführer
Richard Schulze-Kossens.

Schulze-Kossens with Frank
Brandenburg.

Otto Günsche after his release from the Russian prison camp, Friedland, near Göttingen, 1956. (Ullstein)

Molotov signing the 1939 Soviet-German Nonaggression Pact. Behind him, left to right: Marshal Schaposchnikow, Chief of the General Staff of the Red Army; SS-Sturmbannführer Richard Schulze-Kossens; Reich Foreign Minister Joachim von Ribbentrop; Joseph Stalin and an interpreter. (Ullstein)

XXIV

He stared in shock.

The familiar corridor was gone. Instead there was a row of sooty, iron–and–brick ovens, some with their half–moon–topped doors closed, others with the doors ajar.

Slowly, unable to resist their gruesome magnetism, he walked toward them, aware of a gritty, cloying substance under his bare feet. Ashes. And bits of bone left unconsumed.

The crying came from behind one of the partly open oven doors.

Slowly, slowly he opened it, the door grating harshly on its iron hinges.

A monstrous creature tumbled from it to lie writhing at his feet in the ashes on the brick floor. Its mouth was a blackened hole from which the crying sounds flew out like a flight of hungry bats from the opening of a subterranean cave. It was a small animal. No.

It was a baby.

Scorched and twisted limbs, changed by the fire to grotesquely deformed stumps, reached for him as it wailed its soul–searing agony at him. Empty black eye sockets stared at him, the melted eyeballs still moist on the shriveled cheeks.

And the crying, the wailing, the moaning grew louder and louder.

And from every oven charred, misshapen human forms spilled out. Beseechingly they stretched out their scorched and distorted arms toward him, the flesh peeling from the bones. And the flesh crawled with black maggots.

No. Not maggots.

Numbers.

Numbers. Numbers, alive and twisting with malice. Numbers, unerasable and all–consuming. Numbers.

The wailing and crying reached an unbearable crescendo, and the reaching, ghoulish arms embraced him....

With a start he sat up. His heart was racing. He was soaking wet.

The nightmare had possessed him once again. Ever since his visit to Auschwitz, his meeting with the former inmate, and their heart–wrenching tour of the camp, he had had that horrible nightmare. Always the same. Ovens. Women and children crying.

And numbers. Black numbers.

Numbers tattooed on people's arms. Numbers on list upon list of victims. Numbers on cell doors, and ovens, and graves. Numbers...

He took a shower.

Wrapped in his towel he sat on the edge of his bed, sleep forgotten. He thought.

His thoughts were bleak. A feeling of depression clung to him like a musty shroud, heavy with distress. Perhaps his search for his Fatherland's past had best not been undertaken. Perhaps he would have been better off not knowing, not ever having had to look the truth squarely in the eyes. Perhaps...

Unsinn—nonsense. The truth *had* to be faced, even when it hurt. It was the only way not to suffer that hurt again.

He needed to crystalize what he was doing. He needed to give it some serious thought. His original purpose had long since been accomplished; it now seemed quite a childish pursuit. But then at the time he had been a child. He no longer was. The Holocaust *had* happened. He had long since acknowledged that. No vestige of doubt remained in his mind, despite—or perhaps because—of the vehement denials by some of his subjects. Denials that went so far that they became beacons of corroboration.

Should he stop?

He knew he could not. Too many doors had been presented to him. Some open, some ajar, and some closed. His inquisitive mind cried out to know what lay behind those tantalizing, closed doors, and he knew he would have to go on searching for the keys to open them. But his search needed a clearer direction.

There were three main puzzles in his mind. What happened to Martin Bormann? What happened to the *Serail* documents? And finally, what were the facts of the Hess flight?

Those were questions that had never been settled. Not by the people he had talked to, his subjects. Not by the books and the studies and the reports he had read. Not by the journalists and researchers and historians who had pursued them and examined them. Their reports and conclusions were all contradictory and unconvincing. He knew he had to go on by himself.

But he was alone in his quest.

He needed advice. He needed guidance. He needed support. He thought he knew where to find it.

It would not be fair to try to involve his father. He knew that his father would always give him his support, but so far as guidance and advice were concerned, he also knew that his father was neither willing nor able to give him that. And the same held true for the other man to whom he could turn for support, his grandfather. He, too, could give him neither the guidance nor the advice he had to have.

So far his advisors and supporters had been General Wolff and General Baur. But they were also part of his quest. They had their own axes to grind, and he knew he had to be careful not to look to them for the guidance he knew he needed. What he must find was the counsel and insight of someone beyond reproach, someone trustworthy and "in the know."

There was such a man.

Frank had just finished reading a book written by that man, *Ankläger einer Epoche—Prosecutor of an Era*. His name was Dr. Robert M. W. Kempner.

Robert Kempner was born in Freiburg in Germany and had been educated in law both in his native country and in the United States of America, where he had attended the University of Pennsylvania. He became a municipal judge in Berlin in 1927 and counsellor to the Prussian police system. As such, he had recommended the suppression of the Nazi Party and the prosecution of one Adolf Hitler for high treason and perjury.

Kempner left Germany in 1939 and went to the United States. During World War II he was counsel to the Federal courts on espionage and the trials of foreign agents, and expert counsel to the U.S. Department of Justice, the Office of Strategic Services, and the Secretary of War on legal, political, police, and intelligence techniques of European dictatorships and foreign organizations in the United States. He had been a prominent U.S. prosecutor at the Nürnberg Trials of the top Nazi leaders in 1945–46 and deputy chief of counsel for war crimes trials, as well as chief prosecutor of German Reich cabinet members and diplomats, and in the investigation of the Holocaust. In 1961 he had served as special counsel to the Israeli Government in the Adolf Eichmann case. Still a prominent and esteemed international jurist, he was the perfect man for Frank to turn to for guidance and advice.

Frank had been successful in approaching and meeting his Nazi subjects, why not someone from the other side, he thought? If anyone had knowledge of Nazi crimes and Nazi criminals, of the whole Nazi era, it would be Dr. Kempner. If anyone could provide him with a guiding beacon amid a sea of incertitudes, it would be he.

Frank had learned from the publisher of Kempner's book that the jurist, who lived in Pennsylvania in the United States, also maintained a residence and office in Germany. Frank was able to talk to his secretary there, a Frau Stiefel. Briefly he told her why he wanted to meet with Dr. Kempner. She listened and told him that Dr. Kempner was in Königstein, a town just outside Frankfurt am Main, and that she would call him there. An hour later she called Frank back. Dr. Kempner would see him if he could get to Königstein the following afternoon.

He could.

Dr. Kempner stayed in the Hotel Sonnenhof in Königstein, a former Rothschild palace. The jurist was a slight, somewhat delicate–looking man with pure white hair and a pure white moustache, a little shorter than Frank, yet with a bearing undeniably demanding respect. He greeted Frank with Old World courtesy, politely and correctly, but with no cordiality whatsoever. They met in a secluded corner of the all–but–deserted hotel lobby. They had the place pretty much to themselves. Kempner introduced Frank to his two secretaries, a Miss Jane Lester and a Miss Margot Lipton, both of whom had been with him in Nürnberg, Kempner informed him. The women acknowledged the introduction perfunctorily.

Dr. Kempner offered Frank a chair, but he, himself, remained standing, occasionally pacing the floor in front of Frank.

"Now, young man," he said, his voice crisp and impersonal. "Why do you want to see me? What do you want from me?"

Frank felt ill at ease with the jurist's cool, almost adversarial manner. As best he could, he explained his reason for getting involved in the search for his country's past, and his drive to learn as much of the truth as he could. Kempner listened attentively and impersonally to him without interrupting him. When Frank had finished, Kempner stopped in front of him and fixed him with his inquisitive eyes.

"Why are you doing this? What are your reasons?" Kempner shot the questions at him.

As he had done with his father and Herta, Frank did his best to explain why he felt the need to conduct his search.

"When do you do it?" Kempner asked, his voice brusque and short.

"When?"

"Yes. When?" Kempner snapped impatiently. "I presume you have other aspirations than to talk to Nazi war criminals."

"Oh. Yes, sir. I study." He told the jurist about his current studies in Lübeck.

"Very well. Then when *do* you go about your inquiries?"

"During my vacations. And over weekends. Any free time I have."

"Are your studies being neglected?"

"No. My grades are good."

"Have you lost any time because of what you are doing?"

Frank was beginning to feel resentful at the cross–examination carried out by Kempner. If I feel as if I am sitting in the witness chair, he thought, it is only because I am. And that I don't need.

"No," he said, a hint of defiance in his voice. "My studies are progressing exactly as scheduled."

Kempner gave a little snort. Disbelief? Disdain? Frank looked at the jurist.

Kempner returned his look. "And how do you pay for all this— this traveling around you say you do? Your father's money?"

"No, sir." Frank told him how he got money from his subjects themselves, by selling their autographs.

"Whom have you seen?"

Frank mentioned about a dozen of his subjects.

"They are all murderers!" Kempner shot at him. "You realize that?"

Frank nodded.

"Do you admire the people you talk to?"

Frank looked at the old jurist. The witness chair was getting damned uncomfortable. But he decided an honest answer was the way to go. After all, what he wanted from the man was guidance; criticism, if that is what it turned out to be.

"Yes," he said. "In some cases, in some ways. Some of them have exhibited great personal courage, such as Rudel and Galland. Others have contributed to the arts, to culture, such as Breker and Giesler. I have learned a lot by talking to them, but I do not admire, nor condone, what they stand for, and what some of them did. I—I am very often repelled by it. But I do know *what* they did, and what *their* reasons were."

"And you think that is reason enough for hobnobbing with criminals and murderers?"

"My—hobnobbing is a tool for learning, Dr. Kempner," Frank said, perhaps a shade too recalcitrantly. "I do not think that the search for truth, for information, should be limited to—to hobnobbing with only the best people. Nor that it should be condemned."

He had had enough. He was about to stand up, excuse himself for having taken Kempner's time, and leave. The old man obviously was not in sympathy with his search.

Kempner looked at him, a slight smile of amusement on his lips. "That is what you think, is it, young man?" he said.

"Yes, sir. That is exactly what I think," Frank said firmly. He began to get up.

Kempner turned toward his secretaries. "I like that young man," he said brightly. "He is quick on the draw. He has convictions, and he handled my goading well. What do you say we help him out? As best we can?"

The two women smiled at Frank, and voiced their assent.

Frank was taken completely off guard. He sat silently on his chair. Best to see what was going on.

"Very well," Kempner said, his tone of voice no longer that of a courtroom inquisitor. He smiled at Frank. "You have got yourself an advisor, young man," he said. "If not as a jurist, then as a friend. A silent partner, as it were. Very silent. I shall try to answer any questions you may have, any doubts, but one thing you must understand. I will not tell you how to deport yourself, nor will I provide you with names of people for you to talk to. There you are on your own."

"I understand, Herr Doktor."

"Fine." Again Kempner turned to his two secretaries. "Why don't we all have some coffee and cake and get acquainted?"

Kempner and the two women quickly made Frank feel comfortable. The women, and Kempner himself, asked him myriad questions, friendly questions, and seemed genuinely interested in what he had to tell them about his activities.

"You seem to have developed quite a—a rapport with some of your subjects," Kempner remarked. "Karl Wolff, for example. Do you find him sympathetic?"

Frank nodded. "I do," he answered honestly. "Sometimes I feel it difficult to believe the reports about him. And toward the end of the war, he did work with the Americans to surrender his forces in Italy. And he was a witness at Nürnberg, not one of the accused."

Kempner contemplated him for a moment. "You came to me to get advice, Frank," he said. "Guidance. Then let me give you some counsel now. Not by way of censuring you. I do not. I support you. But by way of caution."

He paused for a moment as if to organize his thoughts.

"When you deal with those people, Baur, Rudel, Wolff, do not lose your perspective. Be an observer. Learn. But do not involve yourself. Do not forge ties that you may not be able to break. Stand apart and watch—even that is not without danger.

"It often happens that a bond develops between victim and victimizer. There are all too many documented cases of kidnap victims, for instance, who ultimately identify with their kidnappers. That happens with reporters and researchers and their subjects as well—however unsavory those subjects may be. You must guard against that, Frank."

Frank listened earnestly to the older man. He realized the truth in what he was saying.

"Your friend, Karl Wolff, for instance," Kempner went on. "You like him because he is a sympathetic human being. He *did* do his best to befriend you. And he *did* make a good case on his own behalf. But, do you *really* know the man? Do you know what his involvement in the abysmal crimes of the Third Reich *really* was? Other than carrying out orders?"

He turned to Jane Lester. "Jane," he said. "Let me have those letters we copied for Herr Brandenburg."

The secretary picked up a battered briefcase from the floor and opened it.

"I photocopied two file letters from the Nürnberg Trials," Kempner said, "when my secretary told me that one of the people you were seeing was former Oberstgruppenführer Karl Wolff. On the witness stand in Nürnberg, your friend declared that he had known absolutely nothing about the—'the terrible extermination of the Jews,' as he put it. To every question put to him about Auschwitz, Lublin, Treblinka, he knew absolutely nothing. I am certain he has told you that, too. I have heard the phrase, 'I knew nothing about those camps until after the war,' at least a thousand times. I am certain you have, too."

Jane Lester handed a couple of xeroxed pages to Kempner. He held them out to Frank.

"One is a letter dated 28 July 1942—*1942*, Frank, to Wolff from the acting director of the German Reich Railroads, a man named Ganzenmüller. The other is Wolff's reply to him, dated 13 August 1942. Read them."

Frank took the photocopies. He looked at the first letter. It was signed, *Heil Hitler! Ihr ergebener*—your devoted, Ganzenmüller.

He read the first few sentences, and he could feel the blood drain from his face.

XXV

Berlin W 8, den 28. Juli 1942
Vosstrasse 35
GEHEIM—SECRET

Frank skipped the obligatory salutations. He read on:

"Pursuant to our telephone conversation of 16 July, I am advising you of the following facts regarding my Generaldirektion der Ostbahnen (Gedob)—my General Directorship of the Eastern Railroad in Kracow, for your proper information:

Since July 22, daily trains each carrying 5,000 Jews from Warsaw have been dispatched over Malkinia to Treblinka, and in addition, twice weekly, a train with 5,000 Jews from Przemysl to Belzek. Gedob is in constant touch with the Security Police in Kracow. This organization is in agreement with the fact that the transport from Warsaw over Lublin to Sobibor (near Lublin) be suspended as long as repair work on that stretch of the line makes such transport impossible (to about October 1942)...

In response, Wolff had written Ganzenmüller a letter dated Führerhauptquartier, 13 August 1942, which thanked the man for his letter,

243

both on his own behalf and that of the Reichsführer SS. Frank went on to read:

"It is with special pleasure that I take note of your information that, beginning already 14 days ago, daily trains each with 5,000 members of the chosen people are departing for Treblinka, so that we in that way are able to expedite the flow of that segment of the populace at an accelerated pace."

And Wolff had finished his letter with a request that Ganzenmüller continue to give his attention to the matter.

Frank stood staring at the letter. Special pleasure...5,000 members of the chosen people...Treblinka...

"Personally I had nothing to do with those concentration camps," General Wolff had assured him. "I never had anything to do with the elimination of Jews," he had said. "My duties included many things, but never that!" he had asserted. "The evidence against me was lies made up by the international Jews," he had sworn.

But his letter said "daily trains with 5,000 Jews...to Treblinka...." And at Treblinka Jews were put to death!

Frank was shaken. He felt betrayed, and yet he recognized that he had known it all along. General Wolff could not possibly have held the high position he did, personal adjutant to the instigator of the concentration camps, Reichsführer SS Heinrich Himmler, without being personally involved. But he had not wanted to admit to himself that the general had not been telling the truth. He had believed what he wanted to believe. He had been seeking the truth, but he had not looked it fully in the face when confronted with it. Perhaps *that* was the real danger in his pursuit. Perhaps the danger lay within himself. Perhaps, as Dr. Kempner had admonished him, he must realize fully that the people with whom he dealt were, in fact, criminals and murderers.

He suddenly felt as if he had taken a giant step along the path of his quest.

Without a word he gave the two letters back.

His meeting with Dr. Kempner had been everything he had hoped for and more. He felt he had gained an invaluable ally. He was back on track. He saw his role with greater clarity, and he knew he now had someone to go to for counsel should he need it, someone with whom to talk over matters about which he had had no one to turn to, for so long.

With the exuberance of youth, he felt he had exchanged his tarnished, chipped, and sprung suit of armor for a shining, new, and invulnerable one, and he was ready to venture forth once again.

He had decided to visit General Wolff at his first opportunity and confront him with his just–discovered knowledge. That opportunity came the following weekend.

But his resolve quickly evaporated.

The man who greeted him at the door with obvious pleasure looked gaunt and drawn, not the robust figure of earlier meetings. Frank had known that the general had been sick, and he had sent him a get–well card, but he was not prepared for the wasted appearance of the old man who welcomed him.

Seated in front of a cheery fire in Wolff's living room fireplace, the general leaned over and patted Frank on the hand.

"I am glad you came, Frank," he said. "I always enjoy our little talks. They bring back so many memories." He sighed. "So many fine memories."

He looked at Frank. "I have been a little under the weather, as they say. But I am fine now. Fine." He smiled a wan little smile. "I shall soon be eighty–four years old, Frank. I am almost exactly four times your age. But you have never let that age difference come between us, and I appreciate that at my life's end you have let me share the beginning of yours."

Frank had not had the heart to take him on about his lies. And about his true involvement in the—final solution. He was a little concerned that his resolve to be tough and unrelenting had melted away so quickly. But this was a special circumstance.

Was it not?

"I do not like to feel weak," Wolff complained. "Only once before did I feel as—as weak and helpless as I felt a few weeks ago. That was when I was confined as a prisoner of war. I do not like to feel weak."

Even now, Frank thought. Prisoner of war, not war criminal, which is what he really was. He regarded the old man. Perhaps he really believes what he is saying, he mused. Perhaps he is fooling himself.

"It is a terrible thing to be incarcerated, Frank," Wolff observed. "Locked up. Time suddenly drags out to where a minute becomes an hour, an hour a day, and there are a thousand days in a year." He nodded his head at the memory. "I think perhaps the one of us who suffered the most when the Reich collapsed is the one who deserved it the least," he mused. "Rudolf Hess. All those years. Imprisoned. Alone. It must be hell behind stone walls."

Frank picked up. "I have become very interested in the Hess flight, Herr General," Frank said. "Why? What was the purpose? Who planned it? Do you have any knowledge about this?"

"I was not involved in the affair at all, my boy," Wolff said. To Frank it sounded as if a "but" would follow. When none came he asked:

"But do you know anything about the flight? Some say that the Führer knew all about it, actually planned it with Hess. Others say that Hess planned the flight alone and that the Führer knew nothing about it. Which is true?"

"The Führer was at the Berghof, in a meeting with several of us, including a number of Gauleiters, when the news of Hess's flight to England was brought to him."

"What happened?"

Wolff smiled a sardonic little smile. "The Führer threw a terrible temper tantrum," he said. "He railed in fury at Hess. He shouted about treason and back–stabbing." He gave a little snort. "He put on quite a show."

"A show? Then—did he know about the flight beforehand, or did he not?"

Wolff pursed his lips. "Let us just say that the Führer was an accomplished actor when he wanted to be, and let it go at that." He had a thought. "If you want details about the affair, there are others better informed than I."

"Who?"

"You know General Baur. Why not ask him? That sort of thing was more in his province."

"I will."

"Of course, the Führer did plot some rather impossible missions."

"What do you mean?"

"Well—his kidnapping scheme, for instance."

"What kidnapping scheme?"

"You do not know about it?" Wolff settled back in his chair. "It was in 1943," he began, "in September. The Führer summoned me to a private meeting at the Wolfsschanze. He told me he had a special, top secret mission for me, and he pledged me to total silence about it before he would inform me what it was."

"What was it?" Frank was intrigued.

"The Führer ordered me to kidnap the Pope."

"Kidnap the Pope? Pius XII?" Frank sounded incredulous.

Wolff laughed. "My reaction exactly," he chuckled. "Although I did not express it quite that bluntly!"

"But why? Why on earth would he want you to kidnap the Pope?"

"The Führer wanted me to occupy the Vatican. Secure all its treasures, its library, and its art collections for shipment to the Reich. Arrest the entire papal staff, and all the Jews and anti–Fascists who had taken refuge in the Vatican, 'clear it out,' he said. And he ordered me to bring the Pope himself to Germany, where he would be interned in a special camp."

Frank was fascinated. He let the general speak.

"The Führer's reasons for undertaking an operation of such magnitude and ramifications were rather complex. He did, of course, blame the Pope and his advisors for the downfall of his friend Mussolini, rightly or not, and he did not want the Pontiff to fall into the hands of the Allies for possible propaganda use. He felt the Vatican had become a nest of spies and anti–Nazis, and he thought that by holding the Pope hostage he could insure himself a valuable bargaining chip in future negotiations."

"How could he possibly have justified such an act?"

"He had thought of that too, my boy. He instructed me to be certain to find certain—um, incriminating documents among the Vatican papers, implicating the Pope himself and proving a conspiracy with the Royal House of Savoy and other anti–Nazi factions against Mussolini and against the Führer himself. Goebbels undoubtedly would have delivered impassioned and inflammatory speeches over the radio expounding to the world how the action had put a stop to any further such subversive activities."

"Did you—did you make the attempt?"

Wolff laughed. "Of course not. Some months later, when the entire machinery for the operation was in place, I was able to dissuade the Führer from carrying it out."

"How did you do that?"

"I pointed out to him that the Catholics throughout the world could not be counted on to think rationally, as the Führer did, but emotionally, and might turn their anger at the violation of the person of the Pope against the Führer and his cause at a crucial time. He bought it. However, I did have several meetings with Pius XII, discussing plans to bring peace to Italy."

Frank shook his head in wonder. "Did anyone else know about that kidnapping scheme?"

"No. There were no witnesses to the private conversation between the Führer and me." He looked pointedly at Frank. "Rudolf Hess had no witnesses either."

"It is difficult to imagine what was really in the Führer's mind," Frank mused. "My God! Kidnapping the Pope!"

"You had heard nothing about this before?"

"Nothing."

"I told the press about some of it, years ago." Wolff waved a deprecating hand. "Of course, they got most of it wrong. It is no wonder that so many of us refuse to speak with reporters."

"I know," Frank said. "I had difficulties in talking to some people. Albert Bormann would not even speak to me on the phone. Gauleiter Jordan seemed afraid of every word he uttered, and would not even recognize a photograph of himself from the old days, and Col. Galland, who has, after all, been so much in the public eye, would talk only about mundane, unimportant matters, such as reminiscing about the Führer's dogs, Blondie and Wolf, and that third dog—"

"Muck," Wolf said absentmindedly.

"Muck," Frank repeated. "Was that the third dog's name? Galland could not remember it."

Slowly Wolff turned to look at Frank, his craggy face suddenly ashen. His eyes narrowed as he stared at his young friend.

"You did not know," he said, a statement rather than a question. He answered himself. "Of course not. How could you?"

"Know what?" Frank asked. "That the name of Hitler's third dog was Muck? I never heard it. Until now."

"And now you know," Wolff said heavily.

"Now I know."

"It—it would be best if you did not," the general said, obviously concerned. "But now that you do, be careful, my boy. Be careful."

Frowning, Frank looked at the old man.

"Careful?"

Wolff sighed, a sigh of resignation.

"Perhaps," he said soberly. "Perhaps I had better tell you why."

XXVI

When I gave you my ring," Wolff said. "I told you it would be an 'Open Sesame' for you. *Muck* is a code word, Frank. A password that will gain you entrance into Nirvana or Olympus, Valhalla or the sanctum sanctorum of the brotherhood of the surviving Nazi hierarchy itself. It is a powerful word. A dangerous word. A word that could cost you your life."

He smiled tiredly at Frank. "I am being melodramatic, I know," he said. "But I want to impress on you the real danger of the knowledge you now possess. Had I not been lulled into a feeling of good fellowship and safety being with you, my boy, I would never have divulged that name to you."

Ruefully he again gave Frank a little smile. "You caught me off guard," he admitted. "I am getting old. It would never have happened a few years ago." He sighed. "Never..."

"I—I still do not understand, Herr General," Frank said. "How can knowing the name of Hitler's third dog be so—so important?"

"When the war began to go badly for us," Wolff explained, "some of the highest–ranking men of the Reich realized that the day would come when, if they wanted to escape the vengeance of the victors and avoid giving up their pound of flesh to the international Jews, they would have to scatter throughout the world and—go underground, as they say. The problem then became how to keep in touch without risking discovery. And keeping in touch was important."

"Why?"

"The ideals of the Führer and the Reich could not be allowed to die, my boy. This was their primary pledge. Those ideals, those beliefs must be kept alive and nourished, so that some day they may burn brightly in the world once again. And the keepers of the flame that would set them ablaze would have to be those of us who were still abroad—in both senses of the word. But, again, how to communicate in safety? Not by letter. Letters can be intercepted and read by anyone. Not by telephone or telegraph. Such conversations are, of course, far from private. Codes can be broken, and when overheard create suspicions, with all the attending problems. Communication could be accomplished safely only by messengers. By trusted emissaries. But such emissaries had to be able to authenticate themselves without a doubt. A code would be needed. A very special code. A key word that could easily be woven into the conversation, and yet was a definite code. It was decided that Hitler's third dog be given a name known only by the select few. It was easy and natural to reminisce about the good old days at the Berghof. Or the Wolfsschanze."

As Galland had done, Frank thought, and I did not know the name of Hitler's third dog....

"But that was a long time ago," he protested. "There must be a lot of people who know that code name by now."

"There are many more than the original few," Wolff agreed. "Of necessity so. Yes. We are growing old. But there is a new generation, Frank. A new generation taking our place." The old man gave his young friend a meaningful look. "A new generation. And they are fully as ruthless, fully as dedicated to keeping alive and to protecting what was and is the Führer's."

His eyes bored into Frank. "Make no mistake about it, my boy," he said solemnly. "The knowledge you now possess can be dangerous. Do not reveal what you have learned—but use it wisely and with care."

He sat back in his chair, his face tired and gray.

When Frank left General Wolff's home, he had the feeling he would never see him again.

He was right.

SS-Oberstgruppenführer Karl Wolff died four months later, on July 15, 1984.

Although the memory of his last visit with Karl Wolff stayed with him, Frank had decided that the general had indeed been overdramatic. He appreciated the fact that the old man wanted to save him trouble, if that was really his reason for trying to steer him away from that Hitler's–third–dog business, but no one was going to harm him, much less kill him, for knowing the name of a damned dog! He would go right on with his inquiries.

But it was not until the beginning of his summer vacation that Frank had an opportunity to see General Baur. His studies had kept him busy, although he had been able to get away on a few weekends.

During one of them he had visited SS-Obersturmbannführer Fritz Darges, a front–line officer who had served with distinction in two regiments, the SS–Standarte Deutschland and the SS–Regiment Der Führer in Holland, a former ordnance officer on Hitler's staff and later one of his personal SS-Adjutants; the man about whom Schulze–Kossens had told him.

Darges lived in a tract house in Celle, and had agreed to see Frank reluctantly. "I never talk to reporters and journalists," he had told Frank gruffly. "I do not want my privacy disturbed."

With a Prussian, ramrod–straight appearance he had received Frank in his living room, which was filled with mementos and books from the Third Reich. He had asked Frank a series of questions about himself, and heard him out without interruption. Not until he had satisfied himself about his visitor had he talked.

Using elaborate hand gestures he had told Frank that it would have been a technical impossibility to have killed six million concentration camp inmates; he had first heard rumors about such killings and other atrocities supposedly committed in the camps from refugees from such camps liberated by the Allies, during a time when he was in the field near Budapest. He had dismissed it. The camps had, of course, existed, but the accounts of what had taken place behind their barbed–wire fences were mostly fairy tales. At the Führer Headquarters the subject had never been broached.

As for Martin Bormann, whom he thoroughly disliked and referred to as the "Gray Eminence," he would say nothing, but he did remember the mosquito incident and his banishment to the Russian front. Frank had the impression that the man looked upon the entire period of the Third Reich as one great pulp–thriller adventure.

He had not been impressed.

Because of his growing interest in the Hess affair, he had attempted the impossible—to meet and talk to Reichsminister Rudolf Hess in person—and it had, indeed, turned out to be impossible.

He had, however, established contact with Col. Eugene Bird, the former U.S. Army commandant of Spandau Prison, where Hess was jailed.

At a most pleasant meeting in the lobby of the opulent Kempinski Hotel on the Kurfürstendamm in Berlin, Colonel Bird, a broad-shouldered man in his sixties who spoke German fluently, had told Frank about a series of conversations with Hess he had taped at the request of the U.S. Army. The colonel, who knew Rudolf Hess perhaps better than any other man, had given Frank a fascinating and poignant verbal portrait of the man.

For Hess life had ended in 1941, when he flew to England and was interned.

A man who cried when he had a little fever and seldom smiled or laughed, his sole desire was to be allowed to die—"in freedom rather than as a martyr in jail." But he knew that he would die in Spandau Prison. When Bird had asked him whether, if given the choice of reliving his entire involvement with the Nazi movement, he would do it again, his answer, after a long, soul–searching pause, had been: Yes! He regretted what had taken place in the concentration camps, but it had, of course, occurred after his flight to England.

To Bird's probing questions about that flight, Rudolf Hess had told him that he had wanted to try to benefit mankind and the warring nations by effecting a speedy end to the hostilities. All the hostilities. Through talking and negotiating rather than fighting. His goal had been to bring the gift of peace to the world, and—childlike—he could not understand why the British had brought him to trial at Nürnberg, and to prison in Spandau.

And to Bird's specific question he had told the colonel that the decision to fly to England had been his and his alone. The Führer had had no knowledge of his plans.

Frank and Colonel Bird had parted on most friendly terms, and Bird had suggested that Frank see the former Reich's youth leader, Artur Axmann, whom he knew. When they shook hands to leave, the colonel had said to him, "what you are doing, Frank, more young Germans should be doing!"

Frank had seen Reichsjugendführer Artur Axmann in his apartment on Bregenzerstrasse near the Kurfürstendamm in Berlin. Over a bottle of good German wine Frank had brought, they had talked.

Axmann, who in 1941 had lost his right arm in his first firefight on the Russian front and still wore his old–fashioned rigid prosthesis, had been present in the Führerbunker in Berlin when Hitler shot himself, and he had been the last person to see Martin Bormann alive, according to his testimony at the Nürnberg trials.

"Are you certain the Reichsleiter is dead?" Frank had asked him.

"It is what I told the court," Axmann had replied. "I told them that I had been separated from my group after the breakout from the Bunker. I told them that I ran into Bormann and Dr. Stumpfegger, and I told them that I was knocked unconscious, when a Tiger tank exploded near us. I told them that later on, I again met Bormann, Stumpfegger, Naumann, and some others. They were unharmed. We joined up with them and reached the bridge that leads to the Lehrter railroad station. It was dark and we did not know what was on the other side. Several of us, including Bormann and Stumpfegger, jumped off the bridge down to the ground below—and were surprised to land in the midst of a platoon of Russian infantry sheltering under the bridge. They took us for a bunch of Volkssturm men high–tailing it for home, and made good–natured fun of us. Bormann, who was drunk, was not able to play along with them, and he and Stumpfegger made their escape. The rest of us also got away. When I saw Bormann again, he was lying dead near the bridge, next to Stumpfegger."

"Are you certain he was dead?" Frank had asked once more. "Could he not just have been unconscious? Passed out perhaps? You said he was drunk."

"I could see him clearly in the moonlight," Axmann had answered. "There was not a mark on him and I assumed he had taken poison. I knew he carried a cyanide vial. I did not stay long enough to examine him."

Frank had asked him about his reaction to the fact that in the records of the government office that kept the names of all those killed the name of Ludwig Stumpfegger appeared, but not that of Martin Bormann. If the body of Stumpfegger had been found, why not that of Bormann, supposedly lying next to him? Axmann had merely shrugged, obviously not surprised. Despite his testimony to the court and his reiteration of that statement during their conversation, Frank had felt that Axmann had not really been convinced that Martin Bormann had in fact died during that fateful night in Berlin.

But Frank had been fascinated by another event Axmann had told him about. Even though he was on record as having testified that he heard the shot that killed Hitler, he had actually heard nothing. "No sound could be heard through those security doors," he had said tersely. Why he originally had said he heard it was left unexplained. But he *had* picked up the gun with which the Führer had shot himself, as it was lying on the floor at Hitler's feet. He had put it in his pocket, and he still had it on him when he left the Bunker on the night of the breakout. He had buried it at the Sandkrug Bridge, in an area which today is right on the border between East and West Berlin.

"I sometimes read about agents and spies being exchanged between East and West at the Sandkrug Bridge," he had commented. "And I wonder what they would think if they knew that the gun with which the Führer took his own life might lie beneath their feet!"

About the Hess affair, Axmann had had nothing to say. But then Frank already knew the truth. Straight from the horse's mouth, Rudolf Hess himself, as told to Frank by Colonel Bird. Vaguely, he wondered why a horse always is supposed to tell the unvarnished truth. Could not even a horse on occasion and for good reason tell a lie?

He had also paid a visit to SS-Sturmbannführer Otto Günsche, a Hitler SS-Adjutant and friend of Schulze–Kossens. Günsche had been in the Führerbunker when Hitler committed suicide and was one of the last to see him alive; it was he who had carried the corpse of the Führer to the garden above to be burned. Frank had met Günsche in the reception room of his drug manufacturing firm in Bensberg near Cologne, where many of his products were displayed, including a gaudy mosaic, made of pill boxes, that hung on the wall.

Günsche, a typical Aryan with broad shoulders, a full head of hair, and sharp blue eyes, still carried himself proudly erect, although he was in his seventies. He had been a prisoner of war in Russia for ten years, but he had not lost his admiration for or faith in the Führer, and confidently predicted that some day in the not–too–distant future someone would take over where the Führer had been forced to leave off, and continue his work. And when he had spoken of the Führer he had lowered his voice in deference.

He had been contemptuous of Bormann, who without the Führer to back him would have been a total nonentity, and he refused to speculate on the Reichsleiter's death or escape.

But it was what he said when the question of Hess came up that had startled Frank.

Günsche was convinced, he had said, that the Führer knew of Hess's plan to fly to England. Why did he think so? From conversations between the Führer and others of high rank, which he, himself, had overheard!

It was totally contrary to the statement by Rudolf Hess that Colonel Bird had quoted to him. Had the horse lied?

He suddenly felt he was dealing with a stable full of horses, all mouthing a different truth!

And his confusion had deepened when, during a telephone conversation with Arno Breker, the sculptor had reminded him that he had told him about his impeccable source for the fact that the Führer had not only known of the flight, but approved of it!

As with the Bormann question, the more he asked and the more information he obtained, the more muddled the Hess picture became.

Even Waldi, General Baur's suspicious little dachshund, greeted Frank with enthusiasm when he presented himself at the Baur home in Herrsching am Ammersee.

As soon as the customary amenities were over, Frank came straight to the point.

"General Baur," he said. "I have a question I should like to discuss with you, because—"

"Still chasing rumors about your so-called Holocaust, *mein Junge*— my boy?" Baur chuckled good-naturedly.

Dammit! Frank thought. This was not the time to risk alienating the general by telling him that he was now fully convinced that the Holocaust had indeed taken place, despite the general's denials.

"I have done a lot of research on it since we first talked, Herr General," he said evasively. "I—I have learned a lot." He deliberately left out his trip to Auschwitz. This was not the time. "I—"

"Let it go by, *mein Junge*," Baur said with fatherly tolerance. "Let it go by."

Let it go by? Frank thought. The motto on the wall in his room back home said *not* to let it go by. He was glad he had followed the advice of his motto. Even though the truth was not pleasant, he was glad to have learned that truth. He looked at Baur with sudden insight. It was impossible that a man in his position could not have learned the same facts that he, Frank, had learned. Either at the time they happened, or later. He suddenly realized why General Baur kept denying those facts, denying the truth about the Holocaust. It would be impossible for him to accept the fact that his Führer and his world had been evil. All his life he had worshipped Adolf Hitler. If he now had to admit that his Führer, his *Vati*, had stood for evil and had inflicted that evil on the world, then he would have to admit to having worshipped a monster and having dedicated his life to helping him carry out his evil. And such an admission might well destroy him, and therefore had to be denied.

"As a matter of fact," he said. "I don't want to discuss the Holocaust."

"Oh? What then?"

"The question of Rudolf Hess and his flight to England," Frank told him. "Did or did the Führer not know about it before it took place?"

Slowly Baur nodded his head. "I see. And you think that I might know?"

"I do. If anyone does, it would be you, Herr General."

Baur smiled. "Very well, *mein Junge*. I shall tell you what I do know. It concerns the map."

"What map?"

"It was a—a top secret map, Frank. And I believe the story surrounding it will go a long way toward settling the question for you: did *unser Vati* know of the flight planned by Hess before it was executed or did he not?"

XXVII

There existed a master map," Baur told him, "that showed the exact positions of all antiaircraft gun installations in the Reich and the occupied territories, constantly kept up to date. A complete and detailed flak map. It was in several sections. Since it was impossible to cover the air over every square mile of this huge area, there were zones, corridors if you will, over which an aircraft could fly without the danger of being shot down by ground fire. Because of this fact, the existence of this map was known only to a handful of people who had an absolute need to know. As the Führer's personal pilot, I knew of it. The commander–in–chief of the Luftwaffe, Reichsmarschall Hermann Goering, knew of it, *unser Vati*, of course, and a few other high–ranking and trusted officers. None of them would ever have revealed their knowledge to any outsider. Rudolf Hess was not one of those who needed to have knowledge of this map, nor, indeed, was he supposed to have such knowledge.

"Yet, before his flight to England, Hess came to me in confidence and requested a certain up–to–date section of the top secret flak map. I noticed it was a section that showed the safe flak corridors to reach England. He asked for it by sector and code designation, information

which could only have come from one of the few people in the know—
I presumed the Führer himself, since Hess was his deputy. With that
map Hess could have plotted a safe flight plan to England."

"Did you give it to him?"

"I did. I was certain he was requesting it at *unser Vati*'s behest."

"Could he have obtained the knowledge from someone else? Göring
for example?"

"Possibly. But not without the approval of *unser Vati*."

"Then in your mind there is no doubt that the Führer knew of the
flight from its planning stage? In fact—facilitated it?"

"No doubt, *mein Junge*," Baur said emphatically. "No doubt at all."

A pensive look came over his face. "Of course," he mused, "there
is the possibility that Hess, who was an intelligent man, assumed that
such a map would exist. And took a chance. I thought of that. But
even if that were the case, it would not explain his knowledge of the
correct code designation." He frowned. "Perhaps British intelligence
made the same assumption," he said airily, as if speaking to himself.

"British intelligence?" Frank was startled. "You think they were
in on the flight?"

"What?" Baur was brought out of his reveries. "Oh. No. I—I was
thinking of something else. Please excuse me." He gave a little laugh.
"A rather—ludicrous scheme, which I did not learn of until after the
war."

"What scheme was that?"

"Believe it or not, Frank, the British were planning to bribe me or
in some way force me to abduct *unser Vati* and fly him to England.
Me!" He laughed.

"Could you have done it?" Frank wondered. "I mean, physically?"

"Easily," Baur declared. "After all, *unser Vati* trusted me. And I
did have access to the flak map. But then, the British did not know
me." He thought for a moment. "Or perhaps they did, and that is why
the plot was abandoned."

In his mind Frank recalled the plot to abduct the Pope, which Wolff
had told him about. Apparently, crazy kidnap plots were not the
monopoly of the Führer.

The rest of Frank's visit was spent with pleasant small talk. Baur
told him how gratified, actually overwhelmed he had been that past
Christmas, by the hundreds of cards from all over Germany. Most of
the well–wishers had been strangers, many of them young people not

even born when the Third Reich had been in power. He had been touched by that outpouring of good will. It boded well for the future of the Fatherland. And he had remembered one more erstwhile friend for Frank to visit. Waffen SS-Brigadeführer Gustav Lombard, commanding officer of the 31st SS Division. He, too, lived in Munich.

Before he left the Munich area Frank made a quick visit to Ministerialdirigent Heinrich Heim, this time in his second–floor apartment in an old house on Unertlstrasse, which had escaped damage during the war. In contrast to his cluttered, dismal bunker office on Ungererstrasse, Heim's home was richly furnished, with a grand piano in the high–ceilinged living room and several large oil paintings obviously by fine artists hanging on the walls. Heim, himself, had grown a beard, which made him look considerably older.

To Frank's question, whether he had any knowledge about the Hess flight and the Führer's involvement in the planning of it, he had been evasive and professed to know nothing about either the reason for the flight or its planning.

But he did give Frank one valuable bit of information: the address and telephone number of Ilse Hess, the wife of Reichsminister Rudolf Hess.

On his way back to Lübeck, Frank sought to evaluate what Baur had told him about the Hess affair. It certainly seemed to point to the fact that Hitler had known about the flight from the word go.

But a doubt still remained.

Hess could have learned of the map from someone other than Hitler and without the Führer's knowledge, although it seemed unlikely. But he had to face it. He was still astride the Hess seesaw: now the Führer knew—now he didn't.

Perhaps Ilse Hess would be able to shed further light on the puzzle. He hoped so. He had not had the time to visit her on this trip; he thought he should allow himself enough time to get as much information as he could. He had made up his mind to wait for the summer vacation. Exams were coming up, and he needed to devote himself to his studies.

Reluctantly, he admitted to himself that he was feeling a little discouraged. He seemed to be getting nowhere with his three primary riddles: Bormann, Hess, and the *Serail* documents. Bleakly, he began to wonder if he would ever find the answers he sought.

*   *   *

Ilse Hess lived in the little village of Hindelang in the Allgäu of Bavaria. A white–lettered plaque on the wall of the brown clapboard house proclaimed that the landscape painter Otto Modersohn, who died during the war, had lived and worked there in the early thirties.

Frau Hess, a pleasant–looking elderly lady, wore a kerchief around her snow white hair when she opened the door for Frank. Her eyes were direct and appeared somewhat worried, and a gossamer moustache, also snow white, dusted her upper lip. Inside, in the living room furnished with good, old furniture and adorned with pictures of Rudolf Hess, she removed the kerchief.

"You must excuse my voice," she said as she busied herself arranging in a blue vase the flowers Frank had brought her, "but I am just getting over a summer cold. They are always the worst."

She does sound pretty hoarse, Frank thought sympathetically. "I bear greetings from Herr Heim," he said.

"Thank you." She sat down in a chair a little distance from Frank. "We often see each other. I usually visit with him when I go to Munich to take the plane to Berlin. To go to Spandau." She looked at Frank. "He said you were studying—uh, history. He thought I might tell you something about my husband."

"I should be most interested, *gnädige Frau*," Frank said. "And most appreciative."

Her eyes bleak, she looked at him. "I have not—not touched my husband for forty–three years, Herr Brandenburg. I have seen him. I have talked to him. But I have not been allowed to touch him. Not even to take his hand. Can you imagine what that is like?" She looked directly at him.

Frank did not know what to say. "I—I know it must be difficult for you," he said, appalled at how inane it sounded. "But—I was hoping you could help me clear up a few questions that have puzzled me. I talked to Colonel Bird, Colonel Eugene Bird, I am certain you know him, and he told me that your husband had confided in him that he and he alone planned and carried out the flight to England. To your knowledge, is that correct?"

"Bird!" Ilse Hess said. The way she spat out the name in her hoarse voice it sounded like a swear word. "Colonel Bird has said and written much about my husband, most of it more than simply incorrect. If you rely on what he told you, your research work will be more a fairy tale than history." She sounded hurt and bitter. "What Colonel Bird has to say is hardly reliable. He has not the slightest idea of what my husband was or is, or what he thinks."

"Then, what he told me is not true? Your husband did not act alone?"

For a moment Ilse Hess locked her worried eyes on Frank's. "My husband would not have acted without the Führer's consent," she said firmly, almost angrily. "And the purpose was to offer a separate peace on reasonable terms to the British, so that Germany and England together could defeat the common Bolshevik enemy. If the mission had been successful, the Führer would have taken credit for it, but when it failed, he could not admit to having been part of it, or even knowing about it. How could he have explained it to his Axis allies? the Japanese? the Italians? He *had* to disclaim any involvement. He *had* to denounce my husband. I am certain my husband was aware of that when he made his flight. When he left me that evening, he told me he would be gone for two or three days. Nothing else. I did not know where he was going, or on what mission."

She stopped. Her jaws clenched. "And the British? Having turned down my husband's proposal, they could not admit to the world that they had turned down a chance for ending the war, a chance for peace, but had elected to continue and prolong the terrible slaughter, causing the further loss of countless hundreds of thousands of the world's young men and the destruction of towns and cities and the people in them. No. They had to make a—a war criminal out of my husband."

Angrily she fixed Frank with her disturbing eyes. "And they did, Herr Brandenburg. They did. They made him the scapegoat in their deceitful politics. And all my husband wanted was to bring peace to the world. But the truth will not come out until it is too late. Too late to exonerate him. The British have sealed all the documents of the case until 2017."

Her eyes brimmed. "Forty–three years, young man. Forty–three years since that night, and not a hug, not a kiss, not a single moment alone together. Always someone watching. Someone listening. What was my crime? I only married the man I loved."

Unnoticed, the tears began to trickle down her cheeks as she went on.

"He wrote to the leaders of all the four great powers that had defeated the Reich, pleading with them to allow him to live out the remaining years of his life with his family, giving them his sacred word that he would not speak to anyone about his England mission." She sobbed. "He did not even get a reply. They wanted to be certain that he remained silent. So they kept him locked up."

She glared at Frank, her eyes suddenly flashing.

"But I know the truth," she said with quiet strength. "The England trip was planned by the Führer and my husband. He would never have done what he did without the Führer's commitment. He would never have left me, have left his family behind to bear the fury of the Führer, had he—on his own—embarked on a mission that failed. I know that with as much certainty as if I had been present at their planning sessions. And, as you can see, nothing did happen to us."

"Were you not—"

"Oh, Bormann. He was my husband's bitter enemy. Bormann tried to make life difficult for us. He made me persona non grata. But when I complained to the Führer, it stopped. I am convinced that my husband had elicited a promise from the Führer that whatever happened, his family would be safe."

She looked steadily at Frank. "I repeat, Herr Brandenburg. My husband would never have undertaken the England trip without the Führer's knowledge and full approval. My husband was totally loyal to the Führer. A loyalty that began before their imprisonment together at Landsberg. A loyalty that he will keep to the day he dies!" Rudolf Hess died in Spandau Prison on August 17, 1987.

For a moment they sat in silence.

"Frau Hess," Frank said. "Could you tell me—"

Ilse Hess held up her hand.

"Please," she said. "Forgive me, but I do not feel up to— to talking about all this anymore. I—the cold, you understand."

"Of course."

"But I want you to see my son. I will tell him that you are coming. His name is Wolf–Rüdiger Hess. The Führer, who was his godfather, gave him the name Wolf. It was always one of his favorites." She gave a little sigh, unaware of it. "My son lives in Munich. He can tell you better than I about his father. He can answer your questions. He can give you some further information about his father's flight to the British."

She gave Frank a long look.

"And how the Führer was behind it."

✻   ✻   ✻

Wolf–Rüdiger Hess refused to see Frank.

It was not until later, after Frank's second call to him and after he had had a chance to speak with his mother and possibly check Frank out with Heinrich Heim, whom Frank had given as reference, that the son of Rudolf Hess consented to a meeting at his home in Munich, where he lived with his wife in the Gräfelfing district. When the younger Frau Hess opened the door Frank had the fright of his life.

A huge German shepherd dog leaped at him from the door. It took all his courage and willpower to stand his ground, especially in view of his inherent fear of big dogs. All big dogs. Any big dog.

"Do not be afraid, Herr Brandenburg," Frau Hess said. "He does not bite. He only wants to greet you." Nevertheless, Frank had felt terribly on edge, a feeling that stayed with him during the entire visit.

Wolf–Rüdiger Hess received him correctly and impersonally. The three of them, or four of them, if you counted the dog, sat rather stiffly in the Hess living room, while Hess put Frank through a series of questions about himself and his reason for wanting to talk about his father. Only after completing his own interrogative interview did he consent to answer questions.

"Herr Hess," Frank began, "when did you last see your father?"

Hess did not answer his question directly. Instead he launched into a lengthy history of his father's life, all of which Frank already knew. He listened politely as Hess delivered his lecture.

His father had been born in Alexandria in Egypt, Wolf–Rüdiger told Frank, and he had been severely wounded in World War I, in which he served in the German army.

Soon after the war he heard Adolf Hitler speak, and in 1920 he joined the budding Nazi Party. A friendship sprung up between the two young men, and when Hitler was jailed in Landsberg Prison after the Beer–Hall Putsch in 1923 Hess, who had escaped to Austria, returned and voluntarily shared his Führer's imprisonment. It was during that time that the two men completed Hitler's *Mein Kampf*, Rudolf Hess acting as Hitler's secretary.

In 1932 the Führer made Hess chairman of the Central Political Committee of the NSDAP and he was promoted to SS General. The year after, he was made deputy Führer, and when the war with Poland broke out he was designated Hitler's successor after Göring, the third highest post in the land.

Following his flight to England and his trial at Nürnberg Hess had been imprisoned in Spandau, where since October 1966 he was the only prisoner in the jail, built to house six hundred.

"Perhaps my father's greatest virtue was his loyalty," his son told Frank. "I still remember reading the words he spoke at the trial: 'It was granted to me for many years to live and work under the greatest son my nation has brought forth in its thousand years of history!'"

"I wrote your father a couple of letters," Frank said. "I never received an answer."

"He never saw your letters, Herr Brandenburg," Hess said. "He is not allowed to receive ordinary mail. Only four letters a month. From family. That is all he is allowed. There is little that is allowed him." Hess sounded bitter. "He has not even been allowed to see his grandchildren. He has never seen them. And he is allowed only one hour a month in a supervised meeting with one of his close relatives, my mother. I. And—" He looked suddenly at Frank. "How much has my mother told you?"

Frank related what Ilse Hess had said.

Wolf–Rüdiger nodded. "There is little I can add," he said. "I was four years old when my father flew to England, eight when he went to Spandau Prison. Today my father is to me a man who lives behind a glass partition. That is how we meet now. Separated by a glass partition. My father is a man I never see alone. Always there are other men present, close to him, when he is visited by one of his family. Strangers. Sometimes British, sometimes French, sometimes Russian, and sometimes American, depending on which nation is in charge of the prison that month. Except for those visits and whatever formal prison contacts are necessary, my father lives alone. Totally alone. He eats alone. He sleeps alone. Occasionally he walks in the prison garden alone. He is allowed to read and to look at television at certain times. But no newscasts, no history, no current political affairs. He knows nothing of what is going on in the world outside the prison walls. Nothing. The world has stood still for him since his flight to England in 1941."

"Your mother also told me that she thought your father had made Hitler promise that whatever the outcome of the flight nothing would happen to his family. Do you think that is a correct assumption?"

"I do. Others were not so lucky. After all, Hitler had to make *some* show of retribution. Hildegard Fath, my father's secretary since 1933, was arrested by the Gestapo. My father always called her Freiburg, because that is where she was born. She was really like one of the family. She once told us that my father was the one doing penance for the whole nation. But all she could tell the Gestapo was that she provided my father with the weather forecast over the Channel coast for the time of his flight, not knowing why he wanted it. So, after a few months they let her go, and she went to work for my mother.

"My father's deputies were not that lucky. Some of them were sent to punishment battalions at the front. I do not know their fates, but the survival rate in those battalions was close to nil. And none of them had had any knowledge of the planned flight."

"That flight, Herr Hess," Frank asked. "Was it a unilateral decision by your father? Or did Hitler know about it? What is your opinion?"

"The flight was arranged between my father and Hitler," Hess replied firmly.

"You know this? I heard differently. I heard that your father is supposed to have told Colonel Bird that the decision was his and his alone."

"I am aware of that," Hess said shortly. "The key word is 'supposed.' If indeed he made that statement, it was because to this day he is honoring his oath to his Führer. And the Führer had decreed that the decision to make the flight had been my father's alone. That he, the Führer, had had nothing to do with it. It is that statement my father backed up, in loyalty to the Führer."

He looked straight at Frank.

"But there is another statement, Herr Brandenburg, a statement I, personally, believe mirrors the truth."

Frank remained silent. He knew Hess would go on.

XXVIII

T he statement was made by John Hartman," Hess continued. "For eighteen years he was one of the British censors at Spandau, and one of the few men allowed to talk with my father. Hartman is convinced that Hitler knew of the flight."

"Why?"

"Hartman retired in 1972. And he said that my father told him that the flight had been *authorized*. I believed him. And that authorization, Herr Brandenburg, could have come only from Adolf Hitler himself!"

Frank sat in his room back in Travemünde, where he lived while he was studying in Lübeck. He stared at the lists he had made, one headed "Hitler Did Not Know," the other, "Hitler Knew."

He felt content. He was now convinced that Hitler had been in from the beginning on the planning of the flight to England by Hess, his deputy Führer. His conviction had not come as a cymbal–crashing revelation, but rather it had been built by a growing number of logically convincing arguments and observations, and was therefore all the more persuasive.

The evidence on the negative side was rather suspect. There was Axmann, who himself no longer was certain of having seen Bormann lying dead in Berlin. There was the emotional statement by Jordan that Hess had betrayed the Führer, given during an interview that could be characterized as irrational. And finally there was the statement to Colonel Bird made by Rudolf Hess himself, that he and he alone had been responsible. That should have been the definitive statement, were it not for the fact that it seemed to have been made in an attempt to be loyal to the Führer and protect him.

On the other side of the ledger, however, the evidence was overwhelming.

There was Breker's impeccable source stating that Hitler definitely not only knew of the flight but helped plan it. There was Wolff's "actor" story, there was Baur's account of the flak map, and Hess's knowledge of the secret code designations, which he could have obtained only with the Führer's knowledge. There was Günsche, who personally had overheard conversations about the flight, there were Ilse Hess and her son and their convincing arguments for the fact that Hitler knew, and finally there was Hartman, to whom Hess himself had confided that his flight had been authorized.

The conclusion was irrefutable. He felt completely comfortable with his decision.

It was a little like looking at a tree lying on the forest floor next to a stump, he thought, its branches hacked off. While no one had seen it being chopped down, it was safe to assume that someone had done so.

But he still decided to check out his decision with his new-found advisor. He made arrangements to meet with Dr. Robert M. W. Kempner once again.

"Those are my reasons for reaching the conclusion I have," Frank told Dr. Kempner. They were sitting in Kempner's office. "Do you think I am right? Have I reached the right conclusion?"

Kempner gave a little laugh. "If you haven't," he said, "we're in the same boat. For I have reached the exact same conclusion, although by a different route. As it is, your conclusion strengthens mine, as mine strengthens yours."

Gratified, Frank asked, "How did you become convinced that Hitler knew?"

"As in your case there were several reasons," Kempner answered him. "But the one instance that convinced me without a doubt was my in–depth interrogation of SS-Obergruppenführer, Chef der Ausland Organisation der NSDAP—Chief of the Foreign Organization of the NSDAP, Gauleiter Ernst Wilhelm Bohle."

"Why? What did he say?"

"Bohle, like Hess, who was born in Egypt, was an *Auslandsdeutscher*— a German born abroad. He had been born in England."

"And Bohle thought Hitler knew?"

"He not only thought so, he was utterly convinced of the fact. He was a friend of Rudolf Hess, a protege and close confidant."

"How did he become convinced?"

"It is a long but fascinating story. If you wish, I'll tell it to you."

"Please."

"In October 1940 Hess had summoned Bohle to a private meeting. After having made certain they could not be overheard, he had told him that he was about to reveal something to him which he must swear not to disclose to anyone, not even to Hess's own brother. Bohle did.

"Hess then told him he was confiding in him because of their close relationship, because he had greater confidence in him than in anyone else, and because Bohle was familiar with both the English people and the English language; in this case this was of the utmost importance because the matter to which he referred involved ending the war with England as quickly as possible. And he asked him if he would cooperate in the project, the exact nature of which he was not in a position to divulge to him. Bohle had agreed.

"Hess had then asked him to translate a document from German into English, a written message Hess said he would be handing in person to the Duke of Hamilton. When Bohle looked startled, Hess had explained that he would be meeting the Duke in Switzerland, and that he had made his acquaintance during the Olympics in Berlin in 1936."

Frank listened, spellbound. He did not interrupt with questions.

"Bohle had taken the document and asked when Hess wanted the translation back, but Hess had told him that the document could not leave the room, Bohle would have to make the translation right then and there. A typewriter had already been set up for his use. Bohle set to work.

"Hess had asked him not to ask any questions, because he could not answer them, and Bohle had the distinct impression that Hess had been sworn to secrecy by the Führer. 'That,' he told me, 'would be the only reason for him not to confide in me fully. We were that close.'

"Bohle knew Hess perhaps better than anyone, Frank, and he told me that there was no way Hess would have undertaken a mission of such magnitude and daring without the express permission and cooperation of the Führer. It would have been totally uncharacteristic of him. In his mind there was not the slightest doubt that the flight had been planned by the two of them. And Hess's chauffeur told Bohle that a couple of days before the flight Hess had had a four–hour–long private meeting with the Führer in the Reich Chancellery, a most unusual occurrence.

"As in your case, Bohle brought up many points that tended to prove his contention. Hitler had always known about the 'secret' negotiations carried out by top Nazis with their allied counterparts. Göring's talks with the Swede, Dahlerus; Rosenberg's discussions with the Norwegians; Himmler's contact with British intelligence, and so on. And there was the puzzlement of how Hess had been able to avoid all the *Luftsperren*—the antiaircraft installations."

Frank was about to break in. He knew how. He knew about the Baur flak map. He kept silent. He would tell Kempner about his talk with Baur later.

"Hitler distanced himself from Hess and the mission after the flight failed. He had to. But he took no reprisals against the Hess family, as normally would have been the case. And even though he knew of Bohle's involvement, no action was taken against him either, although his association with the project had been far more significant than that of the secretaries, servants, chauffeurs, and other fringe characters who were imprisoned for a while, in a show of outrage. Bohle was certain he was spared only because his friend, Hess, had made a bargain with Hitler to leave him alone. Later he found out that a warrant for his arrest had in fact been issued, but Hitler had refused to sign it. Pretty convincing evidence." Kempner stopped. He looked at Frank.

"And that, Frank, is why Bohle was convinced that Hitler knew all there was to know about his deputy Führer's flight to England, and why I totally agree with him."

For another half hour or so they chatted, then Kempner stood up.

"And now, Frank, what are your plans now? Back to your flowers? Back to your studies?"

"I never left them. I still have a few years to go before I reach my educational goal. But I am also going to continue my inquiries, find new subjects to interview."

Kempner nodded. "I know. The time and the people of the Third Reich seem to be an irresistible, bottomless abyss to be explored. And not only by historians and researchers. Do you know that I still get letters and calls from the children, and sometimes grandchildren, of the Nazis who were prosecuted and sentenced at Nürnberg? They want to know what their fathers or grandfathers were really like. And since I knew them then, I must be able to tell about them now."

"What do you say?"

"What can I say? I tell them the truth."

Frank nodded. "It is the truth that I want to find, too," he said earnestly. "There are still unanswered questions I want answered."

"Such as?"

"Bormann."

Kempner's face clouded over.

"Bormann," he repeated. "I wish you would go back to your flowers, Frank. I wish you would—stay away from those men." He sighed. "But—if you must continue your venture, be careful."

He took Frank by the shoulders. "Please, be careful."

For most of the rest of the year Frank devoted himself primarily to his studies. He would graduate the following year and go on to study business management at the University of Bayreuth. He looked forward to that, and he wanted to prepare himself as thoroughly as possible.

But he had used some of his weekends to call on several people about whom he had learned from other subjects.

There had been Adolf Eichmann, son of the Adolf Eichmann executed by the Israelis; Werner Grothmann, the officer who succeeded Karl Wolff as Himmler's adjutant; and a telephone call to Else Krüger, Martin Bormann's long–time secretary whom he called "Krügerchen"— Little Krüger—and who after the war had married her British interrogator, Capt. Leslie James, and now lived in Cambridge, England.

He had seen Karl Kattengell, intelligence officer on Göring's staff; Gen. Josef Kammhuber, commanding general of Göring's night fighters; and SS-Standartenführer Dr. Werner Koeppen, Alfred Rosenberg's adjutant.

And he had talked to Eugen Dollmann, Himmler's translator and confidant; Staatssekretär Leopold Gutterer, who with Joseph Goebbels had organized and developed the Propaganda Ministry, and after 1944 was director general of UFA, Germany's most important motion picture studio; as well as Fritz Hippler, who had been an associate of Joseph Goebbels, and Kurt Franz, former commandant of the Treblinka concentration camp.

He had been in contact with Leni Riefenstahl, who had glorified the Führer and his 1936 Berlin Olympic Games on film, and another top Third Reich movie star, Louis Trenker; with Mrs. Albert Speer and Gertrud Junge, one of Hitler's private secretaries, and Max Wünsche, one of his orderlies. He had seen Heinz Linge, the Führer's valet; Herta Schneider, Eva Braun's best friend, and SS Standartenführer Gunter d'Alquen, editor–in–chief of the notorious SS weekly *The Black Corps* and chief of the Wehrmacht propaganda department. D'Alquen—who during their talk had exhibited the disconcerting habit of imitating the voices of those he spoke about—had told Frank that to his knowledge Reichsführer SS Heinrich Himmler himself had not believed that Rudolf Hess, in his flight to England, had acted alone, and thus there was no question of his having committed high treason. To Frank it had been yet another corroboration of his conclusion that the Führer had indeed been implicated in the planning of the operation with Hess, voiced by someone in a high enough position in the Nazi hierarchy to be reliably informed.

None of them had been a source for new information. All of them had been what Frank by now regarded as routine interviews. He was beginning to realize that any investigation is ninety percent wasted effort.

One man he had seen had provided a spark of excitement. His name was Rochus Misch, and Frank had visited him in his apartment on Petunienweg in Berlin. Misch, an SS-Oberscharführer—sergeant—during the war, had been manning the telephone switchboard in the Führerbunker in Berlin on the night the *Serail* plane had been lost. When he told Frank that he remembered a strange telephone call he had received that night from someone whose name he could not remember, but who had gone on about a downed plane, Frank had become excited. It had to be the Westermaier call about the *Serail* plane. But Misch could tell him no details. He remembered the call because of its mysterious urgency and the unorthodox manner in which it was placed, but all he could tell Frank was that he had routed it to the office of Reichsleiter Martin Bormann.

It had been just another dead end.

That Christmas he celebrated with his family in Hildesheim. Ulrike, his sister, wondered when he would give up all that Nazi stuff, but Frank, himself, wondered what 1985 would bring.

He knew he would have to spend a lot of time on his studies at Bayreuth University. But he also knew that he would not give up his search for the truth and for the facts about the *Serail* documents and Martin Bormann. He refused to let it go.

Did it matter?

Perhaps to no one but himself. There were still remnants of the cancer that less than half a century ago had afflicted his country. The past was still part of the present. It must not be permitted to become part of the future as well. "The wish to forget only prolongs the ordeal," he had read somewhere, "the secret of the solution is to remember."

Learn—and remember.

The pain and tears, suffering and death inflicted by the Nazis cannot be recompensed. They can only be tempered by mutual remembrance and mutual trust. And a total rejection of repetition. By every German. Especially the young, such as he.

But first the truth must be known, his quest must be continued.

With youthful self–confidence he felt it was not a matter of whether he would succeed, but of how—and when.

XXIX

I t was a clear, crisp November day when Frank strolled up the avenue toward the Festspielhaus—the Opera Festival Theater in Bayreuth, where he was studying business administration at the University.

The trees lining the concourse stretched their winter–naked branches toward the sky, as if in supplication for warm sunshine and gentle rain, patient and secure in the knowledge that it would come.

Although he was not particularly interested in opera, Frank knew that ever since 1876, when the inauguration of the old Bühnenfestspielhaus had taken place, Bayreuth had been the definitive home of the operas of Richard Wagner. All the great Wagner singers had performed there, from Max Lorenz and Set Swanholm to Lauritz Melchior, and from Anna Bahr-Mildenburg and Ernestine Schumann-Heink to Kirsten Flagstad. All of them had sung Wagner roles under the batons of some of the world's most renowned conductors, from Fritz Busch and Wilhelm Furtwängler to Arturo Toscanini. Ever since, international crowds of opera devotees had traveled the broad avenue toward the grand opera house on top of the hill, there to listen to the music of the man who had been the Führer's favorite composer.

Frank was between classes at the university and had felt the need for some fresh air and the opportunity to stretch his legs. The Festspielhaus avenue was a perfect spot for it: a little strenuous to ascend, easy to descend.

In his mind he took stock of the year about to end. It had been a busy year, much of it of necessity devoted to his studies, the rest to his quest, which continued to grow.

He realized that his activities had interfered badly with his social life, particularly his relationship with Herta, and he always felt a little guilty whenever he thought of it. He always promised himself to rectify the situation, but somehow time just slipped away from him. He knew they were growing apart, and it hurt him, but he could not help himself.

At the suggestion of Ministerialdirigent Heinrich Heim, with whom he had kept in touch and who knew about his desire to find out the truth about the fate of Martin Bormann, he had been in contact with four former secretaries of the Reichsleiter and two former Bormann deputies.

Heim had told him that he, himself, strongly felt that Bormann had survived. The Reichsleiter was a clever man, he had pointed out, a powerful man, and a man who looked after himself. It was inconceivable that he would have allowed himself to be trapped in the Führerbunker in Berlin without a sure way of escaping when the time came. But he, Heim, had no personal or definite knowledge of Bormann's fate.

But he had had an interesting suggestion. He knew of four women who had been secretaries to Bormann, and two of his deputies. Any one or more of them might have knowledge of interest to Frank. Heim had given him their telephone numbers; they all lived in the Munich area.

Frank had started with the secretaries. Secretaries often had knowledge far beyond their status, and it was quite possible that they might know of some arrangement or other Bormann had made to ensure his safety.

The first of the former secretaries he called was a woman by the name of Elisabeth Mundlechner. Bormann, according to Heim, had affectionately called her "Silberhörnchen"—little silver horn.

As soon as the woman had been told why Frank wanted to talk to her, she had grown cold and distant, and insisted there had been a misunderstanding; she had never been one of Reichsleiter Bormann's secretaries! Consequently she had nothing, absolutely nothing, to say. And she had cut the conversation short.

The second woman he called, Margarete Fugger, called "Fugger-inn" by Bormann, according to Heim, also angrily denied ever having been Bormann's secretary and refused to discuss the matter. Frank had been taken aback. Two denials? And when the same vehement denials were voiced by the two remaining secretaries, Erika Schrott and Annemarie Hauser, he began to wonder.

Could he have gotten the wrong names and numbers from Heim for all four of them? Impossible. And why should Heim have given him false information? It made no sense. A more intriguing possibility insinuated itself in his mind. Could it be that they did know something about Bormann's disappearance? preparations? correspondence with foreign lands of possible refuge? anything? And could they all have been sworn to secrecy by their erstwhile master, to whom they still were loyal? or whose wrath they feared, should they violate that oath? It was an intriguing idea. Perhaps he could learn something from the two former Bormann deputies.

The first deputy he called was Hans Müller. Müller had been a deputy in the management of Obersalzberg. Frank had noted the conversation in his file records:

FB: Many of Martin Bormann's associates are still alive, but no one will talk about the Reichsleiter or his fate.

HM: I am one of them, Herr Brandenburg. I have nothing to say. I never did talk about those days. I will not do so now.

FB: Why not, Herr Müller?

HM: I have no intention of inviting trouble.

And he hung up.

There was one name left, Ludwig Schmid. Frank had been determined to talk to the man in person, and he had succeeded.

He had visited Schmid in his home in Oberhaching near Munich, a small, brown, single house. During the uncomfortable interview Schmid's wife, a stony-faced woman, and a large, watchful dog had been present. Schmid himself, an indiscriminate, partly bald man who wore large black-rimmed glasses, had been reticent and cautious.

It had quickly become evident that the man had made inquiries about Frank before consenting to see him, and thought he had found out where his visitor stood. Frank was convinced that without that investigation the man would never have agreed to meet with him. It had strengthened his resolve never to appear to be anti-Nazi to any of the people he interviewed, or his sources of information would quickly dry up completely.

He had done his level best to draw out the former deputy, but the man refused to talk about Bormann at all. Only upon being pressed did he admit that he thought the Reichsleiter had escaped, but he would say nothing more. In fact, it was apparent that he regretted having said that much.

It was a curious development, Frank thought. All six people who had worked closely with Bormann categorically refused to talk about it. Even denied it ever happened.

Why?

During the year he had also visited SS-Brigadeführer and Generalmajor der Waffen SS Gustav Lombard, whose name and address had been given to him by General Baur.

Lombard lived on the third floor of an old apartment house in Schwabing, a suburb of Munich that had survived the ravages of the war. The general had been a hunter, and his apartment held several game trophies and paintings of hunting scenes.

At ninety–one years of age, Lombard had been friendly, charming, and outgoing, a delightful host. He had been talkative, obviously pleased to have an audience, and he had told Frank about his years as a Russian prisoner of war, during which time he had met General Baur.

But most of his reminiscing had been about a Russian named Gregor Boris Simonowitsch, who had been Lenin's translator. Imprisoned by Stalin upon Lenin's death, the man was still an avid communist and had regaled Lombard with schemes and plans for the communists to take over the world.

It had been a pleasant and interesting visit, but a visit that had contributed nothing to his search for knowledge.

Although not entirely so.

Lombard had given him a transcript of the official *Kriegstagebuch*—daily war journal—of the notorious 1st SS Cavalry Brigade. In it were recorded the mass executions of Jews in Russia and other countries occupied by the Nazis, as well as the killing of partisans and "looters." Lombard himself had commanded the 1st Cavalry Regiment of this unit. Copies of all these reports had been forwarded to Reichsführer Heinrich Himmler as early as 1941. And all of them had gone through the approving hands of his adjutant, General Karl Wolff.

With a bleak and let–down feeling Frank had read the war journal: "13,788 killed; own losses, 2 dead, 15 wounded." It was not a battle record, it was the record of a massacre.

And Frank recalled once again that General Wolff had denied any knowledge of any such actions, publicly as well as privately, to Frank, and he realized that this record had also contributed to Wolff's prison sentence. It had not been just the need of the war crimes commission to find "warm bodies" to convict, as Wolff had claimed.

Perhaps his father had been right, Frank thought. Perhaps all the people with whom he now associated did have blood on their hands.

And there had been his visit to Gudrun Burwitz, the daughter of Reichsführer SS Heinrich Himmler, in her third–floor apartment on Blumenauerstrasse in Munich. Both Baur and Wolff had suggested that he talk to her.

Gudrun Burwitz, née Himmler, a graying woman in her fifties who wore her hair in a tight bun, bore an uncanny resemblance to her father, not only in looks but in personality.

She had been reserved and testy, not even thawing a little when he presented her with flowers from the Brandenburg nursery. She had been fiercely proud of her father and vehemently defensive, curtly denying all allegations of wrongdoing on his part. Her father had had nothing to do with the extermination of Jews, she had insisted, such accusations were all lies. It was easy for the living, in order to save their own miserable skins, to accuse the dead, who could not defend themselves. She had pointedly ignored existing documentation; that sort of thing could easily be forged. And when Frank tried to probe deeper, she had querulously warned him to "take much care in your future research." She had freely acknowledged having been active in Stille Hilfe—Silent Help, an organization that helped Nazis and their families escape the Allies. In fact, she had told him defiantly, she was still active in that organization, which still existed, although now it was slanted more toward the vindication of such victims. She had had little use for the *Amis*, bitterly complaining that they had taken everything from her after the war, leaving her to fend for herself.

Through it all Frank had felt ill at ease, sitting stiffly on an old chair that the woman had told him had been her father's favorite.

It had been an eye–opening visit, but not of much use. And as a parting statement, the woman had given him a contribution form for Stille Hilfe.

Finally there had been Käthe Heusermann, the chief MTA—Medizin Technische Assistentin—to Prof. Dr. Hugo Blaschke, Hitler's dentist. Christa Schroeder had almost insisted that he see her. He had not anticipated learning anything new or anything of importance, as the woman had been questioned exhaustively by both the Russians and the Americans. Anything she might have known had undoubtedly been extracted from her long ago. But she lived in nearby Düsseldorf, and he had been curious.

Käthe Heusermann, a timid woman in her seventies with greying hair and lips painted bright red, had greeted him uneasily. Her speech had been hesitant, often confused, and she seemed wrapped in perpetual apprehension, if not actual fear. The legacy of years of gruelling interrogation, Frank thought. Her apartment was tidy and pleasant, with a library containing many books about the war, especially the final days.

Frank had asked her about her patients, who had included the Führer himself, and he had been fascinated by her answers. Hitler was always punctual and polite; Eva Braun was a merry girl, quick to laugh. Of them all, Goebbels had been the worst patient and had had the greatest fear of the dentist, once saying to her, "Every time I see you, Frau Heusermann, I am gripped by the fear of a Jew!" And Himmler was an out and out *Memme*—a coward. Bormann had been an unpleasant man, in and out of the dentist's chair, a nasty martinet, especially when he had a toothache. One night, she told Frank, when the Reichsleiter returned home after a session with Dr. Blaschke, he discovered one of his pictures hanging crookedly on the wall. In a rage, he awakened his entire family and staff of servants, and had them go through the whole house straightening pictures.

She had told him that her boss, Dr. Blaschke, had shared a secret code with the chief of the German Red Cross, Dr. Gravitz, who lived in Berlin, through which he could inform Dr. Gravitz by phone of important decisions made at the Führerbunker without fear of being understood by others.

During the last days of the Reich, Prof. Gravitz wanted to know the facts regarding conditions in Berlin. He and Dr. Blaschke felt that as long as the Führer remained in the city and did not leave for Berchtesgaden the situation was relatively safe. But if he decided to leave, measures for the safety of Gravitz and his family should be taken at once. In that case, Blaschke was to say the code message, "the tooth had to be removed suddenly," on the phone. If the Führer and his entire staff were to leave Berlin, all would be lost, they felt, and Blaschke's code message would be, "the bridge had to be removed suddenly today."

When General Baur's evacuation operation began on the evening of April 20th, Blaschke asked Heusermann to call Dr. Gravitz and give him the second message. She had done so. It turned out to be the wrong message. Instead of leaving, the Führer had stayed and had himself given her a small cyanide capsule and carefully instructed her how to use it. Just put it in your mouth, and bite down. Those had been his very words. But later she had learned that after getting her message Dr. Gravitz had at once killed himself and his entire family. He had assembled them all in a room in his house, loaded with land mines, and exploded them.

Heusermann herself had been captured by the Russians, denounced, she told Frank, by a Jewish dentist she had helped hide and had provided with food ration stamps from the Chancellery. And her interrogation ordeal, so well documented, had begun.

One of the most devastating experiences, she had told Frank, was when the Russians took her under guard to a shack to identify the charred remains of Joseph Goebbels and his wife, Magda, along with those of their six children, Helga, Hilde, Helmut, Holde, Hedda, and Heide, whose lives they had taken before they had killed themselves in the Bunker. She had known them all. She had been shattered.

In 1951 the Russians had finally sentenced her to four years hard labor, in addition to the six years she had already spent in solitary confinement. She had actually welcomed the sentence. She would once again be with other people. She had been accused and found guilty of having helped prolong the war by working on Hitler's teeth, and by neglecting her duty to help the world by not using a heavy water bottle kept in the dentist's office to kill him! These crimes had sent her to Labor Camp no. 27 in Taiga, Siberia, where she had worked for the next four years, producing machinery and instrumentation for submarines and airplanes.

When she finally returned to Germany in 1955 she found out that her husband, having heard nothing from her for five years, had had her declared dead. He had remarried and had two children. By law he was under no obligation to assist her. She had been on her own. And she had had absolutely no assets. But she had used her skills, and she had survived.

Frank had reached the Festspielhaus on top of the hill. For a moment he stood gazing at the stark, imposing opera house, very much in keeping with the music of Wagner being performed inside.

Another year was rapidly coming to an end, too rapidly. He felt he had accomplished nothing to further his search in the year gone by. His venture seemed to be bogging down in a morass of trivia.

He had been asked to join a group of friends in West Berlin to celebrate New Year's Eve. As he stood looking at the shrine to the music of the Führer's favorite composer, he made up his mind to go.

He had no way of knowing it was a decision that would be a turning point in his quest.

Ilse and Wolf-Rudiger Hess at Spandau prison in Berlin. (Ullstein)

Rudolf Hess.

Käthe Heusermann, dental technician who worked on Hitler's teeth and helped identify remains.

Col. Eugene Bird, former Commandant of Spandau prison in Berlin. (Ullstein-Klaus Mehner)

SS-Brigadeführer Gustav
Lombard.

Gustav Lombard with Frank Brandenburg.

Rudolf Jordan. (Ullstein)   Gauleiter Erich Koch.

Medard Klapper's General Gun Store in Karlsrühe.

Frank at the gate to Auschwitz Concentration Camp with a surviving inmate.

Prosecutor Robert M. Kempner at the War Crimes Trials in Nürnberg, 1946.

Frank Brandenburg with the German Bundespresident Richard von Weizsäcker, at the fortieth anniversary of the Bergen-Belsen concentration camp.

XXX

Berlin was festive, noisy, and brightly lit on the eve of ushering in 1986. As the old year ticked away its final hours, one of Frank's friends suggested that they celebrate the arrival of the New Year in a really unusual way. Something to remember. They all piled into a car and drove to Checkpoint Charlie, the famous gateway through the Iron Curtain between West and East Berlin.

Someone had had the foresight to bring a bottle of Champagne, and as midnight approached they sipped wine, threw confetti, sang old songs, and waved at the East German soldiers in the guard towers overlooking the checkpoint. The guards did not wave back.

Frank stood gazing into the city beyond the wall. In his mind he recalled his trip to Börnersdorf. He had been damned lucky. He could easily still be there, in some prison in the DDR, instead of on the free side of the wall dividing his country, sipping Champagne and reminiscing about the past as the year flowed out. He recalled the cemetery and his talk with the farmer, Rost. And he thought of the missing documents. After his telephone conversation with the Westermaier widow, he had tried to find anyone who knew about them. He had had no luck. He had asked everyone he had talked to in the intervening months.

Nothing. But he still had that nagging feeling that there was something else he could do. Something...

His friends were singing an old German folk song from the Schwarzwald: "*es klappert die Mühle am rauschenden Bach*—the mill is clattering on the rushing stream, *klip, klap—klip, klap—klip klap*," they carolled lustily, as the old year was rushing to an end.

One of them poked the pensive Frank.

"Sing!" he shouted. "The new year is almost here! *Klip, klap!— klip, klap!*"

Frank came out of his reverie. "What?"

"*Es klappert die Mühle*," his friend sang, slightly off key, "*klip, klap!—klip, klap!*"

Klappert? Klap, klap...why should that word, that sound, suddenly seem so—so familiar, so intrusive—and yet so out of place?

"*Klip, klap*," everyone bellowed, "*klip, klap. Es klappert die Mühle...*" *Klappert...klappert...klapper*. The word seemed to reverberate in his mind, clamoring to get out.

Klapper...Börnersdorf...DDR...East Germany...

And suddenly he knew.

For a single moment he marvelled at how the mind works. Storing information that is unreachable until some apparently unrelated key is turned, allowing the information to pour out. Klapper. It was a name. It was the name of a man he had read about in an article discussing the fake Hitler diaries. And Börnersdorf. At the time he recalled thinking it was a funny name. He hadn't thought of the old folk song then, but now it had acted as a key. A key, belted out on New Year's Eve. Klapper. He could not recall the man's first name or anything about him, only that he had had something to do with Börnersdorf. What? It escaped him. And there was something else. Now that the floodgates had been opened, he remembered. General Wolff had mentioned the name before he died. Someone to see, he had said. The man had seemed quite unimportant at the time, and Frank had not followed him up.

He resolved that as soon as he could get back to his files in his bunker in Hildesheim he would look up the man named Klapper. Suddenly everyone broke into a cheer. The new year had arrived. Enthusiastically Frank sang at the top of his voice: "*Klip, klap!—klip, klap!—klip, klap!...*"

He had made no special file for the man named Klapper, but he found the entry in Karl Wolff's file where the general had mentioned him, and he found the newspaper article that contained a little information about him.

In 1944, as a seventeen–year–old, Medard Klapper had volunteered for the Waffen SS and had served in the Leibstandarte Adolf Hitler until just before the capitulation. He supposedly had also performed outstanding work as a *V–Mann*—an informer—for the Bundeskriminalamt—the West German Criminal Bureau—and other agencies, all somewhat nebulous, one case having to do with retrieving some paintings stolen from Sans Souci, Frederick the Great's pleasure palace in Potsdam. The article mentioned that the reporter who perpetrated the Hitler diaries hoax had supposedly obtained some documents pertaining to other matters from Klapper. Klapper owned and managed a gun shop in Karlsruhe. His address was not difficult to find.

It was in the early afternoon of January 16, 1986, when Frank stood before the display windows of Medard Klapper's General Gun Store on Sophienstrasse. There were two storefront windows, both of them cluttered with a great variety of items pertaining to guns and weapons in general, all of them modern, no World War II weapons. There were models and posters, boxes of ammunition and rifle scopes. There were military steins and commemorative plates, a large model of an old cannon, even a dart game. The entry to the shop was secured by a locked iron–bar door.

Frank buzzed, and the door clicked open. He entered the shop.

The stout, casually clad, dark–haired man who greeted him appeared to be around sixty years of age. Frank introduced himself.

"*Ach, ja*," the man said expansively. He stuck out his hand to Frank. Frank could not help noticing it was large and fleshy, too large for the rest of the man. He shook it.

"A pleasure to meet you," Klapper said. But the man's sudden wariness belied his words. His eyes kept darting toward the door, as if he were on the lookout for something unexpected to happen. "When you called me on the phone, you said you had some questions you wanted to ask me." He looked at Frank, his eyes guarded. "How can I be of help?"

The tone of suspicion and watchfulness, which Klapper was unable to conceal, made it apparent that his offer was made more out of curiosity than a genuine desire to be helpful.

"As I told you, Herr Klapper," Frank said, "General Wolff, before he died, suggested that I talk to you in connection with my—uh, research." He put his hand in his pocket, aware of Klapper's sudden tension, and showed the man what had been in it.

Klapper's eyes widened slightly. "The general's ring," he said. His eyes darted toward the door and back to Frank. "How do you come into possession of Generaloberst Karl Wolff's ring?"

"The general gave it to me," Frank answered him. "To—to facilitate my studies." He put the ring away.

Klapper nodded. "Perhaps," he ventured, "perhaps it would be better if we did not talk here." He nodded toward the door. "There is a coffee shop in the hotel across the street. We can talk there. They have nice, secluded booths. For security—yours as well as mine." He started for the door. "I can close up for a short while. I can see the shop from across the way. If anything important should happen."

Together they crossed the street, Klapper's eyes flitting up and down—and not only to check on traffic. His attitude toward Frank had changed, but he was still enshrouded in a veil of wariness.

Seated in a booth by themselves, with a clear view of the General Gun Store, Klapper looked with curiosity at Frank. "You knew the general personally, then?" he asked. It was obvious that it was a concept difficult for him to accept.

"I did. We were—good friends."

Klapper nodded. He eyed Frank speculatively. "And he gave you his ring? *Donnerwetter!*—by thunder, that is something!" He peered at Frank, seemingly impressed, but with overtones of doubt. "I never met the general myself," he said. "I saw him, of course. Many times. When I served in the Leibstandarte Adolf Hitler. General Wolff was a very important man, no doubt about that. And I, of course, was not important enough to meet him." He gave Frank a sidelong glance. "But I know the general was often in the company of the Führer himself." His eyes flitted to the window and back to Frank. "And I was told the general was fond of dogs," he continued ingenuously. "That he used to enjoy the Führer's three beautiful shepherd dogs. Blondie. And Wolf. And—and—" he looked straight at Frank with an expression as if he were trying to remember. "What *was* the name of the third dog?"

"The third dog?" Frank repeated.

"Yes. The third dog." Klapper looked at him, eyes narrowed.

"Muck," Frank said, level–voiced.

Klapper's eyes crinkled in a smile. "*Ja*," he said. "*Stimmt*. Correct. Muck!" He settled back in his chair.

"Now," he said. "How can I be of help?" This time the question was asked in quite a different tone of voice. This time he meant it.

"The general told me that you are a man of much knowledge, Herr Klapper," Frank flattered him. "He said that you were a man of importance, of—of crucial involvement in both the—uh, the old and the new."

Klapper seemed to grow a couple of inches. He gave a quick look out the window at his shop across the street. "The general was too kind," he mumbled, with quite obvious insincerity. "What specifically do you want to know about?"

"I was led to believe that you might know something about certain important documents," Frank said. He decided to reveal as little as possible of what he already knew. That way he would not influence what Klapper told him.

Klapper nodded slowly. He let his eyes flit toward the window. "You are referring to the documents in Madrid," he said.

Madrid? Frank thought. "Yes," he said. "What can you tell me about them?"

Klapper shrugged. "It goes back to shortly after the war," he began.

Frank took his little tape recorder from his pocket, and placed it on the table.

Klapper at once stopped talking. He glared at the tape recorder.

"Do you mind if I tape what you tell me?" Frank asked. "It is for my own use only. Do you mind?"

"I do," Klapper said curtly. "I intend to answer your questions frankly and completely. I cannot do this knowing that what I say is being recorded. If you want honest and uninhibited information from me, you must turn it off."

"Of course," Frank said. He started to put the little recorder back in his pocket. Klapper stopped him.

"On the table," he said firmly. "Leave it on the table, where we can both see it. In the off position."

"As I was saying," Klapper picked up where he had stopped, "it was shortly after the war. I was contacted by the Bormann group and

ordered to help arrange for the recovery of certain documents, about
a dozen crates, I was told, that were hidden in Dresden. In the zone
occupied by the Russians."

The *Serail* documents! Frank thought. With growing excitement he
asked, "What do you know about those documents?"

"Only that they had been aboard a plane that had crashed. And that
they had been salvaged from the plane and hidden in Dresden. The
Bormann group instructed me that they were of the utmost importance.
That under no circumstances must they be allowed to fall into Russian
hands. Or any of the other enemy allies. That they must be recovered
by us."

"And they were?"

"They were."

"By you?"

"Not actively," Klapper said. His eyes shifted toward the window
and back. "I was the *Vermittler*—the agent for the operation."

"What happened?"

"Exactly what was supposed to happen," Klapper said testily. "The
documents were retrieved and sent to Madrid. To the Bormann
group."

Frank felt enormously keyed–up. Here was what he had been seeking.
Here was the answer to what had happened to the *Serail* documents.
They had been sent to Madrid. They were in the hands of a—a Bormann
group.

"That Bormann group," he said. "What can you tell me about that?"

"They still have their headquarters in Madrid," Klapper told him.
"Today it is the Mariborsol, and—"

He suddenly stopped and gave Frank a sharp look. "You *are* familiar
with Mariborsol?" he asked.

"I have heard of such an organization," Frank lied, "but—no, Herr
Klapper, I am not familiar with it. Neither General Wolff nor General
Baur mentioned it to me."

Klapper nodded sagely. "They would not know," he said. "They
were not among the—the active. There was no reason for them to
know."

For a moment Klapper studied him. His eyes once more darted
quickly to his shop and back to Frank.

"Such knowledge could be dangerous for you to possess," he said
finally, an ominous tone to his voice. "I presume you realize that."

"Nevertheless, Herr Klapper, it is necessary to my work that I know."

Klapper nodded. "The name is, of course, an acronym. *Mari* from Martin, *bor* from Bormann, and *sol*, the Spanish word for sun." Again he smiled. "The rising sun of our cause," he said. "Mariborsol."

"And—the purpose?"

"To insure that the future will be ours," Klapper said earnestly. "The financial matters, for instance. And they are considerable, even on a world scale. Real estate. Manufacturing plants. All kinds of profitable investments and business ventures, controlled by our people, the people of Mariborsol, both old and new." Again he smiled his disconcerting smile. "Such as you, *nicht wahr?*—not so?"

Frank treated it as a rhetorical question and said nothing.

"And to guard the papers and documents handed down to us from the Führer and the Third Reich to guide us." Klapper went on. "Such as the contents of the crates recovered from concealment in Dresden. The reporters of the popular press have coined the phrase 'The Fourth Reich.' We do not mind. It will be *our* Reich. The future will be ours. Martin Bormann himself may not live to see the organization that bears his name become triumphant," he finished. "But triumphant it will be!"

Frank stared at the man. The *Serail* documents, he thought, the Börnersdorf cache. It may hold a blueprint for the future. A future patterned after the ideology of Adolf Hitler. Now he knew what had happened to them. They had become the guiding gospel of the new Nazi movement.

"The Reichsleiter is convinced of that," Klapper said.

Frank picked up. "*Is*, Herr Klapper? Then Martin Bormann did not die in Berlin? in that tank explosion? He is still alive?"

He was excited. Here might be real corroboration of what had happened to Martin Bormann.

Klapper looked at him as if he had suddenly turned into a simpering idiot. Abruptly he cackled a dry laugh.

"Tank explosion!" he snorted. "Even the driver of that tank survived. He still lives somewhere in the south of Germany. Certainly Martin Bormann." He leaned conspiratorially toward Frank. "I myself had the honor of meeting the Reichsleiter. In Spain."

"When?"

"Less than four years ago. In 1982."

"Are you certain it was Martin Bormann?"

Klapper gave him a stiff look, obviously taking affront.

"Of course," he said curtly. "He was introduced to me. Besides, I had seen him many times when I served in the Leibstandarte Adolf Hitler. And I recognized him, and his voice. It was the Reichsleiter himself! Of course he was an old man. Eighty–two. But still as stocky as ever and amazingly robust."

"Then he did survive," Frank said, not surprised. "He did escape from Germany. Do you know how?"

Klapper shook his head. "No. I do not. But I know of someone who does."

"Who is that?"

"A former ODESSA man. Are you interested?"

"I am. Who is this man?"

"His name is Recher. Martin Recher. He lives in Kempten. In southern Bavaria."

"Do you know him?"

"Only of him. But if you show him General Wolff's ring, I am certain he will give you whatever information he has." He cackled unpleasantly. "He will not know the name of the Führer's third dog, and I suggest you do not entrust it to him. He is not an important man."

Frank nodded. "Thank you. I shall contact him."

Klapper glanced at Frank, a calculating look in his eyes.

"You travel much, Herr Brandenburg," he asked.

"Quite a bit. My research requires it."

Klapper nodded. A decision had been made. "Then this is what must happen," he said. "In a few weeks I shall be going to Madrid. To meet with certain Mariborsol representatives. You will go with me."

"I!" Frank was startled.

"*Genau*—exactly. They must know you. It will depend on what they think of you. Your future will depend on it: whether you will be acknowledged and accepted into one of the most vibrant and active organizations working for our cause. It will be an honor for you. New vistas will be opened for you. As one of us your work will gain new meaning, new importance."

Frank was stunned. Here it was. Here and now he had a decision to make. Was he ready?

"But—how?"

"There is a definite procedure in cases like this," Klapper told him.

"A strict procedure, which must be followed. For the safety of the organization and for your own safety. We must travel...."

Frank's thoughts whirled in his mind. He hardly heard Klapper explain the procedure to him: Secret meeting places...private transportation...blindfolded...body searches...code names...vows of secrecy...a flood of melodrama...

Except it was real.

For an eternal moment he sat in silence. He knew why Klapper wanted him to go with him. It was the culmination, after all, of what he had realized, more and more strongly, as he had pursued his quest. He was being looked upon as "new blood" to be infused into the old Nazi veins. He had been, and was even now, being wooed to join the awakening of a new Reich. Many of the important old–time Nazi leaders were old or elderly men; the current cadre of leaders, who managed the enormous resources available to the movement, were mature men. New, young blood was urgently needed. And he, Frank Brandenburg, was in the process of being recruited.

What to do? He needed time to think.

"The—the neo–Nazi organizations, here in Germany and abroad, which one reads so much about, are you—is the Bormann group— is *Mariborsol* involved with them? Are they being financially supported by funds in the control of—of your organization?" he asked.

Klapper smiled a thin, noncommittal smile. He regarded Frank with hooded eyes. "Do not ask too many questions," he said. "Not just yet." He shrugged. "Figure it out for yourself."

He looked questioningly at Frank.

"I shall need some time," Frank said. "Before I can accept your invitation. I have some other—obligations. But I am honored."

"A few days," Klapper said. He put his finger to his lips and winked broadly at Frank. "And—*maul halten!*" he said, using the vulgar term, "Keep your trap shut! No use providing a welcome mat for trouble."

Again his eyes flitted to his shop across the street. He started. Frank looked.

Two men were peering in through the iron bars of the gate before the entrance to the gun shop. Both were small of stature and seemed to be swarthy–looking, and both wore wide–brimmed hats.

"*Da sind sie!*" Klapper exclaimed. "There they are! The people we were just talking about. I must go at once."

He stood up.

"You will wait here until we have gone into my shop," he said hurriedly. "It is necessary that they not make a connection between us. They are not important people."

He turned to leave, but quickly turned back to Frank.

"You will decide about the trip to Madrid," he said, "and then I will tell you when we go." He threw a quick glance at the two Latin–looking men, still standing at his store. "Meanwhile there is a man I want you to see."

"Who?"

"His name is Stein. Georg Stein. I will give you his number."

With a pencil quickly plucked from his jacket pocket he wrote a telephone number on a matchbook he picked up from the table. He gave it to Frank.

"He lives in Stelle," he said, "near Hamburg."

"Who is he? Why do you want me to see him?"

"Have you ever heard of the *Bernsteinzimmer*—the Amber Room?"

Franks stared at him, thoroughly puzzled.

"It is a treasure," Klapper hurriedly went on. "An entire room made of precious amber. It is worth many hundreds of millions. It disappeared. After the war." His eyes flitted toward the two men waiting impatiently at his shop, and back to Frank. "I have no time to tell you about it now. But—our organization may have a lead to where it is."

"I do not understand," Frank said. "What has that to do with the man Stein you said you wanted me to see?"

"When you see him, he will make that clear to you," Klapper said hurriedly. "Quite clear. It is important."

Abruptly he turned on his heel and hurried from the cafe—leaving Frank to pick up the bill.

As he watched the three men enter Klapper's gun shop, Frank wondered uneasily. Who was the man in Stelle named Georg Stein? And why did Klapper so urgently want him to go see him?

XXXI

Martin Recher, the man Klapper had suggested might know about Bormann's escape from Germany, was not at home when Frank called. He was out of town and not expected back for a couple of weeks, Frank was told.

He decided to use the time to call on the man in Stelle whom Klapper had all but insisted he go see, Georg Stein.

The woman at the Polish Embassy had mentioned a Georg Stein in connection with the imprisoned Gauleiter Erich Koch. Was it the same man?

Frank knew nothing about him. He called Dr. Kempner and asked him about him, but although Kempner recalled hearing the name during the Nürnberg Trials, he had not been familiar with the man. He had, however, suggested that if Stein had in any way been involved with the Trials, his name would appear on the records kept at the Hauptstaatsarchiv Nürnberg—the Main State Archives in Nürnberg, and there might be some information in the files there about him.

The floor in the Archives building in which the Nürnberg records were kept was being renovated, and Frank skirted ladders and scaffolding as he made his way to the information/reception desk, behind which stretched row upon row of sturdy shelving packed with numbered and lettered cardboard boxes.

To a pleasant, efficient–looking woman he explained his interest in the Trials, that he was doing research on some lesser known aspects of them, and that he was specifically interested in a man named Georg Stein.

The woman wrote the name on a slip of paper, asked him to wait, and disappeared into the cliffs of crates.

Presently Frank saw her re–emerge at the far end of one of the aisles. She walked a short distance into the aisle, looking searchingly at the boxes. She finally stopped and wrestled one of them down, placing it on a stool.

Frank saw her open the box, take out some file folders, examine them, and select one of them. She studied it for a brief moment, then placed it back in the box and replaced it on the shelf.

She walked up to Frank.

"*Es tut mir leid*," she said. "I am sorry. But the file you requested is classified."

"I do not want to remove it from here," Frank said. "Only look at it."

"I am afraid that is not possible. The file is marked Secret."

"Is there anyone who might be able to give me permission?"

The woman frowned. "I could possibly speak to the administrator," she said. "Find out if he will see you. But he is not here today. I will not be here tomorrow, but if you can come back the day after, I will see what I can do."

"Thank you very much," Frank said.

"You are welcome," the woman smiled at him. "But do not let your hopes fly too high. It is most doubtful that the administrator will or can let you examine that file."

As Frank left he felt disappointed. There seemed to be no chance for him to find out about Georg Stein at the Archives. He had to walk around a dropcloth spread out on the floor where some painters were working, preparing the walls for new wallpaper.

He suddenly brightened. There was the answer. There was his passport to the secret Stein files!

When Frank returned to the Archives the next morning, he wore paint–splattered white overalls and carried a small, well used dropcloth rolled up under his arm and a paint bucket in the other hand. From his back pocket a paintbrush stuck up and on his head perched a stained painter's cap—all of it borrowed from a local house–painting establishment.

As expected, there was a different woman at the desk of the Nürnberg Trials records room.

With a cheery *"Grüss Gott,"* he breezed right by her and started down among the precipitous shelves.

"Just a moment," the woman sternly called after him. "Where are you going?"

Frank stopped and turned back toward her.

"There is some touching up to be done back there," he said. "I have some time now, and I thought I would take care of it."

The woman looked dubious. "Well, I—I do not think—"

"Oh, that's all right, Fräulein—?"

"—Frau Meissner."

"—Frau Meissner. I can come back another time." He grinned at her. "Just as well. It will mean another day's pay for me, and we can all use that, *nicht wahr?*—not so?" He began to walk back out. "I shall just tell the *Malermeister*—the head painter, that you did not want me to finish it today."

He began to walk away.

"Wait!" the woman called after him. "Will it take long?"

"A few minutes now, Frau Meissner. For the first coat. And a few minutes later on, for the second."

"Very well," the woman sighed. "Just as long as you do not make a mess back there."

Frank looked disappointed. *"Schon gut*—all right," he said. "No extra pay for me." He winked at her. "But I love you all the same."

The woman blushed. "Be off with you, young man," she chided him.

Frank tipped two fingers to his soiled cap and walked down the aisle lined with record boxes.

At the far end he stepped out of sight.

So far so good.

He waited for a few moments, then he peered around the corner at the desk.

Frau Meissner was busy with a man asking information.

Quickly, silently, Frank walked into the aisle where yesterday he had seen the other woman take down the box containing the Stein file. He knew approximately where it was located.

The boxes all had code letters and a list of contents displayed on the front.

There. Stein, Georg.

He glanced back toward the desk. Frau Meissner was still occupied with her visitor. He pulled the box from the shelf and opened it. There, on top, was the folder marked Stein, Georg. He removed it, replaced the box and wrapped his dropcloth around the file folder.

Nonchalantly he walked up to the desk.

"That's it for now," he said. "Be back in half an hour or so. Don't miss me too much!"

Again the woman blushed.

Only a few streets from the Archives building was a self–service photocopying shop. There were a dozen or so documents in the file folder. Frank copied them all. He placed them in a large envelope and sealed it. On his way out he asked the girl at the cash register to keep the envelope for him; he would return within the hour.

Back at the trial records room he waved chummily at Frau Meissner. "Should be ready for that second coat by now," he called to her, as he walked down the aisle.

Once again he waited until the woman was busy with a visitor. Then he quickly replaced the file folder with all the documents.

Back home, having divested himself of the borrowed overalls and splattered painter's cap, Frank spread out the purloined papers on his bed. Inwardly he grinned. It had worked! Just like in the movie. When he had noticed that dropcloth in the hall of the Archives he had remembered a motion picture he had seen recently. The story of a jewel heist. A brazen jewel heist in Paris or another city where many shops close down for a midday rest period. A couple of men in workers' clothing had arrived with a truck at a jewelry shop, put up barriers on the sidewalk to route pedestrians around the shop, and hung a heavy tarp over the display window, from behind which the sound of a paint–scraping machine or sandblaster drowned out all other sounds, such as those made by cutting through the glass and emptying the displays of jewels in the window and the shop. It had worked. Just as his painter ploy, inspired by this film, had worked. Who said going to the movies was a waste of time?

The information contained in the Stein files was disappointing. Either that, or Frank did not recognize the significance of what he read.

There were the obligatory vital statistics about the man. The son of a city official in Königsberg in East Prussia, now Kaliningrad in the USSR, and office–holder in former Weimar Republic Chancellor Gustav Stresemann's right–liberal German People's Party, Georg had served in World War II and been a prisoner of war in Russia. He was now an orchard owner and an amateur historian and art collector, who had concerned himself with tracking down and recovering art treasures that had been lost or stolen during the war.

It was in this connection that his involvement with Gauleiter Koch had occurred, and his interest in the famous eighteenth century *Bernsteinzimmer*—Amber Room, a room constructed entirely of amber from the Baltic Sea and containing priceless treasures, which had been presented to Peter I, Czar of Russia by the Prussian King Friedrich Wilhelm I in 1717 and installed in the Zarskoje Selo Palace near Leningrad. The entire room and its contents had vanished in 1945 and to this day have not been found. While carrying on his investigations and inquiries, Stein had become convinced that Gauleiter Koch was the only living soul who knew what had happened to the magnificent treasure and probably also where it was hidden. One document, dated 1941, described the room and valued it at not less than 200 million marks.

When Frank read that, it at once occurred to him that that was the reason Koch was still in prison. His Polish jailers were still trying to learn his secret and certainly did not want to risk the possibility of having him reveal it to someone else, should he be set free.

An addendum to the Amber Room documents mentioned that the valuable treasure had been and still was the object of investigations and searches by many organizations and individuals besides Georg Stein, from several countries, among them West Germany, the DDR, Poland, and Russia, and including neo–Nazi groups, who wanted to get their hands on the many hundreds of millions the room would be worth today.

Frank was disappointed. He had expected a startling revelation to leap from the pages of the secret documents.

There was none.

The Stein home on Ashausnerstrasse in Stelle was a two–story dwelling painted grey with green shutters, with a tiled roof and the clean lines of a typical Holstein house. The man who received Frank, however, was far from typical, either in dress or appearance.

Clad in a white shirt and bright red corded trousers, he was of average height, partly bald, but with long white hair hanging down his neck from the sides of his head, like a skirt around a decidedly moon–shaped face, the most prominent feature of which was a harelip.

Perfunctorily he welcomed Frank, his speech, strangely, both sibilant and nasal, due to his disfigurement.

Rumpelstiltskin, Frank thought. It had been one of his favorite childhood tales, and he had always tried to visualize what the peculiar little creature would look like.

Stein ushered Frank into his living room, furnished with heavy antique oak furniture loomed over by a very large microfilm reader that seemed hopelessly out of place.

Stein looked at Frank with obvious curiosity. "You told me over the telephone," he said, "that it was important that you see me, but that you did not want to discuss it over the phone. Now—why is it you want to see me?"

"I am here at the express suggestion of Herr Medard Klapper in Karlsruhe," Frank said.

For a moment Stein looked at him. Then he said, "I do not know anyone named Medard Klapper. In Karlsruhe or anywhere else."

XXXII

Frank stared at the strange little man. What the hell was going on?

"Did your friend in Karlsruhe say why he wanted you to look me up?" Stein asked.

"Not specifically," Frank answered him. "But he did mention the—the Amber Room."

Stein gave him a startled look. He rose from his chair and began to pace the room.

"What did he say about the Amber Room, Herr Brandenburg? Tell me. What did he say?" It was obviously difficult for him to contain his agitation, and his speech became even harder to understand. Frank decided to go slowly.

"I am aware of your interest in the Amber Room, Herr Stein," he said. "But I know only a little about it. Would you mind filling me in before we go on?"

Stein gave him a quick look, half impatience, half annoyance, with a dash of "what choice do I have?"

"During the war," he began. He spoke quickly, straining Frank's capacity to understand him. "In 1941. The Zarskoje Sela Palace was within—" He gave Frank a quick glance. "You do know about the palace and how the Amber Room got there?" he asked.

Frank nodded. Stein at once went on.

"The Palace was within range of Russian heavy artillery. Already an air strike had damaged the Great Hall, and the decision was made to dismantle the Amber Room and transport it to safety. This was done, and the room was shipped via Riga to Königsberg in East Prussia, where it was assembled in Room 37 next to the Corinthian Hall in Königsberg Castle, where it was once again being exhibited, under the protection of Gauleiter Koch. The—"

"Did you know Gauleiter Koch?" Frank asked.

Stein nodded impatiently, irritated at having been interrupted. "Our families were friends," he said curtly. "When Königsberg became a major target for air strikes," he went on, "the Amber Room was once again dismantled, packed in several crates—the reported number of them ranges from twenty–seven to fifty–five. Suffice to say that there were supposed to have been several such crates. The room itself was ten by ten meters and six meters to the ceiling. The crates were stored in the deepest dungeons of the castle for safekeeping." He gave Frank a speculative look. "What happened to those crates is the puzzle."

"Up to fifty–five large crates," Frank observed. "It seems difficult to believe they could just have—vanished."

Stein looked shrewdly at him. "I believe they were all wrong," he said. "I believe there were only *four* crates."

"Four?"

"The amber was affixed to wooden plates, Herr Brandenburg. It could easily have been loosened from them. In that case, if only the amber and the amber art objects were packed in crates, four large ones would have sufficed. And that, I believe, is exactly what happened." He gave Frank a sidelong glance. "At least according to a man I tracked down in Berlin, a Prof. Strauss, who was present when the amber was crated!"

"Then—what do you think happened to those four crates?"

"That, Herr Brandenburg, is indeed the question. The riddle so many people have been trying to solve for more than four decades now. Some say they were destroyed when the castle was laid in ruins. I believe they were secretly taken away in 1945, to a place that to this day is unknown."

"Do you think anyone still alive knows?"

Stein nodded. "I am convinced of it."

"Who?"

"I believe Gauleiter Koch knows."

"Koch? The Gauleiter is dead."

Stein shook his head vigorously. "He is still alive. Very much so. He is imprisoned in an old Franciscan monastery prison in Barczewo/Wartenburg."

"The Polish Embassy in Köln told me he was dead."

Stein snorted, a peculiar sibilant sound. "They do not like to admit that they still hold him. That they are still trying to pry his secret from him. No one can see him. But, believe me, Herr Brandenburg, he is there!"*

He stopped his agitated pacing in front of Frank and fixed him with his eyes. "And now, Herr Brandenburg," he said firmly. "What did your friend in Karlsruhe—Klapper, Medard Klapper was it?—what did he say about the Amber Room?"

"He simply said that his organization might have uncovered a lead as to where it is," Frank told him.

A look of apprehension suddenly clouded Stein's face. "Organization?" he said. "What organization?"

"He referred to it as—the Bormann group," Frank said. He thought it best to leave out Mariborsol. For now.

Stein sat down. He rubbed his temples in a circular motion with the thumb and middle finger of his left hand. He looked up at Frank, a trace of worry in his eyes.

"Now I know why you are here," he said. "Now I know why Herr Klapper sent you to me."

"Why?"

"The Bormann group," Stein said. "I know there are such—groups. Powerful groups. Groups of old, and new Nazis. They, too, want to find the Amber Room. The financial bonanza to them would be immense. If Herr Klapper represents such a group, a strong—"

"He does," Frank said. He had decided to reveal whatever he knew to Stein. Klapper could not fault him for doing so, having sent him to see the man himself. Anyway, what if he did?

---

* In November 1986, six months later, Koch's death at the age of ninety was announced by Polish authorities.

Stein gave him a quick glance. "You are certain of that?" he asked sharply.

"I am. Klapper represents an organization of Nazis called Mariborsol," Frank told him. "An organization which he claims is headed by Martin Bormann himself."

Stein nodded. "I have suspected something like that," he said. "I never accepted the claim that the Reichsleiter died in Berlin. Whatever old bones they dug up. And if he did not, he would have been certain to gather a group, an organization around him. Apparently he has."

"But why should Klapper send me to see you?"

"It is evident, Herr Brandenburg," Stein answered him soberly. "My interest in, my investigations concerning the Amber Room and what has become of it are well known. There is even a play, a Russian theater play that is based on my activities in recovering art objects lost or stolen during the war. The character based on me is called Fritz Forst in the play. It has run for six years in Russia by now." He gave a rueful little smile that accentuated his harelip. "They have him murdered in the last scene. Murdered, Herr Brandenburg."

"Then you think it is because of your interest in the Amber Room, your knowledge about it, that Klapper asked me to see you? But why? What did he think would be accomplished?"

"It is more than that, Herr Brandenburg. Much more than that. You see, I too have recently uncovered new leads to the treasure. From Eastern sources." He leaned toward Frank and lowered his voice to a tone of confidentiality if not conspiracy. "I actually have quite excellent connections with certain Soviet sources," he said. "Intelligence sources. I am certain the people of—uh, Mariborsol, your Medard Klapper, have learned of this new development in my search for the Amber Room. That is the reason you are here."

"For what purpose?" Frank was beginning to feel uneasy. "It does not make sense."

"But it does, Herr Brandenburg, it does. Those people do not do things the straightforward way. I have had marginal dealings with other such individuals and groups before. I know. You were sent here as a messenger, Herr Brandenburg, as an intermediary if you wish, either with a guarded invitation for me to collaborate with them in the further search for the treasure—or with a warning."

"What do you mean—warning?"

Stein ignored his question. "What you must now do," he said, "is this. You must return to Karlsruhe. You must see your Medard Klapper, and you must convey to him my willingness to meet with him, to discuss the possibility of my collaboration with—with Mariborsol, in the search for the Amber Room. By combining our knowledge, and our new leads. *Einverstanden?*—agreed?"

Frank stared at him.

"Herr Stein," he said, "I am not a—a messenger, or an intermediary in this matter. Or in any other matter pertaining to Mariborsol. I am not one of their couriers."

Stein contemplated him, an ironic little smile on his deformed lips. "Whether you want to be or not," he said, "you already are one of them. Already you have been used. As a messenger to me. And now you will have to carry my answer back to them. They will expect it."

"I must decline, Herr Stein," Frank said, increasingly ill at ease. "I am a researcher. A seeker of facts. I am *not* a participant."

Stein frowned at him. "I would caution you not to cross them," he said slowly. "It is a dangerous game you play. There are still among them those who will kill."

He looked earnestly at Frank. "You must understand," he said solemnly. "Even though the old Nazis in the organizations such as your Mariborsol are dying out, new ones, young ones, such as you, step into their footsteps. You must realize that they are motivated by fanatic beliefs. They see in you someone who is ready to join the pool of young blood to be infused with their beliefs, shaped in the image of the old guard, ready to take their places. Your life, from the day you do, will be set on a new course, a course that they firmly believe will see the rise of a new Reich, soaring from the ashes of the humiliation and degradation of the old. Like an iron–clad Phoenix to rule the world with absolute power, guided by the mighty ideals of Adolf Hitler—a world that will be theirs."

He stopped. He looked hard at Frank. "Be not deceived by the flowery speech, the fanatic goals, Herr Brandenburg. Those are words from the mouths of the very people you are dealing with even now."

Frank sat silent. For the first time the full realization of how deeply he had become involved in his project surged through him like an icy bolt. He was no longer just looking for information, he was becoming part of the whole unsavory cabal. It was time to call a stop before it was too late.

"Do not take my warning lightly," Stein cautioned him. "The matter in which you have involved yourself, the struggle to find the missing Amber Room, is a dangerous matter. I myself have often been warned. Everyone knows of the dangers. Even the old abbot of a monastery to which my inquiries led me said to me, 'Give it up, Herr Stein. Die in bed, and not with a bullet in your back!'"

Frank stood up. "Thank you for your time," he said. "And the information you have given me. But I must categorically decline any active involvement on my part with the activities of Mariborsol or you."

As he walked away from the Stein house, he made up his mind that his quest had come to an end. It had to. The people he was dealing with would eventually demand commitments from him, commitments he was not prepared to make. He did not want to dwell on what might happen to him should he refuse their "requests."

There was only one loose end to take care of.

A telephone call to Martin Recher, the man Klapper had said would be able to give him the final word on the fate of Reichsleiter Martin Bormann.

Any negotiations, any machinations concerning the Amber Room treasure that Georg Stein wanted to enter into with his Russian sources or with Mariborsol, he would have to handle himself.*

When Frank called Martin Recher the man became positively obsequious on the telephone as he listened to Frank's name–dropping: General Baur and General Wolff; Gauleiter Jordan and Ministerialdirigent Heim, adjutant to Reichsleiter Martin Bormann...

There was no need for the Herr Brandenburg to travel to Kempten, he said. The man the Herr Brandenburg really wanted to talk to about Reichsleiter Martin Bormann was a man who lived in Austria. In the village of Stoizendorf.

A man named Franz Lechner...

---

* A year later, Georg Stein was found murdered in a forest near Munich, naked, stabbed to death with two table knives that were still stuck in his body.

XXXIII

F ranz Lechner ceremoniously placed the gun on the table between them and his grimy hand next to it. He fixed his pale–blue eyes on Frank.

"Now," he said tonelessly. "Now we find out why you are here."

Frank brought himself out of his reverie. How long had he sat staring at the gun? He was suddenly acutely aware of the ominous presence of the foreboding little man who sat across from him and the two huge dogs on the floor, never taking their watchful eyes off him. The room was gloomy, the windows partially obscured by the ears of corn hanging on the walls outside.

Involuntarily, he tensed. This was to be his last interview, his last contact with the people from the past.

Was it to be one too many?

Should he have heeded the warning by Georg Stein?

Should he have passed up this, the last of his interviews?

His last?

His eyes were once again inexorably drawn to the gun on the table, so readily accessible to the grim little man seated opposite him.

"I am waiting, young man," Lechner said, his eyes never leaving Frank, the hand lying close to the gun twitching almost imperceptibly. "What is it you want? How did you get here? How did you find me?" His voice was deceptively quiet, but Frank recognized the menace behind his words.

He tore his eyes from the gun. He dug his hand into his pocket. For a moment his heart stood still. It was not there! He could not find it—

There! Crammed into a corner.

He brought out the SS ring given to him by General Wolff. He handed it to Lechner.

"A friend," he said. "Of ours. Of—Uncle Martin. General Wolff. He gave me this ring. He told me..." He let the sentence hang, still amazed at himself for claiming Bormann as his uncle.

Lechner examined the ring. "Generaloberst Karl Wolff?" he asked. It was a rhetorical question. He turned the ring over in his hand. He peered at the SS emblem on it. He opened the little compartment meant to hold a suicide pill. He gave the ring back to Frank. He nodded.

"Karl Wolff," he said slowly. "*Erstklassig*—first rate."

He pocketed his gun and fixed his water–blue eyes on Frank. "Now, Poldi," he said, using the popular nickname for Leopold as an expression of friendliness, "what do you want to know?"

Frank drew a long breath of relief.

"I want to know what happened to—Uncle Martin," he said. "I want to know what you can tell me about him. When did you first meet him?"

Lechner laughed. "Poldi, Poldi!" he said. "Your uncle was *ein Arbeitskollege*—a colleague in my work."

"What was that?"

"I was an officer z.b.V.—*zu besonderen Verfügung*—on special orders."

"What does that mean?"

Lechner wagged a dirt–soiled finger at him. "Poldi!" he said. Again he laughed. "At the Wolfsschanze I was security officer."

"When did you last see the Reichsleiter?"

"In September. September 1946."

"Where?"

"In Nauders. In Austria. Where I lived. Very close to where the Swiss, the Italian and the Austrian borders come together."

"Nauders was an *Anlaufstelle*—a station on the escape route?"

"*Genau*—exactly. Nauders was a central station."

"And you were involved with that?"

"With the leg between the stations in Nauders and Bozen,* in Italy."

"How did you—uh, get involved with that?"

Lechner shook his head at Frank. "Poldi, Poldi!" he scolded. "I was an officer z.b.V. It was my duty. But I did not serve in any concentration camp. I did not kill anyone."

"So, my uncle showed up in Nauders. How did he get there? Did you pick him up somewhere?"

"*Nein, nein,*" Lechner said. "No. I got a telephone call from a certain Recher—"

"Martin Recher?"

"*Ja.* You know him too, *gell?*—don't you? He called me from Obersdorf. In the Allgäu. He told me he had taken an important escapee to Innsbruck. To a priest there, who helped the Nazis get away."

"And that was the man who then came to *Anlaufstelle* Nauders? That was my uncle?"

"*Genau.* He came by bus. With a blonde woman, who said her name was Rosi. She was about thirty."

"Do you know who she was?"

Lechner shrugged. "Rosi."

"How did you recognize my uncle?"

"I knew him at once. I knew him from the Wolfsschanze."

"Did he give you his name?"

"No one gave his name."

"Could you—describe him to me? What did he look like, then?"

Lechner snorted. "He looked like Reichsleiter Martin Bormann, Poldi, that is who he looked like." He grinned. "And he had *X–Beine*— he was knock–kneed, your uncle. He waddled like a goose."

He laughed, showing a couple of missing teeth.

It was true, Frank thought. Bormann had been knock–kneed.

"Did my uncle tell you how he got out of Berlin?"

"He came to Sonthofen in the Allgäu by way of Nordkirchen."

"Aided by Herr Recher?"

"No, no. A truck driver from Kempten, his name was Wulf, he took him."

"How did my uncle get from Berlin to Nordkirchen?"

* Bolzano.

For a moment Lechner contemplated Frank, then he nodded slightly. "His escape was planned, Poldi," he said. "Your uncle had a small plane concealed. At the outskirts of the city. To the west. A Fieseler Storch. In the middle of the night—"

"When? what date?"

"In early May. On the fifth, I believe."

That would have been two or three days after the breakout, Frank thought.

"*Bei Nacht und Nebel*—under cover of the night, his pilot flew him out."

"Do you know who the pilot was?"

Lechner nodded. "His name was Berliner. Werner Berliner."

"Is he still alive?"

"I do not know. I can tell you nothing more."

"My uncle told you all this?"

"He did."

"And Berliner flew him to Nordkirchen?"

"No, no. He flew him to Kempten. From there he went to Nordkirchen. It is only a few kilometers. Then he went to Sonthofen, and then to Obersdorf."

"What happened after he and—uh, Rosi, came to the *Anlaufstelle* in Nauders?"

"Your uncle was exhausted, Poldi," Lechner said. "He stayed with me for fourteen days. In *der Alten Mühle, no. 6.*"

"In the Old Mill?"

"That is where it was."

"The *Anlaufstelle?*"

Lechner nodded.

"And that is where he told you all this?"

"We talked about the old days."

"How was he dressed?"

"He wore civilian clothes." Lechner grinned and patted the pocket in which he had his gun. "And he carried a gun. A Walther."

"Did he smoke?"

"Like a crematorium chimney," Lechner grinned. *"Und er hat gesäuft, und wie!*—and he drank, and how! Like a camel about to cross the Sahara—and all the water holes dry!"

That was like Bormann, Frank thought. He had the reputation for both smoking and drinking to excess.

"Then what happened?"

"I took your uncle and the young woman to a safe hut in the mountains close to the Italian border. We stayed there overnight."

"And then?"

"Then I guided them over a secret path across the border into Italy, and in the first little town we came to, Reschen it was called, just across the border, we got a car." Again he grinned his toothless grin. "Your uncle was not in the best of shape, Poldi. With the woman alone I would have made better time." He laughed. "In the car I took them to Brixen.* Just as I had done with all the others."

"You helped many others across?"

Lechner nodded proudly. "Many."

"Can you give me any names?"

For a moment Lechner looked speculatively at Frank, then he shrugged. "Richard Glücks," he said. "The Inspector of the KZ—the concentration camps. And Alois Brunner, for example."

Alois Brunner, Frank thought. The notorious SS mass murderer, one of the most wanted Nazi war criminals, who escaped to Syria, and today is reported to be living in Damascus.

"What happened in Brixen?" he asked.

"That is where he got his passport," Lechner told him. "And a driver's license. And papers so he could go to Argentina." He chortled. "Without me."

"He got the papers at the *Anlaufstelle* there?"

"No, no. At the Papal Prefecture. That was where they all got their papers. So they could go to Australia. To Egypt. To Syria and to Argentina."

"At the Papal Prefecture?" Frank asked.

"*Genau.* The escape route we used was called the *Päpstliches Hilfwerk*—the Papal Aid Operation."

The same as the Monastery Route, Frank thought. "Then where did you go?" he asked.

"We took a taxi, Poldi," Lechner grinned. "Your uncle was tired. We took a taxi to the next Papal Prefecture in Bozen. Others took over from there." He looked at Frank. "Your uncle swore me to secrecy, Poldi, and he told me he would never forget the help I had given him; never in his whole life."

* Bressanone

"And from Bozen my uncle went to Argentina?"

Lechner nodded. "I learned that later," he said. "Your uncle was sent to the Genoa *Anlaufstelle*. From there to Istanbul—and Argentina.

"Then you think he reached safety?"

For a long moment Lechner gazed at Frank.

"Yes," he said firmly. "And I should know, *gell?*—should I not? I, who personally took him across the border out of Germany." He leaned across the table, his eyes boring into Frank.

"And a blessing it was, Poldi. *Als wenn heute mein heiss geliebter Führer aufstehen würde!*—as if today my ardently beloved Führer were resurrected!"

Frank walked slowly to his car. A myriad thoughts tumbled about in his mind.

He had heard pros and cons about the survival and escape of Martin Bormann, but no one had been more persuasive than Franz Lechner, who had no profitable or personal motive for lying to him. He believed the testy little man.

Coupled with all the other information he had unearthed about Bormann, Lechner's account of the Reichsleiter's flight convinced him that Martin Bormann had not died in Berlin, but had lived to flee Germany and make his way to South America.

When Frank walked out the gate to the Lechner farmyard the place was dark behind him. It was symbolic, he felt. He had been on a long and dark journey into the dark past.

And yet, a journey that had shed some light. He had been allowed a glimpse behind the scenes of history.

Soberly, he realized that much of what some of the men and women had told him had been told to others before him. It mattered not. He had heard it from their own mouths, and he had looked into their eyes. And into their souls. Again and again he had listened to the malignant credo of the Hitler era defended, rationalized, and approved of by unrepentant Nazis.

The German people must recognize that it is there—and guard themselves against it. History must not be allowed to repeat itself, as the ominous saying goes.

How much of what he had been told these last seven years was true? He had no way of knowing. But he knew that the people who had told him of their beliefs and ideologies, their regrets and their hopes, had wanted him to believe them. And that was the real issue.

And he realized that he may not have learned anything that had not already been known by someone, somewhere. But what he had learned, he had learned for himself.

He was reminded of a story he had once heard, about an inventor who isolated himself in a cabin on a mountaintop for years and invented the typewriter. When he came down off his mountain he found his invention already in use in every office in town.

He, Frank Brandenburg, might just have invented the typewriter.

But he might have come up with a few extra keys.

He might have discovered what did happen to the missing *Serail* documents.

He might have established the existence of a powerful Nazi–oriented international organization called Mariborsol; he might have stumbled upon the secret name of the Führer's third dog—and its significance.

And he might have determined the probable fate of Reichsleiter Martin Bormann.

It was all unimportant.

What *was* important was that the challenge had been there, that he had accepted it—and prevailed.

As he drove away from the Lechner farm, the dogs were barking in the distance.

Epilogue

When the writing of *Quest* was finished I decided to turn the tables on Frank. I sat him down, and *I* interviewed *him*.

"During your quest, Frank, were there times when you felt yourself wanting to believe in your subjects, to 'join' them?"

"Yes. It was impossible not to. Many of the people I talked to were charming and likeable. They flattered me—and all of us are apt to respond at least a little bit to flattery. They extolled the past and minimized its shortcomings. They saw in me a new hope, a new and malleable recruit for their old ideas and ideology, which they could and would not abandon. Many of them had at one time been among the most powerful and influential men in Germany, something which could not fail to impress a young man, even though what they had stood for was to be condemned. But, as they said, such condemnation was unfair. And it had all been in the past, and it was not easy to understand it all immediately, especially since it was presented through their eyes, their interpretations.

"Yes, at times it took a lot of soul–searching and mind–pinching to keep my feet firmly planted in reality. But—I did *not* join them. I only refrained from showing disagreement or disapproval to their faces. Had I done so, had I not seemed sympathetic to them and their cause, my excursion into the past would quickly have come to an end.

"Had I not seen 'The Holocaust,' had I not subsequently traced down as much research material as I could and read it all, had I known only their version of what happened, I might have. And that is the honest truth. But—I *did* see 'The Holocaust.' I *did* have other information, other views—and I could not accept or embrace their ideology.

"Some of my friends would berate me for consorting with old Nazis and convicted war criminals. But how else could I have learned what I *did* learn? Could a researcher working toward finding a cure for cancer steer away from all who were afflicted with cancer? I was, after all, like a reporter doing a story. If that story brought him into contact with a murderer, would he drop it? Would he not go ahead? Of course he would. Just as I did."

"What made you decide to tell your story now?"

"Many people already know much of what I have to say; certainly about what took place during the Third Reich. But I feel people must not forget—especially young people. Unpleasant things have a habit of becoming less and less unpleasant with time. This must not happen in the case of the Nazis. And I want to point to the dangers of totalitarianism—right or left. People must wake up to the fact that these dangers still exist. The Nazis were defeated—but the dangers they represent did not die with them.

"Those seven years of probing and searching were not pleasant. I had to suffer many unhappy times, with friends and family, and in general. But I did learn a lot—not least about myself. I did not swim with the stream, but against it, and that is never easy.

"There are forces, powerful forces, with their roots deeply and firmly planted in Adolf Hitler's Third Reich, and they are working tirelessly toward the rise of a Fourth Reich, if you will. Not with the strutting of goose steps and stiff–armed Hitler salutes—but with the same ideals and goals. People must not sweep this fact under a rug of complacency."

"Do you think the German people have learned from history? Could an Adolf Hitler–type Reich emerge into power in Germany today?"

"We Germans have not as yet conquered the past. Until the present, Germans have always suppressed their Nazi past. *Sie nehmen sich viel zu wichtig!*—they take themselves much too seriously. Another Hitler–type regime? It is always possible, but I doubt it. The world is watching Germany and would try to prevent such a thing from happening. Today the German people say, enough. We have talked enough about and heard enough about Hitler and his times; the guilt the world wants to place on our shoulders. Enough.

"Of course, there is a hard–core cadre of so–called neo–Nazis with the same ideology and the same goals as Hitler, with their leather coats, death's–head emblems and 'Heil Hitler' salutes; pathetic clones of another era. Several thousands of them. They exist in more or less clandestine clusters throughout the world. There are more than twenty–five such organizations in Germany alone. And several in the United States. In fact, much of the financing of the neo–Nazis through-out the world comes from the States. Some of these gangs are violent, but I doubt that they will become politically powerful. Not in Germany. But they can do damage. However, more dangerous by far are the organizations founded and run by the old–time Nazis and their current recruits.

"Most, if not all of these neo–Nazi organizations are outlawed, but as old ones are stamped out, new ones spring up to take their places."

"You don't think Nazism is dead in Germany?"

"How can I say this...Germany has been robbed of her identity. National pride has become a dirty word. The first verse of our national anthem, *Deutschland, Deutschland über Alles,* has become an embar-rassment. People no longer sing it. Only the third verse, *Einigkeit und Recht und Freiheit fur das Deutsche Vaterland*—Unity and Right and Freedom for the German Fatherland, has been declared our national anthem. Ordinances forbid dealing in Nazi art and *Mein Kampf* can only be read for research purposes.

"Do the Germans of today obey those edicts?"

"For the greater part, yes. But it is like forbidden fruit. Something you can't have, something you can't do, becomes more attractive. And there are people who will do those things just *because* they are forbidden. I believe those dictates only perpetuate the forbidden, rather than eliminate it. One cannot legislate thought—or desires. So—is Nazism *dead* in Germany?

"Once Nazism was like a religion to the German people. Hitler was like a god, a new Messiah, although that may not be the right word. And there was a certain mysticism in the air, a hovering of the Germanic spirit.

"If someone could emerge to tap these feelings, which are still there, although suppressed, then I think the people might follow him, even though he might be another Hitler. Hitler himself, after all, came to power when the German people were yearning for lost pride, lost identity.

"I once heard an old saying. It was French. Or Flemish, I think. It went like this:

> When the Hun is out and down,
> He's the humblest man in town.
> But when he mounts and holds the rod,
> He has no love for man or God.

It cut deep, hearing it. Is it true? I do not know. I honestly do not know. It could be."

"What has happened to Frank Brandenburg because of his quest? How has he changed? How has he grown?"

"I learned a lot, of course. The banal thing to say is that I matured. But every young man between the ages of sixteen and twenty–three matures. There is more to it than that. I learned how easy it is to be swayed by convincing arguments and the seduction of flattery. I will never again be as uncritical of people—making mistakes, being misled. I *have* changed. In a way I missed out on a time in my life when most young people experience a certain frivolity. While others were passing through the juvenile phase of their development, I was involved in deadly serious matters, even immersed in them, constantly striving to keep my head out of the darkened clouds above me and my feet on the firm ground of reality. How have I grown? I know myself better. And that is real growth.

"In the past, I have never talked much about all this—about my experiences. I kept it to myself. But it must out. Telling my story is like relieving myself of all the things that have been pent up in me—and must out."

"What is your assessment today of your journey into the past?"

"After I had seen the mind–shattering film *'The Holocaust'* in 1979, I wanted to find out for myself how it had *really* been, by conducting intensive and direct conversations with the people who once wielded absolute power, or had been in immediate proximity to that power, people who had survived the Nürnberg Trials. My layman's naive conception, that I would unearth the 'truth' from these 'pure sources,'

launched me on my way. I was certain that my guilelessness would
be rewarded with exclusive information. I wanted to gain that information because of my own need to know, but I also thought I could
put myself in the enviable position of being able to make new material
available to the learned historians, who all too often were restrained
in their research, and met with skepticism. In my desire to conduct
this research I dreamt of soon being in a position, through this 'oral
history' which I would compile, to augment and enlarge upon what
was taught in the schools and reported by historians; at least to enrich
and possibly correct questionable points in this knowledge.

"Today I know that in some cases, not all cases, but in some cases
I was confronted with defensive statements, evasion, self–exoneration
and prejudiced portrayals of the facts, but when I began my project,
at the age of sixteen, I—naively—had no conception that this might
be the case. Not one of the people I talked to expressed any kind of
guilt, or remorse. Not one of them had regrets or concern for their
victims. Yet, it is easier for me to understand that. Who, in his old
age, wants to admit having committed such misdeeds? To admit that
everything one had believed in, worked for and lived for, had been
corrupt? So must we also understand and accept the fact that so many
young people in Germany are now suppressing and ignoring that
darkest chapter in our country's history. That neglect of the past can
only lead to trouble in the future.

"I do not know if my journey into my country's past has been of
any value. But, despite all of this—for me personally—it worked."

"Is this now the end of it?"

"I shall always retain my interest, but—yes—this is the end of my
active project. It is likely to be the last opportunity anyone will have
to conduct such a project. The old Nazis are dying out. Already several
of the people with whom I talked have passed on. Lina Heydrich
Manninen and Karl Wolff; Heinrich Heim and Georg Stein; Richard
Schulze-Kossens and Hermann Giesler, Nicolaus van Below and Rudolf
Jordan,Werner Best, Hans-Ulrich Rudel and Christa Schroeder; the
list grows daily.

"*Quest* may well have been the last chance to compile an 'oral
history,' or what these old-time Nazi cadres perceived as history.

"My hope is that it has been worth while. I am, after all, a German,
and I love my country."

Frank's activities gained him a certain amount of notice in Germany, and in 1985, when President Ronald Reagan visited Germany, Frank was invited by the Minister President of Rheinland–Pfalz, Dr. Bernhard Vogel, to join a select audience to meet the President and hear him speak at Hambacher Schloss, where he addressed the German youth.

That same year Frank also attended the Fortieth Anniversary of the liberation of the Bergen-Belsen concentration camp, where he met with the German Bundespresident, Richard von Weiszacker.

In June 1987, when President Reagan spoke at the Brandenburg Gate in Berlin on the occasion of the birthday of the city, Frank was once again invited to attend the ceremonies, this time by the Mayor of Berlin.

But this was not the only kind of attention Frank's activities generated.

There were thinly veiled threats and vilifications delivered by telephone, and in April of 1988 Frank had a curious and disturbing experience.

Out of the blue he was visited in his home in Hildesheim by a grim, forbidding gentleman by name of Hebel, who identified himself as an agent of the Spionabgewehr DDR in Niedersachsische Innenministerium von Hannover—the DDR Counterspy Corps of the Lower Saxony Interior Ministry of Hannover.

Frank had been anonymously denounced as an East German spy! The kind of denunciation that was common during the Third Reich.

He was accused of meeting regularly with international agents in Prague, Stockholm, and Vienna—all places where he had actually been—with a special interest in art objects stolen by the Nazis.

The agent was well informed about Frank and his activities. The denouncer had been, as well. Hebel mentioned the Amber Room specifically, and other treasures, such as one supposedly concealed near Guben in East Germany. And the informant had apprised him of the fact that Frank had a friend in government circles, a young woman from whom he ostensibly was trying to elicit confidential information.

It was true that Frank knew a woman in Bonn, in the CDU, the governing party in West Germany, but they had the name wrong. The letter denouncing Frank had called her Heidi. Her real name was Ines.

After lengthy interrogation and investigation of Frank's files and records, the agent finally departed, satisfied that the denunciation had been made "out of spite."

But Frank wondered who felt it necessary to try to destroy him in that manner.

Hebel left with an admonition to Frank not to mention the incident to anyone. It would be the only way his organization would possibly have to apprehend the denouncer.

As he left, the counterespionage agent turned his grim face to Frank. "Be careful," he said. "Be very careful."

TABLE OF EQUIVALENT RANKS

US ARMY	WEHRMACHT (German Army)	SS and WAFFEN SS
General of the Army	Generalfeldmarschall	Reichsführer SS
No Equivalent	Generaloberst	SS-Oberstgruppenführer Generaloberst der Waffen SS
General	General	SS-Obergruppenführer General der Waffen SS
Lieutenant-General	Generalleutnant	SS-Gruppenführer Generalleutnant der Waffen SS
Major-General	Generalmajor	SS-Brigadeführer Generalmajor der Waffen SS
Brigadier-General	Oberst	SS-Oberführer
Colonel	Oberst	SS-Standartenführer
Lieutenant Colonel	Oberstleutnant	SS-Obersturmbannführer
Major	Major	SS-Sturmbannführer
Captain	Hauptmann Rittmeister	SS-Hauptsturmführer
First Lieutenant	Oberleutnant	SS-Obersturmführer
Second Lieutenant	Leutnant	SS-Untersturmführer
Sergeant Major	Hauptfeldwebel	SS-Sturmscharführer
Master Sergeant	Oberfeldwebel	SS-Hauptscharführer
Staff Sergeant	Unterfeldwebel	SS-Standartenjunker Scharführer
Sergeant	Unteroffizier	SS-Unterscharführer
Corporal	Obergefreiter	SS-Rottenführer
Pvt First Class	Oberschütze	Sturmmann SS-Oberschütze
Private	Schütze	SS-Mann SS-Schütze

INDEX